Classroom-Ready
RICH MATH TASKS

GRADES
4–5

Classroom-Ready
RICH MATH TASKS

GRADES
4–5

Engaging Students in Doing Math

Beth McCord **KOBETT** • Francis (Skip) **FENNELL** • Karen S. **KARP**
Delise **ANDREWS** • Sorsha-Maria T. **MULROE**

CORWIN Mathematics

FOR INFORMATION:

Corwin

A SAGE Company

2455 Teller Road

Thousand Oaks, California 91320

(800) 233–9936

www.corwin.com

SAGE Publications Ltd.

1 Oliver's Yard

55 City Road

London, EC1Y 1SP

United Kingdom

SAGE Publications India Pvt. Ltd.

B 1/I 1 Mohan Cooperative Industrial Area

Mathura Road, New Delhi 110 044

India

SAGE Publications Asia-Pacific Pte. Ltd.

18 Cross Street #10-10/11/12

China Square Central

Singapore 048423

President: Mike Soules

Associate Vice President and Editorial Director:
  Monica Eckman

Publisher, Mathematics: Erin Null

Associate Content
  Development Editor: Jessica Vidal

Production Editor: Tori Mirsadjadi

Copy Editor: Linda Gray

Typesetter: Integra

Proofreader: Scott Oney

Indexer: Integra

Cover Designer: Scott Van Atta

Marketing Manager: Maura Sullivan

Printed in the United States of America.

Library of Congress Cataloging-in-Publication Data

Names: Kobett, Beth McCord, author. | Fennell, Francis M., 1944- author. | Karp, Karen S., author. | Andrews, Delise, author. | Mulroe, Sorsha-Maria T., author.

Title: Classroom-ready rich math tasks, grades 4-5 : engaging students in doing math / Beth McCord Kobett, Francis (Skip) Fennell, Karen S. Karp, Delise Andrews, and Sorsha-Maria Mulroe.

Description: Thousand Oaks, California : Corwin, [2021] | Includes bibliographical references and index.

Identifiers: LCCN 2020052691 | ISBN 9781544399164 (paperback) | ISBN 9781071841068 (ebook other) | ISBN 9781071841075 (ebook) | ISBN 9781544399171 (adobe pdf)

Subjects: LCSH: Mathematics—Study and teaching (Elementary) | Mathematics—Problems, exercises, etc. | Fourth grade (Education) | Fifth grade (Education)

Classification: LCC QA139 .K625 2021 | DDC 372.7/2—dc23

LC record available at https://lccn.loc.gov/2020052691

This book is printed on acid-free paper.

21 22 23 24 25 10 9 8 7 6 5 4 3 2

Contents

Visit the companion website at
resources.corwin.com/classroomreadymath/4–5
for downloadable resources.

Preface

We know that teachers work incredibly hard to make their mathematics lessons meaningful, challenging, and accessible to their students. We were inspired by a teacher we worked with who made this comment:

> *It seems like I spend a lot of time, often in the evenings, thinking about and then creating or locating, and usually revising, math tasks for my students. Having my students engage in challenging mathematics tasks is important to my planning and teaching—every day!*

> *(Elementary school teacher)*

We also know how valuable time is and how many, if not most, teachers find it to be in very short supply. For some time, we have felt that teachers need to have access to mathematics tasks that fully represent the most important mathematical topics and standards they are responsible for teaching and that will truly engage their students in doing the mathematics they are learning.

This book is designed to address these concerns! Here's our plan: We begin by unpacking a *doing-math task* (Chapter 1). The chapter defines and addresses the importance of *doing-math tasks* and why such rich, engaging, and high-level tasks are important. The chapter then considers issues related to planning for task implementation, with particular emphasis on task selection and implementation.

In Chapters 2 and 3, we address major planning and instructional issues relative to the use of rich mathematics tasks, the importance of which, to an extent, pushed us to write this book and the companion Grade K–1 and Grades 2–3 volumes. Our point, our concern—it's not just the task! We have been in too many classrooms and had too many conversations with our teacher and teacher leader colleagues and friends about the need—the necessity—to truly recognize and value the importance of planning for and implementing such tasks. Planning considerations include ensuring that every math task addresses important mathematics standards and related mathematical practices. We also discuss the characteristics of effective mathematics teaching practices, including, for example, the use of multiple representations. Our approach is to address issues related to planning (Chapter 2) and instruction (Chapter 3) using a task template. In Chapters 4 through 15 we present 54 *doing-math* task-based lessons, which as noted, consider much more than just locating and presenting a mathematics task.

As the title of Chapter 2 indicates, the chapter lays the groundwork for teaching with rich, *doing-math task*, with attention to planning-related essentials. These features include mathematics vocabulary, materials, grouping approaches, strategies for engaging your students in the task, and other anticipatory considerations related to preparing to implement a task-based lesson. We also note the importance of setting norms for task-based inquiry and provide specific planning and teaching-related suggestions regarding the importance of student and task access and equity; opportunities for productive struggle as your students engage *doing-math task*; alternate learning environments, including online teaching; and strengths spotting—that is, being able to recognize student strengths and considering them the launch point for your work with rich, *doing-math tasks*.

Chapter 3 is all about implementing a *doing-math* task-based lesson. This process begins with suggestions regarding the launching of a task-based lesson, which includes, but is not limited to, the following techniques: See, Think, and Wonder; Notice and Wonder; and the Three-Read Protocol. The facilitation of a *doing-math tasks* lesson includes classroom considerations related to grouping students for engaging in the task; classroom discourse, including the use of purposeful questioning; and monitoring the task lesson's progress using the following five classroom-based formative assessment techniques: observations, interviews, Show Me, hinge questions, and exit tasks. Our task-based lesson template considers lesson closure as an opportunity to make the mathematics that students learn visible. The chapter suggests teaching strategies to involve students in sharing their work and learning from each other. Finally, the chapter discusses the importance of taking time to reflect on the planning and implementation of each *doing-math task* lesson.

Chapters 4–15 are chock-full of 54 rich, *doing-math tasks* that your students will want to engage in as they make sense of the mathematics they are learning. The tasks provided address important mathematics standards within the content strands appropriate for Grades 4 and 5 and are presented using the task-based lesson template discussed earlier and described in Chapters 2 and 3.

Finally, Chapter 16, titled Your Turn, is your opportunity to reflect on what *you* have learned, review the tasks you have implemented, and explore recommendations for selecting, adapting, and creating tasks in the future. The chapter also examines responses to a sampling of frequently asked questions teachers have when teaching with mathematics tasks.

Well, let's move on! Get ready for some lively, cooperative, mathematical discussions that are sure to reveal your students' unique and powerful mathematical insights as you and they become immersed in *doing-math tasks*.

Acknowledgments

From Beth McCord Kobett: It is an impossible task to describe my gratitude to the people who have supported and lifted me up to do things that I never thought I could do, but here it goes.... I am forever grateful to my husband, Tim, who from the beginning has patiently supported and championed my interests and passion for education. My deep appreciation to our daughters, Hannah and Jenna, for their enduring love and support. To an incredible author team, I express my gratitude to Skip and Karen, for anchoring this project with their marvelous wisdom and expertise, and to Delise and Sorsha for their diligence and brilliance in making this work come alive. To my preservice teachers, graduates, and colleagues, I am in constant awe of your dedication, creativity, and passion for teaching and learning—thank you for inspiring me every day.

From Francis (Skip) Fennell: To Nita, Brett, Heather, and Stacey for all of the support and patience! And to all of my former students and colleagues at McDaniel College, thanks for regularly providing me with the support, feedback, and opportunity to, I hope, make a difference. I would also like to thank all co-authors, with particular thanks to Dr. Beth Kobett for her vision and diligence related to the importance of defining and implementing *doing-math tasks* lessons.

From Karen S. Karp: I wish to thank the coauthors of this book from whom I have learned a great deal throughout the writing process. I especially would like to thank Beth Kobett for inviting me to participate and being our courageous leader.

From Delise Andrews: I wish to thank Dr. Beth Kobett for inspiring this work and giving me the opportunity to be a part of it; Ms. Sally Dunham, who taught me everything I know about teaching; Dr. Matt Larson and Dr. Jim Lewis, both pivotal mentors to me in mathematics education; and most of all my parents, Jerry and Kay Andrews, who faithfully trained me up in the way I should go.

From Sorsha-Maria T. Mulroe: I wish to thank the students, families, and staff at Running Brook Elementary school, who are an honor to serve each and every day; Dr. Beth Kobett and Dr. Skip Fennell for cultivating my knowledge and agency as a mathematics coach; Dr. Frank Lyman for nurturing my understanding of collaborative learning; my parents Jolyon and Carmen Tiglao for love and support my husband Kevin Mulroe for stretching my mind and letting me dream; and my daughters Alexa and Bella who energize, inspire, and fill me with pride.

From the authors: We are very thankful for our publisher at Corwin, Erin Null. She championed this work many years ago when this project was just a nub of an idea. Erin's superhero ability to first navigate hefty, somewhat unformed ideas and target what is practical and thoughtful with a laser-like focus is truly a marvelous talent to behold. We also want to thank Jessica Vidal for her enduring commitment and devotion to transmitting this book from start to finish and making the work shine. To the entire Corwin team, we thank you for your careful eyes and hands each step of the way.

We are grateful to students, teachers, and families everywhere who show up to learn and teach mathematics in an uncertain world. We hope that you will take a moment to celebrate the brilliance and strengths that each of you hold individually and collectively.

Publisher's Acknowledgments

Corwin gratefully acknowledges the contributions of the following reviewers:

Karla Bandemer
Grades 3–5 Mathematics Teacher Leader
Lincoln Public School
Lincoln, Nebraska

Nicole Bell
Teacher
Canada

Cheryl Berkuta
RTI Interventionist
Old Bridge Township Pubic Schools
Monroe Township, New Jersey

Lynn Mitzel
Secondary Mathematics Teacher/Instructional Coach
West Fargo, North Dakota

Bronwyn Papasideris
Mathematics Learning Coordinator K–8
Thames Valley District School Board
London, Ontario, Canada

Oliver Woollett
Elementary School Teacher
St. Leonard's College Melbourne
Melbourne, Victoria, Australia

About the Authors

Beth McCord Kobett is professor in the School of Education at Stevenson University, where she teaches and supports early childhood, elementary, and middle preservice teachers in mathematics education. She is a former classroom teacher, elementary mathematics specialist, adjunct professor, and university supervisor. Beth also serves as the Director of the First Year Seminar program at Stevenson University. She is currently serving a three-year term as an elected Board Member for the National Council of Teachers of Mathematics and was the former president of the Association of Maryland Mathematics Teacher Educators (AMMTE). She is a recipient of the Mathematics Educator of the Year Award from the Maryland Council of Teachers of Mathematics (MCTM) and the Johns Hopkins University Distinguished Alumni Award. Beth also received Stevenson University's Rose Dawson Award for Excellence in Teaching as both an adjunct and a full-time faculty member. She believes in fostering a strengths-building community with her students and strives to make her classroom space inviting, facilitate lessons that spark curiosity and innovation, and invite positive productive struggle. Beth is a coauthor of *Strengths-Based Teaching and Learning in Mathematics: 5 Teaching Turnarounds for Grades K–6*; *Formative 5: Everyday Assessment Techniques for Every Math Classroom*; and The Mathematics Lesson-Planning Handbook Series for Grades K–2, 3–5, and 6–8.

Francis (Skip) Fennell is emeritus as the L. Stanley Bowlsbey Professor of Education and Graduate and Professional Studies at McDaniel College in Maryland, where he also directed the Elementary Mathematics Specialists and Teacher Leaders Project. He is a former classroom teacher, principal, and supervisor of instruction and is past president of the Association of Mathematics Teacher Educators (AMTE), the Research Council on Mathematics Learning (RCML), and the National Council of Teachers of Mathematics (NCTM). He is a recipient of the Mathematics Educator of the Year Award from the Maryland Council of Teachers of Mathematics (MCTM), the Glenn Gilbert National Leadership Award from the National Council of Supervisors of Mathematics (NCSM), the Excellence in Leadership and Service in Mathematics Teacher Education Award from the Association of Mathematics Teacher Educators (AMTE), the James W. Heddens Distinguished Service Award from the Research Council on Mathematics Learning (RCML), and the Lifetime Achievement Award from the Maryland Council of Teachers of Mathematics (MCTM) and the National Council of Teachers of Mathematics (NCTM). In 2018, he received an honorary Doctor of Humane Letters degree from McDaniel College.

Karen S. Karp has been a professor in the EdD program in the School of Education at Johns Hopkins University since 2015. Previously, she was a professor of mathematics education in the Department of Early and Elementary Childhood Education at the University of Louisville where she received the Distinguished Teaching Award and the Distinguished Service Award for a Career of Service. She is the author or coauthor of approximately 23 book chapters, 50 articles, and 40 books, including *Strengths-Based Teaching and Learning in Mathematics: 5 Teaching Turnarounds for Grades K–6*; *Elementary and Middle School Mathematics: Teaching Developmentally*; *Student Centered Mathematics*; and *Developing Essential Understanding of Addition and Subtraction for Teaching Mathematics*. She is also a member of the author panel for the updated What Works Clearinghouse Practice Guide *Assisting Students Struggling With Mathematics: Intervention in the Elementary and*

Middle School Grades for the U.S. Department of Education Institute of Science. She is a former member of the board of directors of the National Council of Teachers of Mathematics (NCTM) and a former president of the Association of Mathematics Teacher Educators. Recently, she received the Lifetime Achievement Award from the National Council of Teachers of Mathematics. She holds teaching certifications in elementary education, secondary mathematics, and K–12 special education.

Delise Andrews is the 3–5 Mathematics Coordinator for Lincoln Public Schools in Lincoln, Nebraska. During her career, she has worked in both rural and urban districts and has taught mathematics to students at every age from kindergarten through the eighth grade, undergraduate math methods, and graduate-level courses for teachers of mathematics. Delise is a recipient of the Presidential Award for Excellence in Mathematics and Science Teaching and a Robert Noyce Master Teaching Fellow. She is also an active member of NCTM, serving as a past member and chair of the Professional Development Services Committee, member of regional conference committees and chair of the St. Louis annual conference committee, and an NCTM Professional Services facilitator.

Sorsha-Maria T. Mulroe is a mathematics coach at Running Brook Elementary School in Howard County, Maryland. She is nationally board certified in mathematics: early adolescence. Prior to her current role, Sorsha served as a fourth- and fifth-grade Gifted and Talented Resource Teacher and also a second- and third-grade classroom teacher. She has two years' experience teaching overseas in Alexandria, Egypt. She was selected to be part of the visioning and development panel for the NAEP Mathematics Framework, 2025.

Doing-Math Tasks

What Are They, Why Are They Important, and How Do I Plan for Implementation?

In this chapter, you will explore the idea of *doing-math tasks* and their importance in an instructional model that includes engaging, high cognitive demand tasks as part of your overall mathematics teaching. By the end of this chapter, you will

- Understand the need for and importance of *doing-math tasks*

- Explore how *doing-math tasks* increase your students' mathematical understandings

- Explore the research behind selecting and implementing mathematics tasks

As students learn mathematics, they must be actively involved in learning experiences that both challenge and engage them. The work students do—which is, in practice, defined by the *tasks* teachers assign—determines how they think about solving problems. This level of engagement is how they come to understand concepts and ideas; it's how they give meaning to mathematics. But tasks are essentially how we would want to picture students actually "doing math," right? We want to see students truly engaged in activities—every day—that help them to connect with concepts and skills and deepen their understanding of the mathematics they are learning. One way to do this is by providing experiences that develop the learner's ability to apply their mathematical knowledge in novel problem-based settings, a life skill expected of 21st century learners (National Research Council, 2012). Such learning opportunities are best supported with what we, in this book, describe as *doing-math tasks*. Stated briefly, *doing-math tasks* require your students to explore yet also to self-monitor their thinking as they mentally retrieve prior instructional experiences while working through a task. And yes, such

> **The ways students think about solving problems are governed by the tasks we assign.**

> **Doing-math tasks** require your students to explore yet also to self-monitor their thinking as they mentally retrieve prior instructional experiences while working through a task.

tasks should challenge and involve your students in relevant contexts (National Council of Teachers of Mathematics [NCTM], 1991; Smith & Stein, 1998). The classroom environment where students are *doing math* by engaging in meaningful tasks is anchored in the critical role of teachers in creating, locating, and implementing them. We'll explore the elements of such tasks in more depth and demonstrate how this book supports your role in becoming a connoisseur and developer of high-quality tasks yourself. Then we will share an amazing collection of tasks that will absorb your students in regularly *doing math!*

Here's the challenge. *Doing-math tasks* are typically not what you may find in your school's prescribed set of mathematical instructional materials, which is why this book's focus on *doing-math tasks* is so important. *Doing-math tasks* require student exploration. They help students develop and implement solution strategies that draw on their prior knowledge and learning experiences and translate them into use for new situations (Smith & Stein, 1998). That said, let's consider the reality of the classroom. A recent RAND Corporation study of 2,873 U.S. teachers found that almost 100% reported that they used instructional materials "I developed and/or selected myself" (Opfer et al., 2017). Such curation of curriculum from a wide array of resources can actually result in entirely different lessons within the same grade, certainly a potential for curricular confusion, as well as a possibly mismatched set of mathematical progressions across an entire school. In addition, the online or print gathering of a self-selected collection of lessons is certainly not a reliable path to a clear, cohesive, or equitable instructional plan. This concern is addressed very directly within NCTM's (2020) *Catalyzing Change in Early Childhood and Elementary Mathematics* document:

> The danger of teachers creating their own daily lessons with instructional resources found at random through search engines is that mathematics topics are treated as isolated containers of ideas to master in a lesson or to experience through a "fun" activity. The likely result is instruction that is not deep, coherent, or aligned with a carefully crafted developmental learning sequence. The progressive nature of mathematics learning demands coherent instructional experiences that build and connect to one another, which is best accomplished through high-quality mathematics instructional materials. (p. 39)

Like you, we recognize the importance of students being engaged in doing the mathematics they are learning. We also know that locating, developing or adapting, planning for, and implementing such *doing-math tasks* can be a daunting and time-consuming task on top of all the other subject areas you are planning for. If you are one of the hundreds of thousands of elementary classroom teachers who spend hours searching online for truly engaging mathematics activities or if you want to differentiate more to meet the needs of your students or if you fret over the fact that you simply *don't have the time* to do all "this"—this book's for you! The mathematical tasks presented in Chapters 4 through 15 are intended to be integral elements of mathematics lessons at the grade levels you teach. These task-based lessons are neither intended to replace your major curriculum resources—textbook or otherwise—nor to be used every day, but they are intended to be "distinctive tasks" that will engage your students as they explore, understand, analyze, apply, and yes, more than occasionally, productively struggle while they truly are *doing mathematics*.

> In this book, you will find fifty-four 4th- and 5th-grade tasks with accompanying resources.

What Is a *Doing-Math Task?*

Long-term research about the use of well-designed mathematical tasks as an important component of mathematics classroom or schoolwide instruction led to the development of an influential guide for evaluating the quality of such tasks (Figure 1.1) This guide, designed by Smith and Stein (1998, p. 110), outlines characteristics of effective tasks on a continuum from low-level cognitive demand to high-level cognitive demand.

Figure 1.1 Mathematics Task Analysis Guide

Level of Demands

Lower-level demands (memorization):

- Involve either reproducing previously learned facts, rules, formulas, or definitions or committing facts, rules, formulas, or definitions to memory

- Cannot be solved using procedures because a procedure does not exist or because the time frame in which the task is being completed is too short to use a procedure

- Are not ambiguous. Such tasks involve the exact reproduction of previously seen material, and what is to be reproduced is clearly and directly stated.

- Have no connection to the concept or meaning that underlies the facts, rules, formulas, or definitions being learned or reproduced

Lower-level demands (procedures without connections):

- Are algorithmic. Use of the procedure either specifically called for or evident from prior instruction, experience, or placement of the task.

- Require limited cognitive demand for successful completion. Little ambiguity about what needs to be done and how to do it.

- Have no connection to the concepts or meanings that underlie the procedure being used

- Are focused on producing correct answers instead of on developing mathematical understanding

- Require no explanations or explanations that focus solely on describing the procedure used

Higher-level demands (procedures with connections):

- Focus students' attention on the use of procedures for the purpose of developing deeper levels of understanding of mathematical concepts and ideas

- Suggest explicitly or implicitly pathways to follow that are broad general procedures that have close connections to underlying conceptual ideas as opposed to narrow algorithms that are opaque with respect to underlying concepts

- Usually are presented in multiple ways, such as visual diagrams, manipulatives, symbols, and problem situation. Making connections among multiple representations helps develop meaning.

- Require some degree of cognitive effort. Although general procedures may be followed, they cannot be followed mindlessly. Students need to engage with conceptual ideas that underlie the procedures to complete the task successfully and that develop understanding.

Higher-level demands (doing mathematics):

- Require complex and nonalgorithmic thinking—a predictable, well-rehearsed approach or pathway is not explicitly suggested by the task, task instructions, or a worked-out example

- Require students to explore and understand the nature of mathematical concepts, processes, or relationships

- Demand self-monitoring or self-regulation of one's own cognitive processes

- Require students to access relevant knowledge and experiences and make appropriate use of them in working through the task

- Require students to analyze the task and actively examine task constraints that may limit possible solution strategies and solutions

- Require considerable cognitive effort and may involve some level of anxiety for the student because of the unpredictable nature of the solution process required

Source: These characteristics are derived from the work of Doyle on academic tasks (1988) and Resnick on high-level-thinking skills (1987), the *Professional Standards for Teaching Mathematics* (NCTM, 1991), and on the examination and categorization of hundreds of tasks used in QUASAR class-rooms (Stein, Clover, and Henningsen, 1996a; Stein, Lane, & Silver, 1996).

Here are examples of a task in each level of demand category at the 4th- and 5th-grade levels (Fennell et al., 2017):

Lower-level demands – Memorization

- *Grades 4–5: What is the formula for the area of a rectangle?*

Lower-level demands – Procedures Without Connections

- *Grades 4–5:* $\frac{3}{4} + \frac{1}{2} = ?$

Higher-level demands – Procedures With Connections

- *Grades 4–5: Use a number line to show* $\frac{1}{4} \times \frac{1}{2} = ?$

Higher-level demands – Doing-Mathematics

- *Grades 4–5: Create a word problem for the following:* 6×0.25 *Solve the problem. Then be prepared to discuss how you might solve the problem using mental math.*

> **Your conscious decision-making about the tasks you select and use in the mathematics classroom makes a demonstrable difference in student learning!**

Your conscious decision-making about the tasks you select and use in the mathematics classroom makes a demonstrable difference in student learning! Your choice of high-quality tasks and implementation using high-quality instructional strategies results in high student learning gains (Stein & Lane, 1996), as seen in Figure 1.2.

Figure 1.2 Eventual Learning Results of Differing Levels of Task Quality and Implementation

Task Quality	Implementation	Results
Low	High or low	Low
High	Low	Moderate
High	High	High

Source: Kobett, B. & Karp, K. (2020). *Strengths-based Teaching and Learning in Mathematics: 5 Teaching Turnarounds for Grades K-6.* Newbury Park, CA: Corwin and Reston, VA: NCTM.

When you expect to regularly implement high-level tasks, the quality of the task is important. Similarly, the actual classroom implementation of a high-quality, *doing-math* task is of related consequence. For example, if the task is of low quality the results will be low, regardless of how masterful your instruction is. By low-quality tasks, we mean reduced cognitive demand, which is potentially watered down, focused on memory or procedures, and generally lacking connections to important ideas. Low implementation means there is little questioning, a lack of attention to students sharing their thinking, and a surface level of attention to developing the mathematical meaning. Similarly, you can have a high-quality task combined with low implementation, which also doesn't produce what you want. The highest-level results come from the combination of a high-level task and high-level implementation. So what do teachers who are using high-level tasks with high-level implementation "look and act like?" These teachers

- ask questions that have an elevated cognitive demand,

- promote both student-to-teacher discourse as well as student-to-student discussion,

- arrange students in groups to compare solution strategies, and

- make the mathematics evident and visible by using their students' own mathematics thinking to advance their students' understanding.

But let's be cautious. Stein et al. (1996) suggest that sometimes with the best intentions, we think the ideal approach to implementing a challenging task might be to reduce the cognitive demand. This approach can sometimes inadvertently result in overexplaining, focusing on procedures without emphasizing their meaning, jumping in to demonstrate or model for students before they have opportunities to fully explore the problem, or dissecting a task into such small bits that the larger task vanishes. Situating students as "thinkers" as well as "doers" during lesson implementation creates an environment that promotes success and likewise positions students' strengths as the forefront of task design. That's precisely what the tasks in this book are positioned to do.

> "Situating students as "thinkers" as well as "doers" during lesson implementation creates an environment that promotes success and likewise positions students' strengths as the forefront of task design."

WHY IS THE SELECTION OF HIGHER LEVEL *DOING-MATH TASKS* IMPORTANT?

The first step in this process is the selection of these higher-level tasks, so let's look at why that is of great consequence. Figure 1.3 breaks down the research on how effective use of *doing-math tasks* is both as a curricular and an instructional essential. Then it describes the implications to consider as we plan for and implement these tasks, including specific examples from the tasks in this book.

Figure 1.3 From Research to Practical Examples

Research	Classroom Implication	Task Examples
Student learning of mathematics is greatest in classroom settings where the tasks encourage high-level student thinking and reasoning. The learning is least in classrooms where the tasks are typically procedural (Boaler & Staples, 2008; Hiebert & Wearne, 1993; Stein & Lane, 1996).	This finding validates the importance of selecting mathematical tasks that challenge your students. The tasks provided in this book are, very deliberately, designed to engage your students in *doing mathematics* at a high level of challenge.	In Task 28, **Artistic Arrangements** (p. 154), students explain their understanding using a area model. The task is clear yet open-ended and prompts students to apply their understanding to create original designs. *Mr. Pica's 4th-grade art class is learning about the use of positive and negative space in art. Their assignment is to cover $\frac{3}{4}$ of the area of the square below, using it as their positive space (main focus of a picture). They need to leave the rest of the area blank for their negative space (background).* *Complete Mr. Pica's assignment using your choice of colors. You may add additional lines and shapes inside the square to suit your design. You must explain how the positive space in your artwork is equivalent to $\frac{3}{4}$ of the whole area of the art using words, pictures, and equations.*

(Continued)

Figure 1.3 (Continued)

Research	Classroom Implication	Task Examples
Tasks should vary in opportunities for student thinking and learning (Hiebert et al., 1996; Stein et al., 2009).	Each task you locate, create, or adapt is perceived differently by the intended audience—your students. So when considering access and equity for each and every child, you want to provide relevant and sometimes modified tasks tailored specifically to student needs without reducing the rich features of the task. Modifications could include changing contexts to reflect students' experiences, using sentence stems to support language access, and providing choice of solution pathways.	In Task 7, **Rectangle Relay** (p. 74), students are strategically grouped to see how prime and composite numbers are different and why the number 1 is neither prime nor composite. Students will also engage in multiple opportunities to apply the commutative property of multiplication. Collaborative tasks like this one encourage multilingual learners to discuss the task and represent their understanding using visual representations. *Create a poster showing area models representing all possible rectangles for a given area from 1 square unit ($1u^2$) to 100 square units ($100u^2$). Analyze patterns in the resulting collections of rectangles.*
Mathematical tasks should promote and challenge thinking. This expectation often makes higher-level cognitive demand tasks more intensive to plan for and implement (Smith & Stein, 2018; Stein et al., 1996; Stigler & Hiebert, 2004).	High-demand tasks may take more time to implement. Because these tasks often involve using procedures with connections and they may include use of new instructional tools and different mathematical representations, plan for them to take the majority of your daily mathematics instructional time.	In Task 12, **The Sequence Game** (p. 95), students work collaboratively to find the relationships between the students' patterns and use reasoning to justify their solution pathways. *Kay and Jerry were playing a game making number sequences. Kay and Jerry decided to start both of their sequences with the number 10. Then Kay used the rule "add 5" to build her sequence and Jerry used the rule "add 8" to build his sequence. Kay noticed a relationship between the two lists. She said that the next number in Jerry's sequence would be 15 more than the next number in Kay's sequence.* **Kay's sequence:** 10, 15, 20, 25, 30, (rule: add 5) **Jerry's sequence:** 10, 18, 26, 34, 42, (rule: add 8) *Do you agree with Kay? What pattern do you think she noticed?*

Reflect

1. As you read the research, classroom implications, and examples, what resonated with you? Why?

2. When you think about the phrase *doing mathematics* as specifically applied to 4th- and 5th-grade students, what does it mean to you?

3. How do you address student access to mathematics learning? Ask yourself:

   - How can this task be accessed by each of my students?

   - Will this task fully engage each of my students in *doing math*? Consider the students' strengths and needs.

   - What are the task's entry points for my students?

4. What issues do you face as you plan for and implement mathematics tasks with a high cognitive demand?

How Do I Plan to Implement a *Doing-Math Task*?

As you recognize the importance of *doing-math tasks* that truly engage your students, the question of "How do I do this—more frequently?" logically emerges. One teacher told us this: *I understand the importance of mathematics tasks but wonder how I can literally "find" such tasks on a regular basis.* Fortunately, we have written an entire book of tasks that address important mathematics topics in 4th and 5th grade. But if you still find yourself tempted to hunt for more, there are several steps to finding and selecting—or adapting—and then implementing these kinds of tasks. The first two steps go hand-in-hand and must happen concurrently.

SELECTING THE TASK

First, let's consider the following decision points around task selection. These choices include answering the questions in Figure 1.4.

Figure 1.4 Making Decisions About Task Selection

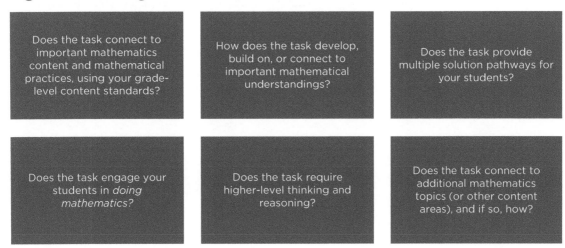

Next, consider how you would answer the following questions as you prepare to implement the task in your classroom (Figure 1.5).

Figure 1.5 Task Implementation

How will you position the task within a lesson? How much time is needed for your students to engage with the task during the lesson's launch, for your facilitation of the task experience, and for the lesson's close?	How and when will students use different representations (e.g., physical, pictorial, symbolic) as they engage in the task?	How and when will you make the mathematics visible by explicitly connecting student representations and other examples of student work to the task?

How will students present their solution strategies and the task's actual solution(s)?	How and when will you build in feedback to students regarding their performance on the task?

Summing Up

Mathematical tasks that engage students in actually *doing math* provide reasoning and problem-solving opportunities that are integral to the development of student thinking and understanding. Such high-level or *doing-math tasks* must become everyday opportunities for all students.

Where are we in the process and what's next? This chapter began by noting the importance of mathematical tasks, considered the levels of demand of mathematics tasks and research findings on the need for their use, and in particular highlighted this book's specific area of focus: *doing-math tasks*. You reviewed important considerations related to the use of math tasks, instructionally. Finally, you examined classroom implications and challenges related to your selection and implementation of *doing-math tasks*. This chapter's focus on defining the importance of *doing-math tasks* and presenting considerations for their use naturally leads to the intent of the next chapter (Chapter 2), which focuses on a careful consideration of the elements of our task-based instructional model, and Chapter 3, which zeroes in on the implementation of the *doing-math tasks* we have provided.

> In the tasks we have created for this book, we have designed structures that address these important selection and implementation questions, but you may still need to ask yourself how these structures and questions fit into your classroom environment. Chapters 2 and 3 consider task selection and implementation in more depth. Chapter 16 explores options for adjusting or adapting the tasks to fit the specific needs of your students.

Professional Learning/Discussion Questions

Read and discuss the following questions with your grade-level teaching team or with teams across multiple grade levels.

- In your own words describe the benefits of engaging your students in high cognitive demand mathematics tasks.

- What is most important to consider as you select/create and implement a mathematics task in your classroom?

- How do you find the mathematics tasks that you currently use in your classroom?

- What is a *doing-math task*?

- What concerns you about locating, creating, or adapting mathematics tasks?

- What is the importance of your whole grade level or school using *doing-math tasks* as a team effort?

Laying the Groundwork for Teaching With *Doing-Math Tasks*

In the first chapter, we explored what a mathematics task is and what it means when students are thoughtfully and meaningfully engaged in mathematics learning through the use of targeted tasks that align with mathematics standards. In this chapter, we will walk further down that path through some of the foundational elements that need to be in place in order for *doing-math task*-based instruction to meet its maximum potential. We will introduce and familiarize you with the components of the task template we use throughout the book to present the *doing-math tasks*. For this chapter, we explore all of the components that you will need to know to prepare to teach a *doing-math task*. Later, in Chapter 3, you will learn all about the components that have to do with implementing a *doing-math task*. In this chapter, you will

- Explore mathematics content through grade-level standards and the mathematical practices and processes

- Understand the important role of mathematics vocabulary for students to know or develop

- Explore how lessons and materials based on *doing-math tasks* support students in representing their mathematical thinking

- Unpack task preparation by investigating the importance of strategically grouping students for *doing-math tasks* and establishing group and classroom norms

- Determine how attention to access and equity, productive struggle, alternate learning environments, and student strengths spotting is addressed in the mathematics tasks

Once you move into Part 2 of this book, you will find 54 *doing-math tasks* reflecting important mathematics topics and standards that are central for Grades 4 and 5.

Effective Mathematics Teaching Practices

We can't consider the selection of mathematics tasks or begin to think through their implementation without first looking at the importance of specific teaching practices that have the potential to make a difference in students' learning and performance. This emphasis is needed because student learning of mathematics "depends fundamentally on what happens inside the classroom as teachers and learners interact over the curriculum" (Ball & Forzani, 2011a, p. 17). These "high-leverage" practices (Ball & Forzani, 2011b), reconceptualized in the National Council of Teachers of Mathematics' (NCTM's) *Principles to Actions* (2014b) as Effective Teaching Practices (Figure 2.1), are research-informed practices that promote students' mathematical learning. The NCTM Effective Teaching Practices guided the development of the tasks and the task-based lesson format used in this book.

> In this book, several components of the mathematics teaching practices are integral to each of the tasks and task-based lessons.

Figure 2.1 NCTM's Effective Mathematics Teaching Practices

Effective Mathematics Teaching Practices	
Establish mathematics goals to focus learning.	Effective teaching of mathematics establishes clear goals for the mathematics that students are learning, situates goals within learning progressions, and uses the goals to guide instructional decisions.
Implement tasks that promote reasoning and problem-solving.	Effective teaching of mathematics engages students in solving and discussing tasks that promote mathematical reasoning and problem-solving and allow multiple entry points and varied solution strategies.
Use and connect mathematical representations.	Effective teaching of mathematics engages students in making connections among mathematical representations to deepen understanding of mathematics concepts and procedures and as tools for problem solving.
Facilitate meaningful mathematical discourse.	Effective teaching of mathematics facilitates discourse among students to build shared understanding of mathematical ideas by analyzing and comparing student approaches and arguments.
Pose purposeful questions.	Effective teaching of mathematics uses purposeful questions to assess and advance students' reasoning and sense making about important mathematical ideas and relationships.
Build procedural fluency from conceptual understanding.	Effective teaching of mathematics builds fluency with procedures on a foundation of conceptual understanding so that students, over time, become skillful in using procedures flexibly as they solve contextual and mathematical problems.
Support productive struggle in learning mathematics.	Effective teaching of mathematics consistently provides students, individually and collectively, with opportunities and supports to engage in productive struggle as they grapple with mathematical ideas and relationships.
Elicit and use evidence of student thinking.	Effective teaching of mathematics uses evidence of student thinking to assess progress toward mathematical understanding and to adjust instruction continually in ways that support and extend learning.

Source: National Council of Teachers of Mathematics. (2014b). *Principles to Actions: Ensuring Mathematical Success for All*. Reston, VA: Author.

To learn more about the mathematics teaching practices and standards for mathematics practices, check out the following resources:

 CHECK THESE OUT

Principles to Actions: Ensuring Mathematical Success for All   NCTM (2014b)
Principles to Actions: Professional Learning Toolkit Sources   www.nctm.org/PtAToolkit/   NCTM (2017b)
Taking Action: Implementing Effective Mathematics Teaching Practices in Grades 6–8   NCTM (2017d)
Routines for Reasoning: Fostering the Mathematical Practices in all Students   Kelemanik and Lucenta (2016)
Putting the Practices Into Action: Implementing the Common Core Standards for Mathematical Practice, K–8   O'Connell and SanGiovanni (2013)
Beyond Answers: Exploring Mathematical Practices With Young Children   Flynn (2017)

Now that we have explored the critical elements for developing powerful mathematics teaching and learning experiences, let's take a look at how the *doing-math tasks* template is designed for you to begin task implementation right away. We will explore the first half of the *doing-math task* template (see Figure 2.2), which includes the following:

- Mathematics Standard(s)

- Mathematical Practice(s)

- Task

- Vocabulary

- Materials

- Task Preparation

The second half of the *doing-math task* focuses on implementing and reflecting on the task, which we explore in depth in Chapter 3.

Figure 2.2 Components of the *Doing-Math Task*

Grade Level

Task Title

Task Topic

Mathematics Standard(s):	
Mathematical Practice(s):	
Task	
Vocabulary	Materials
Task Preparation:	
Launch:	
Facilitate:	
Close: Make the Math Visible	
Post-Task Notes: Reflection & Next Steps	

online resources This online resource can be found in Appendix A and is available for download at **resources.corwin.com/ClassroomReadyMath/4-5**

What's the Mathematics Standard?

The mathematics focus we highlight here incorporates the mathematics content standard(s) and practices or processes that define students' expectations at each grade level. Whether your state relies on the Common Core State Standards for Mathematics (CCSS-M), an adapted version, or mathematics standards unique to your state, the large majority of states use a collection of standards grounded in research-based learning progressions that highlight what is known about how students develop mathematical knowledge, skills, and understandings. Regardless of each state's mathematics standards, using mathematics content and practice or process standards to drive curriculum and instruction represents a renewed focus on strategies for teaching that cross specific topics or big ideas. This emphasis within each grade level allows teachers to cohesively deepen the way they use their time and energy in the classroom. Teachers are central to students' success: "Teachers need to understand the big ideas of mathematics and be able to represent important mathematical topics as coherent and connected" (NCTM, 2000, p. 17).

> " Teachers are central to students' success. "

The dual use of our language for the Standards for Mathematical Practices (SMPs) and the mathematical processes allows us to be inclusive of many states who have made different decisions along the way. Here we focus on how mathematical practices and processes align so you can make informed decisions about using the tasks in this book. While the mathematics content standards focus on the important mathematics that students should learn, the NCTM (1989) process standards were developed first and then revised (2000) and draw attention to the idea that the implementation of the content is critical to developing students' mathematical understanding. The process standards (NCTM, 2000) are as follows:

1. **Problem Solving:** Students use a repertoire of skills and strategies for solving a variety of problems and situations.

2. **Reasoning and Proof:** Students apply inductive and deductive reasoning skills to make, test, and evaluate statements to justify steps in mathematical procedures.

3. **Communication:** Students use mathematical language, including terminology and symbols to express ideas precisely.

4. **Connection:** Students relate concepts and procedures from different topics in mathematics to one another and make connections between topics in mathematics and other disciplines.

5. **Representation:** Students use a variety of representations, including graphical, numerical, algebraic, verbal, and physical to represent, describe, and generalize.

The SMPs (National Governors Association & Council of Chief State School Officers, 2010) were heavily influenced by both the NCTM process standards and the strands of mathematical proficiency specified in *Adding It Up* (National Research Council, 2001). The following SMPs highlight the thinking processes, dispositions, or habits of mind that students should exhibit while engaging in mathematics learning experiences:

1. **Make sense of problems and persevere in solving them.** Students work to understand the information given in a problem and the question that is asked. They use a strategy to find a solution and check to make sure their answer makes sense.

2. **Reason abstractly and quantitatively.** Students make sense of quantities and their relationships in problem situations.

3. **Construct viable arguments and critique the reasoning of others.** Students explain their thinking, justify their conclusions, and communicate those conclusions both orally and in writing.

4. **Model with mathematics.** Students use and apply multiple representations, models, and symbols to make sense of the mathematics.

5. **Use appropriate tools strategically.** Students use a variety of concrete materials and tools to represent their thinking when solving problems.

6. **Attend to precision.** Students learn to communicate precisely with each other and explain their thinking using appropriate mathematical vocabulary.

7. **Look for and make use of structure.** Students look for and discover patterns and structure in their mathematics work.

8. **Look for and express regularity in repeated reasoning.** Students notice if calculations are repeated. Students use patterns to make generalizations.

> In this book, the mathematics content standards and SMPs (we know that those of you who use the process standards will be able to make the connections) have been identified for each mathematics task that is presented. However, you may want to consider and then select different SMPs that you feel need to be emphasized depending on the needs of your students. As you teach a task, you may want to ensure that the students are exhibiting these SMPs as they engage with the task.

The SMPs and the process standards are particularly important in task-based teaching; the expectation is that you want to teach mathematics by having students analyze relationships, communicate mathematical ideas by engaging in discourse, develop multiple solution pathways, articulate and justify their mathematical reasoning, and apply mathematics to real-world situations.

Vocabulary

The role of vocabulary in a mathematics lesson is quite unique to the mathematics classroom.

Mathematics vocabulary can be highly specialized, and students may encounter particular vocabulary only in a mathematics classroom because it is not likely to occur in everyday conversation. For example, think about the last time the word *radius* came up in casual conversation! Student success hinges on knowing and using academic vocabulary, so having only surface-level knowledge of vocabulary does not promote conceptual competence (Thompson & Rubenstein, 2000).

> **"** Student success hinges on knowing and using academic vocabulary. **"**

Instruction related to mathematics vocabulary requires special attention— different from the way vocabulary is taught in a reading lesson, which often focuses on direct instruction of word meanings before students read a passage or book. In mathematics, however, a focus on presenting the word first may lead to partial or even incorrect understandings. For example, Celena decided to pre-teach the definition of a *triangle* by showing a picture of a triangle (Figure 2.3) and stating, "A triangle is a shape with three sides and three angles."

Figure 2.3 Triangle

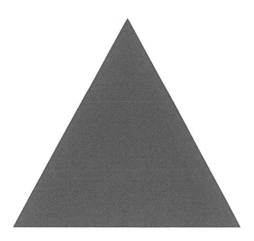

Later in the lesson when students were asked to sort triangles, many did not identify the shapes in Figure 2.4 as triangles because they "looked different" from the original example provided.

Figure 2.4 Set of Three Triangles

The next day, Celena decided to ask students to sort the triangles first and then develop a definition for a triangle using the students' experiences. The students constructed a class definition (Figure 2.5) that encompassed a variety of significant ideas.

Figure 2.5 Students' Ideas for a Triangle Definition

"The shape can be skinny or fat."

"The point on the triangle can point anywhere!"

"Three sides—but the sides don't all have to be the same."

While the student definitions are not standard textbook definitions, they do reflect their emerging understanding of the characteristics of the triangle and demonstrate how students exhibit SMP 6: Attend to precision. Mathematically proficient students try to communicate precisely to others. They try to use clear definitions in discussion with others and in their own reasoning (National Governor's Association & Council of Chief State School Officers, 2010).

In this book, important mathematics vocabulary is highlighted for all tasks. However, you know your students and your curriculum best and may want to loop in additional vocabulary. You can support students' building of mathematical vocabulary by asking them to explain their ideas throughout the lesson and, particularly, at the close of the task lesson as you are making the mathematics learning visible to the students. As your students develop new understandings within a task-based lesson, add new words and corresponding visual representations, student definitions, examples, and non-examples to an interactive mathematics word wall.

To learn more about developing mathematics vocabulary, check out the following resources:

CHECK THESE OUT

"Supporting Math Vocabulary Acquisition," *Teaching Children Mathematics*   Bay-Williams and Livers (2009)
The Math Pact, Elementary: Achieving Instructional Cohesion Within and Across Grades   Karp et al. (2021)
"Vocabulary Support: Constructing (Not Obstructing Meaning)," *Mathematics Teaching in the Middle School*   Livers and Bay-Williams (2014)
"'Weigh' to Go! Exploring Mathematical Language," *Mathematics Teaching in the Middle School*   Lott Adams et al. (2005)

Materials

Materials such as manipulatives, chart paper, technology, or other means to represent ideas central to a *doing-math task*-based lesson support students in developing their understanding throughout the instructional experience. These materials are key as they provide students with the tools to create a variety of ways to represent their thinking. When students can see the connections between multiple representations, it is a signal that their conceptual understanding is in place.

CHOOSING AND USING MULTIPLE REPRESENTATIONS

When choosing representations, consider the types of manipulatives (physical or digital), drawings, equations, tools, and other resources that you may need to support student learning. The primary reason for using multiple representations in the classroom is to help students understand and access abstract mathematics concepts through three fluid stages; concrete, semi-concrete, and abstract (CSA) (Dougherty et al., 2016; Heddens, 1986; Laski et al., 2015; Van de Walle et al., 2019). Representations such as manipulative materials, for example, help students understand new mathematics concepts because "they serve as analogies; the things manipulated are symbols for the new, to-be-understood idea" (Willingham, 2017, "Why Do Manipulatives Help?" para. 7). At first, this may seem contradictory to the idea that manipulatives are concrete, and therefore, learners will immediately be able to understand abstract ideas through the use of manipulatives. But as Ball (1992) stated in her classic article "Magical Hopes," there is an issue in believing that students immediately develop the ideas we hope they will from the use of manipulatives alone. The act of connecting CSA representations *together* is what can help students meaningfully associate a physical model to a visual representation of the mathematics situation *and* to the corresponding equation. The explicit linkages between these different representations in the CSA approach help develop students' mathematical ideas, and when students can articulate the relationships, this approach helps teachers know if the concept or procedure is understood.

> " **When students can articulate the concrete, semi-concrete, and abstract relationships, it reveals whether they understand the concept or procedure.** "

Teachers need to strategically plan for movement between the representations (Fyfe et al., 2014) to explain that mathematics instruction on a particular topic often begins with concrete manipulatives and then gently moves to a greater focus on just the abstract. However, we need to remember that we

In the tasks in this book, students are invited to use many different representations aligned with the CSA approach to represent mathematical ideas (e.g., regional fraction models, number lines, sketches, tables with numbers). As you plan for and prepare to teach the tasks, consider your students' needs and the suggested representations as you strategically select the most meaningful tools to develop important mathematical understandings throughout the lesson.

are asking students to use representations to represent ideas and integrate contexts within visuals, expressions, equations, and word problems. Teachers must strike a balance between ensuring that their students understand the purpose of the representation for the task but without being too rigid in how students use the representation (Carbonneau et al., 2013). So teachers might say, "Our task is about a quantity of markers. Consider using the base ten materials or cubes or drawings to represent the number of markers in the task."

To learn more about representations, check out the following resources:

🔍 CHECK THESE OUT

"Representation: An Important Process for Teaching and Learning Mathematics," *Teaching Children Mathematics*

Fennell and Rowan (2001)

"Star Students Make Connections: Discover Strategies to Engage Young Math Students in Competently Using Multiple Representations," *Teaching Children Mathematics*

Marshall et al. (2010)

"Facilitating Mathematical Practices Through Visual Representations," *Teaching Children Mathematics*

Murata and Stewart (2017)

Clothesline Math

clotheslinemath.com/

Shor (2017)

Teaching Student-Centered Mathematics: Developmentally Appropriate Instruction for Grades 3–5

Van de Walle et al. (2017)

The Mathematics Lesson Planning Handbook, Grades 3–5: Your Blueprint for Building Cohesive Lessons

Harbin Miles et al. (2018)

Task Preparation

All worthwhile lessons based on a task require some level of preparation! As a part of the hundreds of decisions you make each day, you decide on the materials and representations you will use to support your students as they develop mathematical understandings. You also decide how you will group your students to best highlight their learning strengths and needs and establish norms for how students will work together to use strategies and develop solution pathways.

GROUPING YOUR STUDENTS TO ENGAGE IN THE TASK

In the words of one of our preservice teachers, Em, "Grouping students without data is just crazy!" We won't waffle; we strongly recommend that you strategically arrange students in heterogeneous learning groups or groups based on varied strengths to engage in the book's tasks while you circulate to both observe and facilitate students' mathematical thinking and reasoning. We call this kind of instruction mixed-strength group instruction, meaning that the students are situated in a variety of small groups within the whole group and are instructed to complete the same or similar differentiated tasks while the teacher circulates the room, observes and facilitates thinking, and advances learning through probing questions (Kobett & Karp, 2020). During this time, students will have an opportunity to engage with partners or small groups throughout the lesson. Back to Em's point, however, teachers need to use data (see the section on Formative Assessment in Chapter 3, page 37) about what students already know about this topic and the solution pathways they tend to use to strategically assign students to work in pairs or small groups so that their individual strengths shine and, at the same time, support one another to reason about the mathematics they are learning.

In this book, you will find that we recommend pairs or small-group work for every task-based lesson! In preparing for the task work, consider taking Em's advice to strategically prepare student groups to solve tasks as you engage in the task preparation.

We are aware that many school districts across the country recommend or even require whole-class or targeted small-group homogeneous instruction. Research evidence demonstrates that the practice of fixed-ability grouping based on student performance—either in whole classrooms or in small groups—is not associated with increased student achievement (Ellis, 2008; Hattie, 2009; Yeh, 2019) and that students arranged into heterogeneous learning groups actually learn more and achieve at higher rates (Boaler, 2006).

To learn more about grouping students using mixed-ability strengths, check out the following resources:

🔍 CHECK THESE OUT

Strengths-Based Teaching and Learning in Mathematics: 5 Teaching Turnarounds for Grades K–6
Kobett and Karp (2020)

Reimagining the Mathematics Classroom: Creating and Sustaining Productive Learning Environments
Yeh et al. (2017)

SETTING NORMS FOR TASK-BASED WORK

The task-based lessons in this book require students to work positively and collaboratively to solve problems, share their own ideas, listen to the ideas of others, and offer thoughtful and helpful feedback that moves mathematical understanding forward. But the classroom must be set up for these behaviors to occur. Classroom and task-based norms are the behavioral and cognitive expectations, stated with positive strengths-based language, that promote equitable student participation. When teachers establish norms for task-based work, they help students to learn how to productively work together to engage in the mathematics. First, many teachers find it helpful to co-construct the norms with the students to develop ownership. Teachers can do this by asking students, "What does it look like and sound like when your group is working together to solve problems?" Second, it is essential to strategically teach the norms to students and allow them to reflect on how they are enacting those norms each day, even sometimes discussing or role-playing counterexamples. Some of the norms can be used universally for group work when students are sharing their ideas whereas other norms are specific to mathematics task work. Note how the Mathematics Task Norms in Figure 2.6 reflect the SMPs.

Figure 2.6 Developing Group and Task Norms

Universal Group Norms	Mathematics Task Norms
• We respect everyone's learning in our class. We do this by praising each other and helping each other.	• We talk about our mathematical thinking.
• We ask questions to understand ideas.	• We persevere when solving problems.
• We take turns when sharing ideas.	• We use multiple representations to show our understanding.
• We encourage each other to keep going by saying, "You can do this!"	• We use multiple strategies to solve problems.
• We make sure that everyone in the group participates.	• We use mathematics vocabulary.
• We listen to each other's ideas and give eye contact when they are explaining their ideas.	• We critique each other's thinking by asking, "How did you decide on that strategy?"
• We appreciate all ideas, even if we don't agree.	• We ask questions to make sense of the math we are learning. We say, "Why did you _____?" And "How did you _____?"
• We ask for help when we don't understand something.	
• We keep trying, even when we make mistakes.	

 Because the tasks in this book invite students to work in pairs or small groups, if your students don't regularly work together to solve problems or discuss their thinking in small-group and whole-class discussions, you may find it beneficial to develop the norms before introducing the task-based work. You should provide ample opportunities for students to reflect on how they used and applied the norms while solving problems.

To learn more about developing and using norms in your mathematics class, check out the following resources:

CHECK THESE OUT

Setting Up Positive Norms in Math Class
www.youcubed.org/wp-content/uploads/Positive-Classroom-Norms2.pdf
Boaler (2014)

Co-Creating Classroom Norms With Students
illustrativemathematics.blog/2019/08/02/co-creating-classroom-norms-with-students/
Illustrative Math (2019)

"Norms and Mathematical Proficiency," *Teaching Children Mathematics*
Kasberg and Frye (2013)

When we attend to the selection and implementation of tasks, we also need to make sure that we support students' access, promote productive struggle, consider alternate learning environments, and attend to students' strengths. Therefore, we have designated special places within a task's implementation to call attention to ways that you can promote these important teaching moves.

Student Considerations for Planning *Doing-Math Tasks*

Before we leave this chapter in which we unpacked the first half of this template, let's explore some important ideas and teaching moves that will enrich students' learning experiences while engaged in *doing-math tasks*. These will be highlighted throughout the tasks as appropriate:

- Access and Equity

- Productive Struggle

- Alternate Learning Environments

- Strengths Spotting

ACCESS AND EQUITY

Knowing your students is the first step in providing equitable learning opportunities and access to high-quality mathematics instruction. NCTM's (2014a) Access and Equity Position Statement states:

> Creating, supporting, and sustaining a culture of access and equity require being responsive to students' backgrounds, experiences, cultural perspectives, language, traditions, and knowledge when designing and implementing a mathematics program and assessing its effectiveness. Acknowledging and addressing factors that contribute to differential outcomes among groups of students are critical to ensuring that all students routinely have opportunities to experience high-quality mathematics instruction, learn challenging mathematics content, and receive the support necessary to be successful. Addressing equity and access includes both ensuring that all students attain mathematics proficiency and increasing the numbers of students from all racial, ethnic, linguistic, gender, and socioeconomic groups who attain the highest levels of mathematics achievement. (para. 1)

Without equal opportunities to access strong, thoughtful mathematics instruction, students' access to learning is limited. Students' learning challenges can be the result of our instructional challenges as we grapple with our teaching decisions regarding how to best meet our students' needs. Frankly, our beliefs about our students' learning potential influence how we plan, what we plan, the questions we ask, how and when we assess, and the feedback we provide. Simply put, we enact teaching that reflects what we believe. If we believe that our students possess deficits and will likely struggle, we may prevent them from engaging in high-quality instruction by reducing the rigor of the tasks we select and implement. Perhaps more concerning, we may break the task down into tiny, bite-size pieces in an effort to make the task accessible, which ultimately prevents our students' access to solve problems using deep mathematical thinking and may make it harder for them to put those pieces back together to see the bigger idea on their own. Our instruction needs to focus on teaching the way that students learn. Pedro Noguera powerfully states the following in an interview (Gonzalez, 2018, "Teach the Way Students Learn," para. 2):

> " We enact teaching that reflects what we believe. "

> Class time needs to be work time for kids.... It's only when they're working that a teacher can see who's getting it, who's not, who needs more support. We need to move away from a teacher-centered approach and move toward a student-centered approach. Kids learn through experience. Kids learn through mistakes. Kids learn by asking questions, through interaction. If we taught kids the way they actually learn, our classrooms would look very different than they do right now.

Instruction centered on rich, *doing-math tasks* does just that! NCTM defines equity-based mathematics teaching as the "practices that take into account the way(s) mathematics education perpetuates oppressive norms and therefore actively seeks to erase them, so that *all* students can

In this book, the tasks have been designed to promote access and equity for each and every student through designated opportunities marked with a special icon.

participate meaningfully in mathematics learning and create their own mathematical knowledge" (NCTM, 2020a, para 2). These teaching practices include reflecting, noticing, and engaging in a classroom community. Reflecting includes teachers' openness to cultures and perspective, awareness of personal culture, beliefs, and prior experiences, and commitment to Culturally Responsive Mathematics Teaching (NCTM, 2014a). Noticing and attending to your students' mathematical thinking promotes their belief that they are mathematical learners, which in turn promotes the positive development of their identities. Further, teachers can foster a positive and productive classroom community by facilitating rich student discourse where students can reason about mathematics and explain their thinking (Chapin & O'Connor, 2013) using home languages (Turner et al., 2013) and multiple forms of representation.

To learn more about providing access and equity for your students, check out the following resources:

CHECK THESE OUT

The Impact of Identity in K–8 Mathematics: Rethinking Equity-Based Practices   Aguirre et al. (2013)
Catalyzing Change in Early Childhood and Elementary Mathematics: Initiating Critical Conversations   NCTM (2020a)
Countering Deficit Myths of Students With Dis/Abilities and Conceptualizing Possibilities: A Culturally Responsive and Relational Approach to Mathematics   TODOS Live!   vimeo.com/353856573   Yeh (2019)
Rehumanizing Mathematics for Black, Indigenous, and Latinx Students   Goffney et al. (2018)

PRODUCTIVE STRUGGLE

Productive struggle in learning mathematics is the process of developing a positive, perseverant mindset for both approaching and pursuing solution pathways when solving problems. When students productively struggle through tasks, they apply prior learning to their new mathematical situations and persistently engage in higher-level thinking (Kapur, 2010). This idea of productive struggle is featured prominently in both the SMPs (National Governor's Association & Council of Chief State School Officers, 2010) and in the research-based teaching practices featured in *Principles to Actions* (NCTM, 2014b).

The first of the eight SMPs focuses on helping students *make sense of problems and persevere while solving them* (National Governor's Association & Council of Chief State School Officers, 2010). Students' opportunities to experience productive struggle depend, in large measure, on a teacher's instructional decisions. Students cannot develop the ability to productively struggle if they are not presented with consistent opportunities to engage thoughtfully, and yes, productively, when they are learning mathematics. Teachers cannot force students to productively struggle, but they *can* cultivate an environment that nurtures students' stamina and builds their tolerance for pushing through that uncomfortable feeling that materializes between not understanding and understanding. Facilitating productive struggle can be challenging for teachers because they may have been taught to "rescue" children, and this approach that encourages struggle initially may feel indifferent or uncaring. With a few simple moves, you can be on your way to developing a flourishing mathematics classroom environment where students routinely engage in productive struggle as they grow to greater independence (Figure 2.7).

Figure 2.7 Facilitating Productive Struggle

Productive Struggle Move	What Teachers Do	What Students Do
Provide a safe environment.	Co-create group norms with students.	Students ask questions to the teacher and one another, share ideas with their classmates as they solve problems, and encourage each other to try out new ideas and approaches.
Use *doing-math tasks*.	Select and adapt tasks that encourage multiple solution pathways.	Students don't immediately know how to solve a problem or task. They try different strategies and revisit the task to make sense of the problem.
Offer flexible thinking opportunities.	Encourage multiple solution pathways and the use of multiple representations. Ask questions such as, "What might be another way to solve this task?" and "What other representations will help you understand this problem?"	Students use multiple strategies to flexibly solve problems. They select and apply representations by attending to the types of problems in the task.
Create a strengths-based classroom.	Celebrate students' strengths and successes.	Students know their strengths and use these assets to solve problems and support their classmates in the problem-solving process.

The opposite of the disposition of productive struggle is one of destructive struggle, which is when students are in a negative cycle and can't move past their frustration or through feelings of helplessness. Some indicators that students are in a destructive cycle include the following:

- Disengaging in the task by not participating or physically showing signs of giving up

- Choosing an alternate activity that is off task

- Retreating and getting quiet, avoiding the teacher's gaze

- Expressing frustration or anger at the task, other students, or the teacher

Your role as a teacher is critical for turning this destructive cycle around; you "greatly influence how students perceive and approach struggle in the mathematics classroom" (NCTM, 2014b, p. 50). Instead, select and adapt tasks that will target that special space of harmonious balance where students are free to persevere and take risks—a place where they want to work hard. Support your students' move away from any form of destructive struggle and instead consistently point to productive struggle by trying these teacher moves (Figure 2.8).

Figure 2.8 Language to Move Students Toward Productive Struggle

Moving Students Toward Productive Struggle →	
Acknowledge your students' feelings while they are learning mathematics.	"I see you are not sure where to start. What have you thought about trying?"
Name perseverance when observed.	"I see you tried three strategies to solve the task, Jenna. You are showing perseverance and flexibility by trying new strategies."
Promote collaboration among students.	"I see you are having trouble getting started on this task. Who would you like to work with?"
Explain that being good in mathematics is about problem solving rather than getting answers quickly.	"I know we sometimes feel like we should solve problems quickly, but today we are going to spend the whole class talking about one task!"
Encourage student discourse.	"Talk with a partner about your ideas for getting started on this task. Then each pair will share their ideas with another pair."
Ask students to share stories of perseverance in other contexts (e.g., video games, athletics).	"Tell about a time when you felt frustrated and then you persevered to accomplish your goal."

 In this book, the tasks and lessons have been designed to promote productive struggle. Look for the ! icon to promote opportunities for your students to engage in productive struggle.

To learn more about productive struggle, check out the following resources:

🔍 CHECK THESE OUT

Productive Math Struggle: A 6-Point Action Plan for Fostering Perseverance SanGiovanni et al. (2020)
"Productive Struggle for All: Differentiated Instruction," *Mathematics Teaching in the Middle School* Lynch et al. (2018)
"Productive Struggle in Action," *Mathematics Teacher: Learning and Teaching PK–12* Baker et al. (2020)

ALTERNATE LEARNING ENVIRONMENTS

We recognize, understand, and support the fact that learning happens in many environments, including outside the traditional classroom. Particular events such as the COVID-19 pandemic that impacted the world beginning in 2020, weather conditions, individual student medical or mental health conditions, religious observations, or other issues may prevent students from learning inside a classroom. Instruction may occur in online formats, in remote settings, through one-on-one teaching, or through small-group instruction in a nontraditional location. We also recognize that when schools and families cocreate learning opportunities, students consistently benefit.

To find resources that support mathematics instruction in alternate learning environments, check out the following resources:

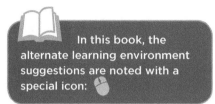

" When schools and families cocreate learning opportunities, students consistently benefit. "

In this book, the alternate learning environment suggestions are noted with a special icon:

CHECK THESE OUT

Moving Forward: Mathematics Learning in the Era of COVID-19
www.nctm.org/uploadedFiles/Research_and_Advocacy/NCTM_NCSM_Moving_Forward.pdf
NCTM and NCSM (2020)

The Math Learning Center: Free mathematics applications for virtual manipulatives, including number lines, clocks, geoboards, base ten materials
www.mathlearningcenter.org/resources/apps

Pear Deck: A communication platform used to provide individual feedback to students
www.peardeck.com/remote-learning

Desmos: Digital mathematics activities that can be assigned and created
www.desmos.com/

Google Suite: A full suite of collaborative documents, slides, whiteboard tools
edu.google.com/products/gsuite-for-education

STRENGTHS SPOTTING

When teachers promote their students' strengths, both teachers and students flourish. All students possess strengths in mathematics and often showcase those strengths when they get excited about an idea they have or a strategy they are trying. To best identify students' strengths, we must first look for strengths within the individual student, not in comparison to other students. Students demonstrate their strengths when they persevere through a task, use manipulatives, or create representations to show their mathematical understanding, communicate their ideas, seek conceptual understanding by asking "why" when learning mathematics, and collaborate with classmates to solve problems. Teachers recognize and cultivate students' strengths by carefully observing and listening to their students as they make sense of the mathematics they are learning.

There are four steps for strengths spotting, as seen in Figure 2.9.

Figure 2.9 Four Steps for Strengths Spotting

1. Notice the strength.	Teachers plan to recognize their students' strengths. They observe and record the strengths they see. Some teachers use checklists; others use journals.
2. Name the strength.	Teachers articulate the strength to the student by first recognizing the strength when they see students demonstrating the strength. For example, teachers might say, "I see Imani is using a number line to compare decimal values." Then they state, "She is using her mathematics representation strength."
3. Translate the strength.	Teachers explain how the strength helps students learn mathematics. Teachers might say, "Imani is showing a mathematics strength by using a representation to make sense of the value of decimals."
4. Appreciate and value the strength.	Teachers can appreciate the strength, or they can call on other students to explain how the student's strength is valuable to them. For example, a teacher might say, "When I see K-Shaud persevering through the task, I am encouraged to keep persevering too. Thank you K-Shaud for helping me want to keep trying."

 In this book, the strengths spotting suggestions are noted with a special icon:

To learn more about strengths spotting, check out the following resources:

🔍 CHECK THESE OUT

Strengths-Based Teaching and Learning in Mathematics: 5 Teaching Turnarounds for Grades K–6
Kobett and Karp (2020)

"Assembling the Puzzle of Students' Mathematical Strengths," *Mathematics Teaching in the Middle School*
White et al. (2018)

"Supporting Teacher Noticing of Students' Mathematical Strengths," *Mathematics Teacher Educator*
Jilk (2016)

Summing Up

Preparing to teach a *doing-math task* requires time and thought to effectively plan. In this chapter, we explored the mathematics process standards, mathematical practices, vocabulary, materials, and the task preparation needed to prepare to teach the tasks located in Chapters 4 through 15. In Chapter 3, we turn our attention to implementing the task.

Professional Learning/Discussion Questions

Read and discuss the following questions with your grade-level teaching team or with teams across multiple grade levels.

- Which of these planning components of the task template are most challenging for you? Why?

- What are some of the shifts in your practice you feel you need to make? What do you already have in place?

- Why is preplanning so important to this work? What would you need to add to your planning process that you haven't tried before?

- How do you anticipate when your students might be engaged in productive struggle within a task?

- What do you notice about your students when they are engaged in math tasks?

- As you think about preparing to implement a task, how will you use strengths spotting to prepare for your class to engage in the task?

CHAPTER 3

Implementing a *Doing-Math Task*-Based Lesson

In this chapter, we move from planning to action, from thinking about and selecting *doing-math tasks* to implementation. We will use this chapter to elaborate on the second half of the task template—Launch, Facilitate, Close, and Reflection—which is all about instructional actions. We recognize that actual task implementation is a significant step. In this chapter, we provide the information we all wish we knew and had access to when we started teaching. By the end of this chapter, you will

- learn how to launch a *doing-math task*-based lesson by capturing the students' attention and inviting and affording access for all students;

- understand the dynamics of lesson facilitation by focusing on grouping practices, discourse moves, purposeful questioning, and formative assessment;

- explore the most important elements of task lesson close; and

- consider the importance and significance of recording post-task notes and reflecting about teaching *doing-math tasks*.

Launching a Mathematics Lesson

The lesson launch is very much like those first few paragraphs or pages of a new book you open. The words either grab your attention and summon you to turn the page to learn more, or sadly they cause you to abandon the book in disinterest. The *doing-mathematics* task lesson launch is no different! The way teachers choose to launch the task sets the lesson in motion and, in many ways, establishes the tone for the entire experience. From the first powerful moment, "Students make conscious or unconscious decisions about whether they will engage in a lesson" (Kobett, Harbin Miles, & Williams, 2018, p. 136).

Additionally, an effective task launch promotes access and equity for students because it helps students engage in tasks from multiple entry points, capitalizing on both their prior mathematics knowledge and personal funds of knowledge to make sense of what they are experiencing. Leveraging the launch requires careful attention to what researchers Jackson et al. (2012) identify as the four critical elements that should be considered when launching rich mathematics tasks:

1. **Discuss the key contextual features:** Contexts that are unfamiliar to students create barriers because the effort they expend trying to understand the context overworks their working memory (Sweller, 1988). This overextension leaves the students, in essence, less cognitive space to solve the task.

2. **Discuss the key mathematical ideas:** Students need to know and understand the learning goal for the task. Warning! This element does not mean that the task is unpacked with so much detail that students do not have to think to solve the task. Rather, teachers need to be able to "discuss the key mathematical ideas without hinting at particular methods or procedures that should be used to solve the task" (Jackson et al., 2012, p. 27).

3. **Develop a common language to describe the key features:** Teachers carry out this element by asking open-ended questions that encourage students to talk about the task rather than the teacher's telling students about the task. When teachers solicit students' ideas and pose questions about the task, they support students' development of a common language about the task, mathematical ideas, and potential solution pathways.

4. **Maintain the cognitive demand:** A task's degree of cognitive demand was described in detail in Chapter 1 as the level of effort, or mathematical rigor, that students use to solve the problem (Stein et al., 2009). Teachers can do a lot to promote the cognitive intensity of the task in the launch portion of the lesson by prompting students to generate and use multiple solution pathways. In turn, teachers must be careful not to mandate or promote a particular method because that "robs them [students] of the opportunity to develop mathematical understanding as they generate their own solution methods and representations" (Jackson et al., 2012, p. 28).

You can launch tasks using a variety of techniques that captivate students. The launch techniques in this book all share one common theme: They promote students' critical thinking about the problems they are solving. The tasks students encounter are all problems to be solved within particular contexts that connect to specific topics and standards within the grade level. The launch should support, not detract from, the goal and should always allow the mathematics task to be problematic. Hiebert et al. (1996) explain that

> **Launches should captivate students.**

allowing the subject to be problematic means allowing students to wonder why things are, to inquire, to search for solutions, and to resolve incongruities. It means that both the curriculum and instruction should begin with problems, dilemmas, and questions for students. (p. 12)

The launch builds curiosity and a desire to solve rich, thoughtful problems.

LAUNCH TECHNIQUES

The following launch techniques are used in Chapters 4 through 15:

- Discussion-Centered Launches

- See, Think, and Wonder

- Notice and Wonder

- Three-Read Protocol

- Which One Doesn't Belong?

We'll introduce you to them here, briefly, to familiarize you with them and give you a hint of what you will see in the tasks. You may already be familiar with some of these launches and incorporate them already. If some are new, they can be added to your toolbox!

Discussion-Centered Launches

Students need opportunities to process and discuss their ideas before moving toward solution pathways. Every task-based lesson in this book provides multiple opportunities for students to engage in mathematical discussions in pairs, small groups, and in a whole group using a variety of approaches. These discussion techniques are described in detail and may include *Turn and Talks*, *Turn and Learns*, *Think-Pair-Share*, and *Pair-to-Pair Share*. Explanations and examples of these techniques are described in detail in this chapter in Figure 3.1, Grouping Structures and Techniques.

See, Think, and Wonder

The See, Think, and Wonder launch ignites students' curiosity and engages students in an inquiry cycle that prepares students to ask mathematical questions (Ritchhart et al., 2011) using visual images, graphs, and video. Students are invited to recall what they think about the content before being directed to engage with the math in particular ways. This launch technique is particularly helpful for students who are learning mathematics in a language that is different from their home language. See Task 5, p. 66 for an example of See, Think, and Wonder in action.

To learn more about See, Think, and Wonder, check out the following source:

 CHECK THIS OUT

Making Thinking Visible: How to Promote Engagement, Understanding, and Independence for All Learners
Ritchhart et al. (2011)

Notice and Wonder

Similar to See, Think, and Wonder, the Notice and Wonder launch protocol (Math Forum, 2015) also summons students' observations and ideas about what they are seeing. Using visual images, videos, graphs, and/or manipulatives, students are prompted with these questions: "What do you notice?" "What do you wonder?" Teachers record what students notice and wonder on a chart and then use the students' ideas to present the task. See Task 12, p. 95 for an example of what Notice and Wonder looks like within a task.

To learn more about the Notice and Wonder launch protocol, check out the following sources:

 CHECK THESE OUT

"Beginning to Problem Solve With 'I Notice and Wonder'"
www.nctm.org/Classroom-Resources/Problems-of-the-Week/I-Notice-I-Wonder/Math Forum (2015)

"Capturing Mathematical Curiosity With Notice and Wonder," *Mathematics Teaching in the Middle School*
Rumack and Huinker (2019)

Three-Read Protocol

Teachers facilitate this launch technique by asking students to read the problem stem from the task three times with a different purpose for each read (Erikson Institute, 2018):

1. Read 1: The teacher reads the problem stem (not the question) orally without reading the final question and asks, "What is this problem about?"

2. Read 2: The teacher conducts a class choral or partner read of the problem stem (not the question) and asks, "What are the number values in this task?" The teacher can record all the students' ideas.

3. Read 3: The teacher conducts a class choral or partner read of the problem stem and asks, "What are all the mathematics questions we might ask?" The teacher can record students' questions. Finally, the teacher reveals the question for the task. See Task 1, p. 49 for an example of the Three-Read Protocol.

 CHECK THIS OUT

To learn more about the Three-Read Protocol, check out the following:

Three-Read Protocol

earlymath.erikson.edu/exploring-3-reads-math-protocol-word-problems/

Erikson Institute 2018

Which One Doesn't Belong?

Fashioned after the old Sesame Street song and corresponding visual activity, *Some of these things are not like each other, some of these things are kind of the same* (Raposa & Stone, 1972), these lesson launches ask students to look at four visual images, representations, numerals, or expressions to name and explain how one is different from the others (or how some are the same). These launches work best when each of the options can be identified as viable responses for the one that does not belong. These launches invite students to construct viable arguments, use mathematical vocabulary, incorporate prior knowledge, and make connections. See Task 28, p. 155 for an example of this launch.

To learn more about the Which One Doesn't Belong? launch technique, check out the following:

 CHECK THESE OUT

Which One Doesn't Belong?
wodb.ca/
Barousa (2013)

Which One Doesn't Belong? A Shapes Book and Teacher's Guide
Danielson (2016)

Facilitating the Lesson

Facilitating a *doing-math task*-based lesson is so much more than merely assigning a task for students to complete! Teachers must weigh and regularly consider many factors as they facilitate a task that will maximize the students' learning opportunities. Throughout each of the tasks provided, you will find suggestions that include considerations of the following:

- How students will be grouped to engage in and solve the task

- How and when students will engage in discourse

- Purposeful questions you may ask that will challenge the students or move them to the next stage

- Classroom-based formative assessment techniques you may use to understand student thinking

> In this book, you are encouraged to facilitate grouping your students in multiple ways (Figure 3.1). Don't be discouraged if initial grouping attempts are challenging. Keep working at it to find flexible grouping structures that work for you and your students!

GROUPING STUDENTS

In Chapter 2, you read about grouping students for task work. We strategically placed the grouping discussion in task preparation because grouping structures that are decided ahead of time avoid grouping decisions that don't capitalize on students' strengths. As noted, students who work in mixed-strengths groups are able to contribute their strengths as a cooperative group to solve problems. As you gain comfort implementing *doing-math tasks*, consider how you can flexibly group your students in pairs or groups of three or four to best support their learning on a particular task. Observe which students work best together, make notes, and adjust the grouping as needed.

Figure 3.1 Grouping Structures and Techniques

Group	When to Use This Grouping Structure	Techniques
Pairs	Pairs work well for engaging students in all launch techniques, brainstorming solution pathways during the facilitate, and revealing solutions during the close activities.	*Turn and Talk:* Turn and share your ideas with a partner. *Turn and Learn:* Ask your partner a question about their thinking. Be prepared to share your partner's ideas in the whole group discussion. *Pair-to-Pair Share:* Pairs first share ideas together and then join another pair to share and discuss their ideas. *Pair-to-Pair Interview:* Pairs examine another pair's work and then confer to decide on questions they will ask about the students' work.

Group	When to Use This Grouping Structure	Techniques
Threes	Groups of three can brainstorm ideas during the launch and facilitate part of the lesson. Groups of three can be particularly effective when students are creating multiple representations.	*One Stay, Two Stray:* After a group has worked together to brainstorm ideas or solve a task, the teacher asks one person in the group to stay and the two others to "stray" and join another person who has "stayed" to share ideas. Once new groups are formed, the students share their groups' ideas or answer a new question. This approach can be facilitated by assigning each student a number. For example, Number 1 stays, Numbers 2 and 3 stray (find another group).
Fours	Students can work fluidly in groups of four or can be assigned particular roles in the group.	*Two Stay, Two Stray:* After a group has worked together to brainstorm ideas or solve a task, the teacher asks two people in the group to stay and the two others to "stray" and join another pair who has "stayed" to share ideas. Once new groups are formed, the students share their groups' ideas or answer a new question. This approach can be facilitated by assigning each student a number. For example, Numbers 1 and 2 stay, Numbers 3 and 4 stray (find another group).

Grouping students can be challenging as students build skills in cooperating with one another, explaining their ideas, and attentively listening to one another. For more ideas about establishing group norms, check out pages 19–20 in Chapter 2.

DISCOURSE

A classroom that is rich in mathematical discourse does not happen by accident. It happens with careful and thoughtful planning and the conviction that all students can engage in meaningful communication! The Standards for Mathematical Practice (National Governors Association & Council of Chief State School Officers, 2010), Process Standards (NCTM, 2000), and the Effective Mathematics Teaching Practices (NCTM, 2014b) all emphasize the importance of facilitating student discourse to promote students' mathematical understanding of important concepts and skills (Figure 3.2). Note how the responsibility of this discourse is placed squarely on the shoulders of the students.

> " A classroom rich in mathematical discourse does not happen by accident. "

Figure 3.2 Crosswalk Between Standards for Mathematical Practice, Process Standards, and Effective Teaching Practices

Standards for Mathematical Practice (CCSSO, 2010)	Process Standards (NCTM, 2000)	Effective Mathematics Teaching Practices (NCTM, 2014b)
Construct Viable Arguments . . . (pp. 6, 7) • Mathematically proficient students understand and use stated assumptions, definitions, and previously established results in constructing arguments. They make conjectures and build a logical progression of statements to explore the truth of their conjectures. They justify their conclusions, communicate them to others, and respond to the arguments of others. • Mathematically proficient students are also able to compare the effectiveness of two plausible arguments, distinguish correct logic or reasoning from that which is flawed, and—if there is a flaw in an argument—explain what it is. • Elementary students can construct arguments using concrete referents such as objects, drawings, diagrams, and actions. Such arguments can make sense and be correct, even though they are not generalized or made formal until later grades.	Communication (pp. 60–63) Students: • Organize and consolidate their mathematical thinking through communication. • Communicate their mathematical thinking coherently and clearly to peers, teachers, and others. • Analyze and evaluate the mathematical thinking and strategies of others. • Use the language of mathematics to express mathematical ideas precisely.	Facilitate Meaningful Mathematical Discourse (p. 35) Students: • Present and explain ideas, reason, and represent to one another in pair, small-group, and whole-class discourse. • Listen carefully to and critique the reasoning of peers, using examples to support or counterexamples to refute arguments. • Seek to understand the approaches used by peers by asking clarifying questions, trying out others' strategies, and describing the approaches used by others. • Identify how different approaches to solving a task are the same and how they are different.

Without opportunities to question, discuss, share, critique, and defend their ideas, students won't experience the richness and beauty of mathematics. Quite simply, discourse helps students discover and make their own connections to the mathematics they are learning. *Principles to Actions* (NCTM, 2014b) explains this important idea in the teaching practice, Facilitate meaningful mathematical discourse: "Effective teaching of mathematics facilitates discourse among students to build shared understanding of mathematical ideas by analyzing and comparing student approaches and arguments" (p. 10). Planning for and teaching in ways that support student discourse requires a clear examination of the teacher and student roles in the classroom. By examining the ratio of teacher-to-student talk, we can get a good idea about the opportunities for discourse that we provide for our students. Students should be discussing their ideas at every phase of the task-based lesson but particularly during the facilitate component of the lesson as they engage with their partners or small groups to share their ideas. We can ask a series of questions to better understand how we are promoting discourse in our classrooms.

Are we

- productively grouping students to engage in meaningful discourse?

- highlighting meaningful student discourse when we hear it and see it?

- ensuring that students have time to grapple with mathematical ideas?

- using class norms that promote students as authors of their own mathematical ideas?

- asking questions that promote meaningful discourse?

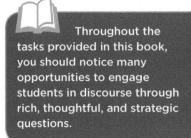

Throughout the tasks provided in this book, you should notice many opportunities to engage students in discourse through rich, thoughtful, and strategic questions.

To learn more about providing rich discourse opportunities, check out the following resources:

🔍 CHECK THESE OUT

Classroom Discussions: Seeing Math Discourse in Action, Grades K–6
Anderson et al. (2011)

Number Talks: Whole Number Computation, Grades K–5
Parrish (2014)

Number Talks: Fractions, Decimals, Percentages
Parish and Dominick (2016)

The 5 Practices in Practice: Successfully Orchestrating Mathematical Discussions in Your Elementary School Classroom
Smith et al. (2019)

Intentional Talk: How to Structure and Lead Productive Mathematical Discussions
Kazemi and Hintz (2014)

PURPOSEFUL QUESTIONS

The kinds of questions that teachers ask during a lesson hold the opportunity to move students' mathematical understanding forward in deep and powerful ways. The NCTM *Principles to Action* (2014b) states, "Effective teaching of mathematics uses purposeful questions to assess and advance students' reasoning and sense making about important mathematical ideas and relationships" (p. 35). As teachers develop questions that will prompt students to think deeply about the mathematics they are learning; make conjectures, generalizations, and conclusions; and extend their curiosity about the task (Van de Walle et al., 2019), they should consider the five question types (see Figure 3.3; NCTM, 2014b, 2017b) to ensure that students are engaged in a variety of levels of mathematical thinking. Beyond Bloom's *Taxonomy of Educational Objectives* (1956), the five question types in Figure 3.3 illustrate how strategic questioning can move students' learning forward:

Figure 3.3 NCTM's Five Question Types With Examples

Question Type	Teachers ask these types of questions to . . .	Task Examples (with page numbers)
Gathering Information	Elicit procedural information that has right and wrong answers.	From Chapter 7, Task 14, p. 104: "How many times greater is 7,000 than 7?"
Probing Thinking	Encourage students to demonstrate their reasoning by explaining their ideas and strategies	From Chapter 10, Task 32, p. 174: "How could you show the same strategy using a number line?"
Making the Mathematics Visible	Support students to recognize patterns, connect mathematical ideas, and understand the underlying structure of the mathematics content they are learning.	From Chapter 6, Task 12, p. 96: "How did Kay know that the next terms would have a difference of 15? Do you think the same kinds of patterns might show up if you used different starting numbers or different rules?"
Encouraging Reflection and Justification	Develop mathematical arguments and justify their solution pathways with deep explanations and representations.	From Chapter 9, Task 28, p. 154: Focus the discussion on justifications about how each suggested design encompasses $\frac{3}{4}$ positive space and highlight these as groups discuss their work or their peers' work.
Engage With the Reasoning of Others	Encourage students to construct a viable argument, listen to the reasoning of their peers, and ask questions of their peers.	From Chapter 8, Task 21, p. 129: "Can you think of an example of two even factors that proves Talia's conjecture is true?" "Can you think of a counterexample, an example of two even factors that proves Talia's conjecture is false?"

In this book, some questions have been provided for you in the tasks, but certainly you will decide other robust and rich questions that you could ask in the task lesson. To ensure that you are asking questions from all of the question type categories, consider using the chart shown in Figure 3.3 to plan your questions as you facilitate the task.

To learn more about the importance and use of questioning, check out the following resources:

CHECK THESE OUT

"Teacher Questioning to Elicit Students' Mathematical Thinking in Elementary School Classrooms," *Journal of Teacher Education*
Franke et al. (2009)

Good Questions: Great Ways to Differentiate Math Instruction in Standards-Based Classrooms
Small (2017)

FORMATIVE ASSESSMENT

Classroom-based formative assessment, also known as formative evaluation (Hattie, 2009), is assessment *for* learning because it centers on collecting information about student understanding while you are teaching and using that information to respond to students in real time—at the moment you are facilitating the task. The formative assessment research presented below provides a powerful reminder of the effects of collecting student responses and data and using it to influence planning and instruction. Formative assessment, when used regularly and strategically, advances student learning.

Wiliam and Thompson (2008) identified five research-informed formative assessment strategies that, when implemented, foster student learning. These include the following:

1. Clarifying and sharing learning intentions and criteria for success

   What: Teachers let students know what they will be learning, how they will be learning it, and how they will know when they are successful using student-friendly language. Sometimes it is appropriate to withhold the exact content of the task to allow students to make their own connections and conjectures. In such cases, it is appropriate to let students know that, for example, they will be solving a problem using multiple representations.

   When: Teachers discuss the learning intentions and success criteria at the beginning of the task and throughout the task.

2. Engineering effective classroom discussions, questions, and learning tasks that elicit evidence of learning

   What: Teachers do this throughout the task's implementation by asking questions, probing student thinking, and asking students to use multiple representations and solution pathways to demonstrate their understanding.

   When: Teachers promote this strategy throughout the facilitation and close portion of the lesson.

3. Providing feedback that moves learning forward

   What: Feedback that attends, responds, and is crafted to target students' understanding in the moment for individual students, small groups, and large groups in an effort to advance students' mathematical thinking.

   When: Teachers provide feedback throughout the facilitation and close portions of the task-based lesson.

4. Activating students as owners of their own learning

   What: Teachers bolster their students' mathematical competence and identities by communicating confidence to them regarding their ability to solve tasks. They turn over mathematical authority to their students by asking them to share ideas and lead discussions with peers.

When: Teachers can and should activate student ownership throughout the entire lesson.

5. Activating students as instructional resources for one another

What: Students do this when they support one another by asking questions, offering new or alternative ideas, and sharing their solution pathways.

When: Students need opportunities to serve as a resource while solving tasks together during the facilitation part of the task-based lesson and in the lesson close when the teacher is helping students strategically bring mathematical ideas together.

> " When used strategically, the Formative 5 Assessments support teachers in collecting important indicators of students' understandings. "

> Throughout the task's Facilitate section, you will find the Formative 5 techniques indicated in bold along with a prompt or question.

Five classroom-based formative assessment techniques, also known as the *Formative 5*, when used strategically throughout a lesson, support teachers in their ongoing collection of important indicators of the mathematical understandings of their students (Fennell et al., 2017). The five techniques are Observations, Interviews, Show Me, Hinge Questions, and Exit Tasks (see Figure 3.4). The first three techniques—Observation, Interview, and Show Me—are used often and seamlessly during mathematics task-based work and may be used in the launch, facilitate, and close portions of the task lesson. Teachers will often use a hinge question as a task-lesson check for understanding/proficiency at a particular point in the lesson. Student responses to these techniques may also inform a decision to drive the lesson in a different direction or point to a different or adapted task. The exit task will be implemented less frequently because the students will have already been engaged in a *doing-math task*. By using these techniques, the student responses and resulting data enable teachers to provide strategic and thoughtful feedback that moves student learning and instruction forward, as well as helping to guide teacher planning and instructional decision making.

Figure 3.4 describes the Formative 5 assessment techniques and provides selected examples of where each technique is used in a task in this book. Each task will feature the use of the Formative 5 techniques. The tasks also refer to a formative assessment tool to record observations and collect student responses from interview and *Show Me* prompts.

Figure 3.4 Formative 5 Assessment Techniques

Formative 5 Technique	Description	Task Examples (with page numbers)
Observation	Strategic observation of students while working individually, in pairs, or in groups. Typically, students are demonstrating their solution pathways with multiple representations that include manipulatives and mathematical sketches or drawings. Teachers record their observations using observation tools and use observations to ask strategic questions as well as inform their planning and teaching.	From Chapter 7, Task 17, p. 115: **Observe.** Listen carefully for students to make conjectures or notice relationships. Record them on the board. For example, students may say things like the following: • It doesn't matter which number we pick because the place values might be different. • We want you to tell us the place value first! • The only way it matters which number is greater is if they have the same place value.

Formative 5 Technique	Description	Task Examples (with page numbers)
Interview	Teachers conduct a brief interview when students are working to learn more about their thinking. These are the kinds of questions that invite students to share their ideas and reasoning. Teachers can collect interview data by recording students' responses on recording tools (find interview tools for individual students or small groups in Appendix B).	From Chapter 5, Task 6, p. 71: **Interview.** Ask the following: • Which of these expressions has the least value? Why? • Which has the greatest value? How do you know? • How did you decide that this expression has a greater value than this one *(based on two cards students have ordered)*?
Show Me	The Show Me technique is "a performance response by a student or a group of students that extends and often deepens what was observed and what might have been asked in an interview" (Fennell et al., 2017 p. 63). Students most often display their responses using some type of representation. Whole-class "Show Mes" can be conducted using whiteboards and technological tools.	From Chapter 12, Task 40, p. 211: **Show Me.** Remind students that in third grade they learned how to represent this kind of data on a line plot. Ask students: • Show me on your paper/marker board what a line plot looks like. • Show me how you could represent the data from the shoe store on a line plot. • How did you decide on the labels for your line plot?
Hinge Question	The hinge question is a particular type of question that is used at a strategic or pivotal moment in the lesson that will likely assess student progress with the lesson and drive the lesson in one direction or another (Wiliam, 2011).	From Chapter 10, Task 33, p. 177: **Hinge Question.** Della thought about it differently from everyone! Della thought of the expression $(3 \times 4) \div 9$. What was Della seeing and thinking?
Exit Task	The exit task is a "capstone problem or task that captures the major focus of the lesson for that day or perhaps several days and provides a sampling of student performance" (Fennell et al., 2017 p. 109). Unlike an exit ticket, the exit task is "meatier" (more demanding) and provides a full range of student thinking about the mathematics topic or perhaps extends the task-based lesson of the day.	From Chapter 7, Task 20, p. 125: **Exit Task.** Change one digit in the number 5.18 so that Becky's estimate of $6 + 1 = 7$ will be closer to the actual sum than Aaliyah's estimate of $5 + 1 = 6$.

Although some Formative 5 techniques are included for you in each task, we encourage you to construct your own prompts for each of the Formative 5 techniques. Use the tool templates provided at the companion website (**resources.corwin.com/classroomreadymath/4-5**) to formulate your own Formative 5 prompts.

To learn more about the Formative 5 techniques and formative assessment, check out these sources:

 CHECK THESE OUT

The Formative 5: Everyday Assessment Techniques for Every Math Classroom Fennell et al. (2017)
"Classroom-Based Formative Assessments: Guiding Teaching and Learning." In C. Suurtamm and A. Roth McDuffie (Eds.). *Annual Perspectives in Mathematics Education* (pp. 51–62) Fennell et al. (2015)
A Fresh Look at Formative Assessment in Mathematics Teaching Silver and Mills (Eds.) (2018)
Mathematics Formative Assessment: 75 Practical Strategies for Linking Assessment Instruction and Learning Keeley and Tobey (2011)

Close the Lesson: Make the Mathematics Visible

Ask any teacher, instructional coach, or leader and you will likely find that they seemingly all agree that lesson closure is a critical part of lesson planning, yet it often gets pushed to the side in favor of additional instructional time (Ganske, 2017). Not providing lesson closure or even rushing its implementation, however, means that students lose opportunities to make connections between and among mathematical representations, discuss solution pathways, consider which strategies are most efficient, and leave with important mathematical understandings, as well as a sense of what's happening next. Effective and thoughtful close activities improve student retention of material (Pollock, 2007), particularly those close activities that ask students to think, respond, write, and discuss concepts (Cavanaugh et al., 1996). Consider the important role that a hinge question or exit task may play within a lesson's close. In general, close activities deepen student thinking, offer opportunities for students to make sense of the mathematics they are learning, see how peers are thinking about the task, make generalizations, identify patterns, clarify emerging mathematical understandings, and advance their thinking as they consider more complex mathematical ideas. Such close activities also provide major signals about your next steps with regard to planning and instruction.

There may be two parts to a lesson's close. The first part of the close, which is the term we are using in our task-based lesson template, often provides opportunities for students to share their solution pathways and review classmates' strategies.

Once the students have had opportunities to review one another's work, the teacher makes the mathematics from the task visible by orchestrating productive discussions (Smith & Stein, 2018) using students' strategies and solution pathways from the task. During the close of the task lesson, the teacher focuses on the last three practices proposed by Smith and Stein. The first two practices, anticipating students' solutions to the mathematics task (referenced in Chapter 1) and monitoring (described in the facilitation portion of this chapter under formative assessment, particularly the use of observation) inform the teacher's decision-making in the close. The final three practices, selecting, sequencing, and connecting, are key practices that may be implemented during the close. Consider the following:

- **Selecting:** After observing and monitoring student work, teachers select the student work they will highlight during the close. They choose student work that represents a variety of solution strategies, ideas, and representations.

- **Sequencing**: The teacher then strategically sequences the students' work to share with the class as it aligns to the mathematics goal for the task. For example, teachers might have three different students share their work reflecting a variety of representations moving from the concrete to the abstract. Or the teacher may sequence the sharing by highlighting the most common strategy to the most unusual.

- **Connecting**: Finally, the teacher connects the students' approaches, unpacks the underlying mathematics, and connects the students' strategies and solution pathways back to the mathematics goal of the task and task lesson.

> In this book, the close activities for the task lessons are designed to be robust and full of varied representations and rich student discourse that make the mathematics from the task visible to the students.

As you plan to implement a task lesson's close activities, consider the amount of time you and the students will need to participate in deep discussions that unpack the mathematics of the task. Students and teachers may be asked to engage in one or more of the following close activities that prompt students to review the mathematics concepts, strategies, and ideas developed during the task lesson's work (Figure 3.5).

Figure 3.5 Task-Based Lesson Close Techniques, Descriptions, and Examples

Close Technique	Description	Where Can I Find Examples?
Open Gallery Walk	Student work is displayed around the classroom. Students are asked to walk around the classroom to look at their peers' strategies and solutions. The teacher uses the student work to strategically discuss the mathematics goal for the lesson, making the mathematics learning visible.	See • Chapter 5, Task 6, p. 72 • Chapter 12, Task 40, p. 210
Something Similar and Something Different Gallery Walk	Student work is displayed around the classroom. Students are asked to walk around the classroom to find peers' work that is similar to and different from their own work. Students place a sticky note or a colored dot on the work to indicate that the work is similar (e.g., pink dot) or different (e.g., green dot). The teacher begins the discussion by reviewing the students' sticky dots, asking the students to share how others' work is similar to and different from their own in terms of strategies and solution pathways. The teacher then strategically points to the mathematics goal for the lesson.	See • Chapter 4, Task 1, p. 49 • Chapter 10, Task 35, p. 184 • Chapter 14, Task 52, p. 262

(Continued)

(Continued)

Close Technique	Description	Where Can I Find Examples?
Notice and Wonder Gallery Walk	In this Gallery Walk, students write their notices and wonders on sticky notes and place them on the student work. The teacher begins the discussion by reviewing the students' sticky notes asking the students to share what they noticed and wondered about the strategies and solution pathways and then strategically pointing to the mathematics goal for the lesson.	See • Chapter 5, Task 7, p. 76 • Chapter 5, Task 8, p. 80
Select, Sequence, and Connect	During the facilitate portion of the lesson, teachers look for student thinking and identify specific ideas that will be shared in the lesson close. Teachers ask specific and strategic questions to highlight students' strengths and reasoning about the mathematical ideas. Then, teachers gather students together for a whole-group discussion. Teachers strategically select student work to display and then ask other students to share their strategies and representations. Teachers "focus students' attention on the structure or essential features of mathematical ideas" (NCTM, 2014b, p. 24) to make the mathematics visible. Teachers also facilitate discussions about efficient and novel strategies by encouraging and coaching students to share solution pathways and make connections among representations.	See • Chapter 6, Task 11, p. 93 • Chapter 10, Task 34, p. 180 • Chapter 5, Task 5, p. 68

To learn more about close techniques and strategies, check out these sources:

 CHECK THESE OUT

Five Practices for Orchestrating Productive Discussions

Smith and Stein (2018)

5 Practices in Practice: Successfully Orchestrating Mathematics Discussions in Your Elementary Classroom

Smith et al. (2019)

Talk Moves: A Teacher's Guide for Using Classroom Discussions in Math

Chapin et al. (2013)

Lesson Reflection

Teacher reflection is key to sustained and continued success. Consistent reflection helps teachers understand the *why* behind the events that happen in their classroom and promotes professional growth (Danielson & McGreal, 2000; Dewey, 1933). Without reflection about how our teaching decisions connect to student understandings, we are left with teaching through imitation rather than through strategic intentionality (Lortie, 1975). This intentional and strategic approach capitalizes on both the mathematics content and your students' strengths and needs. You can support your own reflection process by recording your thoughts in a journal, asking students to give you feedback, or asking a colleague to observe or listen to the story of your lesson. When teachers reflect on their lessons, they learn more about their teaching practice and make connections about how their teaching decisions influence students' learning (Danielson, 2008).

> " Without reflection, we are left with teaching through imitation rather than teaching through strategic intentionality. "

In this book, we include, at the end of each task, an opportunity for you to provide post-task notes regarding your reflective comments as well as thoughts related to your next steps (in both revised planning and instructional modifications).

To learn more about teacher reflection, check out these sources:

🔍 CHECK THESE OUT

Ten Ways to Become a More Reflective Teacher
Terry Heick (2019), TeachThought.com
www.teachthought.com/pedagogy/reflective-teacher-reflective-teaching/

Math Workshop: Five Steps to Implementing Guided Math, Learning Stations, Reflection, and More
Lempp (2017)

Using This Book to Get Started With *Doing-Math Tasks*

This book's collection of *doing-math tasks* is organized by mathematics topics for 4th and 5th grade into chapters. Each chapter includes a chapter opener that describes the mathematics standards and topics, per task, and considerations for anticipating student thinking about those standards, as well as anticipating the task's implementation. As you consider the mathematical topics, it is very helpful to anticipate student thinking to make the most of your task implementation.

ANTICIPATING STUDENT THINKING

Before setting out on a run, cross-country runners visualize the entire racecourse, anticipating every twist, turn, and hill. They don't just think about the race—they embody it. While they visualize, they also imagine their response to each of the racecourse elements. They know that there will still be surprises on the course, but their prior anticipation allows them to respond to expected challenges with expert, almost automatic responses that provide space to handle those unexpected, unanticipated challenges.

Similarly, when teachers anticipate how students will engage in a task, they need to imagine the lesson. Where are the hills that need momentum or the sharp turns that need a slower pace? By mixing their knowledge of their students with their teaching experience, teachers are prepared for and can respond to students with thoughtful questions, prompts, and probes that will advance their students' thinking. While students will sometimes still catch them by surprise with their wonderful and unique thinking, the more prepared teachers are the more likely they can respond with appreciation, and the less likely they are to shut student thinking down. This approach also helps them avoid correcting students before they have had a chance to engage in sense making or convince teachers with logical arguments. It is natural for teachers to focus on what students don't know and frankly, teachers worry about what students don't yet understand. However, a deficit mindset about naturally developing mathematical understanding can harm students because teachers may respond with corrective feedback rather than with curiosity or questions. Teachers purposely do not use the word *misconception*, instead focusing only on student thinking, without judgment, so that they may focus on how they can gracefully advance students' thinking and understanding.

There are several key teaching moves you can make to anticipate student thinking:

1. **Do the task!** Engaging in the task first will allow you to think about the nuances of the task components, including the mathematics, context, vocabulary, strategies, and solution pathways.

2. **Anticipate student responses.** Write down the ways that your students may respond and write a question you will ask in reply to that student's thinking.

3. **Think about students' strengths.** Leverage students' strengths and consider their challenges.

Additional support, including student pages, can be found on the book's companion website.

As you consider your next instructional steps, you may have some technical questions.

Q: Where should I start?

A: We suggest that you begin with a mathematics standard that is particularly important to you and select a task to try first. If possible, pick a teaching partner to plan with, and check back with one another to share your experiences!

Q: Where do I find the student pages?

A: The student pages can be found at **resources.corwin.com/classroomreadymath/4-5**

Q: How much time do I need to teach the tasks?

A: We recognize that the time allotted to teach mathematics varies greatly across this nation. As you read the task lesson note that the launch may require up to 10 minutes, the facilitate portion will likely require 30 minutes as student groups work together to formulate strategies and solutions, and the close will require at least 10–15 minutes and sometimes much more to fully unpack the mathematical understanding. Of course, these are all estimates.

 CHECK THESE OUT

Every Math Learner, Grades K–5: A Doable Approach to Teaching With Learning Differences in Mind
Smith (2017)

"Three Strategies for Opening Curriculum Spaces"
Drake et al. (2015)

Summing Up

In this chapter, we considered important components of task implementation, including the lesson launch, lesson facilitation, and lesson close. Task lesson launches provide opportunities for students to attend to and demonstrate curiosity about the task. As teachers facilitate lessons, they focus on grouping practices and student discourse opportunities, pose purposeful and thoughtful questions, and use formative assessment to assess student understanding. The task lesson close is particularly important when implementing a *doing-math task* as teachers strategically use students' solution pathways to make the mathematics visible to students.

Professional Learning/Discussion Questions

Read and discuss the following questions with your grade-level teaching team or with teams across multiple grade levels.

- Why is a task lesson launch important?

- Which of the task lesson launch techniques have you already tried?

- What is the role of questioning in a task lesson?

- How does formative assessment during the lesson help you support students' learning?

- Why is the close a critical step in teaching a mathematics task lesson?

CHAPTER

4

Operations and Algebraic Thinking

Expressions, Equations, and More

TASK 1: GRADE 4: BOOKS, BOOKS, AND MORE BOOKS

Solve multistep word problems posed with whole numbers and having whole-number answers using the four operations; represent problems using equations with a letter standing for the unknown quantity.

TASK 2: GRADE 5: MITCHELL'S MARKERS

Use parentheses, brackets, or braces in numerical expressions, and evaluate expressions with these symbols.

TASK 3: GRADE 4: TEACHERS GO SHOPPING

Interpret a multiplication equation as a comparison, e.g., interpret $35 = 5 \times 7$ as a statement that 35 is 5 times as many as 7 and 7 times as many as 5. Represent verbal statements of multiplicative comparisons as multiplication equations.

Multiply or divide to solve word problems involving multiplicative comparison, e.g., by using drawings and equations with a symbol for the unknown number to represent the problem, distinguishing multiplicative comparison from additive comparison.

TASK 4: GRADE 5: KARLA'S PHOTO ALBUM

Use parentheses, brackets, or braces in numerical expressions, and evaluate expressions with these symbols.

Anticipating Student Thinking: The algebraic thinking tasks in this chapter all engage students in connecting their understandings with whole numbers to algebraic reasoning. In Task 1, students solve multistep word problems using equations to represent the problems. All the Chapter 4 tasks involve equations with a symbol for an unknown number, or expressions, and are foundational to future, and more formal, applications involving algebra. As students encounter equations and using letters (variables) to represent unknown quantities within the equations and symbols used in evaluating expressions, consider using drawings or manipulative materials to represent the expressions and equations. The use of individual or small-group interviews and Show Me prompts will also provide you with a sense of student understanding as they solve equations or evaluate expressions.

THINK ABOUT IT

How will you provide access to the representations you may want students to use (e.g., drawings, number lines, manipulative materials, online tools) to support how they evaluate expressions or solve equations?

Grade 4

Mathematics Standard

- Solve multistep word problems posed with whole numbers and having whole-number answers using the four operations; represent problems using equations with a letter standing for the unknown quantity.

Mathematical Practices

- Make sense of problems and persevere in solving them.
- Reason abstractly and quantitatively.

Vocabulary

- multistep problem
- equation
- unknown (in an equation)

Materials

- Word Problem task cards
- chart paper
- markers
- sticky notes (optional)

Task 1
Books, Books, and More Books

Write equations with variables to represent a situation

TASK

Books, Books, and More Books

Write equations to represent each problem and use a letter to stand for an unknown quantity:

1. The librarian at Miller Library received two shipments of books. On Monday, she received one shipment of 10 boxes, with 32 books in each box. On Wednesday, she received another shipment of 30 boxes, with 12 books in each box. On which day did she receive more books?

2. Cassian collected 250 more rocks than Makai. Stella collected three times the number of rocks Cassian collected. Makai collected 158 rocks. How many rocks did Stella collect?

3. Chairs in the school cafeteria need to be set up in 10 rows, with 25 chairs in each row. In the media center, 8 tables with 16 chairs per table need to be arranged for math night. How many chairs are needed for the day?

4. 1,258 students participated in a school science fair. There are 7 locations for displaying the science fair projects. If the gym can hold 250 projects, how many student projects can be equally distributed among the other 6 locations?

TASK PREPARATION

- Be prepared to group students for partner work. Think about students who can work collaboratively with sense-making. Consider the needs of multilingual learners for interactive conversations and review the context of the task so that you are ready to support students in understanding the meaning of particular words or concepts.

LAUNCH

1. Present the following numberless problem to students:

   Isabella is preparing for the spelling bee. Her teacher gave her two lists of words to study. The Level A list contains ____ words and the Level B list contains ____ words. She wants to spend ____ days studying all the words.

2. Use the Three-Read Protocol. For the first read, have students visualize the problem and ask, "What is happening in the problem?" Invite students to make a sketch of their idea.

3. Have students do a second read and ask, "What questions might you ask about this situation?" (Possibilities include questions about the total number of words Isabella needs to study, how many more words there are in one list compared to the other, the number of words to be studied each day.)

4. Reveal the problem, with the quantities and question shown. Have students do a third read and focus their attention on the relationship between the quantities:

   Isabella is preparing for the spelling bee. Her teacher gave her two lists of words to study. The Level A list contains 230 words, and the Level B list contains 250 words. She wants to spend 4 days studying all the words. She wants to study the same amount of words each day. How many words does Isabella need to study each day?

5. Inquire about what is known (label the quantities) and unknown in this situation (the total number of words Isabella needs to study; the number of words she needs to study each day). Explain that we can use a letter to represent the unknown in an equation. Add that we can also use two different letters to represent two unknowns in a multistep problem.

6. Assign student partners for pair work.

7. Ask, "What equations can you write for this situation?" Have pairs Think-Write-Share (with another pair).

8. **Observe**. Listen for students who explain what each part of the equation represents and who correctly identify the unknowns in their equations. Call on two pairs to share their thinking.

FACILITATE

1. Present the task cards to pairs, reminding students that for these four problems, they need to write equations.

2. Distribute chart paper and markers.

3. Probe student thinking by prompting students to **Show Me** how equations represent the problem.

4. Monitor pair work, noting which pairs were able to explain how their solution steps and quantities were related. Also note the varying strategies students used to solve the word problems.

! PRODUCTIVE STRUGGLE

Support sense-making by encouraging students to reread and visualize the problem. Ask questions to focus students on the relationship between the quantities.

Note: Consider using the Observation, Interview, and Show Me tools to help organize responses and possible next steps (see Appendix B).

CLOSE: MAKE THE MATH VISIBLE

1. Invite students on a Something Similar Something Different Gallery Walk, emphasizing that they look at their peers' equations and solutions.

2. Ask students what they noticed that was similar and what questions they have.

3. Based on pair responses from Show Me, select pairs of students to explain their equations to the whole class. (See Figure 4.1.) You may want to use different colored markers to make visible for students how each part of the equation is related to each word problem. For example:

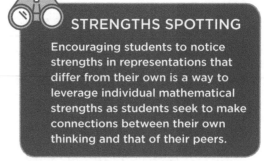

STRENGTHS SPOTTING

Encouraging students to notice strengths in representations that differ from their own is a way to leverage individual mathematical strengths as students seek to make connections between their own thinking and that of their peers.

The librarian at Miller Library received two shipments of books. On Monday, she received one shipment of 10 boxes, with 32 books in each box. On Wednesday, she received another shipment of 30 boxes, with 12 books in each box. On which day did she receive more books?

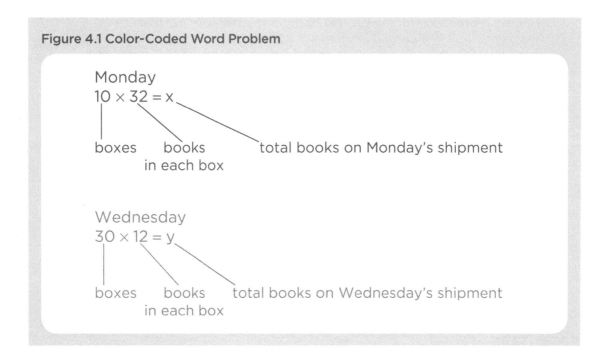

Figure 4.1 Color-Coded Word Problem

Monday
$10 \times 32 = x$

boxes   books   total books on Monday's shipment
         in each box

Wednesday
$30 \times 12 = y$

boxes   books   total books on Wednesday's shipment
         in each box

TASK 1: WORD PROBLEM TASK CARDS

online resources ▸ To download printable resources for this task, visit **resources.corwin.com/ClassroomReadyMath/4–5**

POST-TASK NOTES: REFLECTION & NEXT STEPS

Mathematics Standard

- Use parentheses, brackets, or braces in numerical expressions, and evaluate expressions with these symbols.

Mathematical Practices

- Reason abstractly and quantitatively.
- Look for and make use of structure.

Vocabulary

- expression
- parentheses

Materials

- marker boards
- Counting Marker Collection cards

Mitchell's Markers

Write expressions with parentheses to represent a situation when addition or subtraction is the second step

TASK

Mitchell's Markers

Mitchell keeps all of his markers in a drawer. He has _____ boxes with 10 markers in each box and _____ loose markers. How can he figure out how many markers he has?

TASK PREPARATION

- Have physical boxes of markers and loose markers (crayons/pencils/etc. would also work) to show students a representation of Mitchell's collection. Toss these into a box or drawer so they are not organized. Students should not be able to readily see how many boxes or loose markers are in the collection.

- Print the Counting Marker Collection cards. Have these readily accessible to students.

- Consider how you will partner students for the task work.

  » During the Launch, have students share with a partner or small group before allowing ideas to be shared with the whole class. Think about how you will arrange students for this part. Will they come up to the carpet? How will they know who their discussion partner(s) will be?

  » During the Facilitate phase of the task, students should be organized into small heterogeneous groups (2–3).

LAUNCH

1. Share the story with students and show them a collection of markers.

2. Ask students to turn to a neighbor and tell about how many markers they think might be in the collection. Ask them to tell their partner how they made the estimate.

PRODUCTIVE STRUGGLE

This is not a formal "round then compute to estimate." Here, we are asking students to think about reasonableness.

» **Observe.** Pay attention to how students justify their estimates; are they noticing, for example, that they can see *at least 5 boxes and lots of loose markers, so there have to be at least 60 markers*?

3. On the board, record all predictions about the number of markers in the collection. Encourage students to think about reasonable and unreasonable answers.

   » Ask, "If Mitchell said he had 9 markers in all, would that make sense? Why not? What are some other counts that wouldn't make sense? Why?"

4. Ask the class to think about how Mitchell could find the actual number of markers in the collection. Direct them to talk in small groups; then have a few students share their group's idea with the class.

   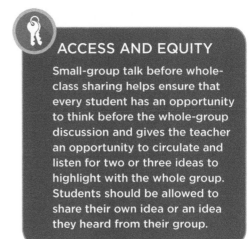

   ACCESS AND EQUITY

   Small-group talk before whole-class sharing helps ensure that every student has an opportunity to think before the whole-group discussion and gives the teacher an opportunity to circulate and listen for two or three ideas to highlight with the whole group. Students should be allowed to share their own idea or an idea they heard from their group.

   » Ask, "How can we find out how many markers Mitchell has?" Elicit from students that Mitchell needs to find out how many markers are in boxes and how many are loose. These two quantities can be combined to find the total number of markers.

   » Sketch a diagram on the board to represent this idea. Use a representation for an additive relationship that will be familiar to your students. Figure 4.2 gives a couple of examples.

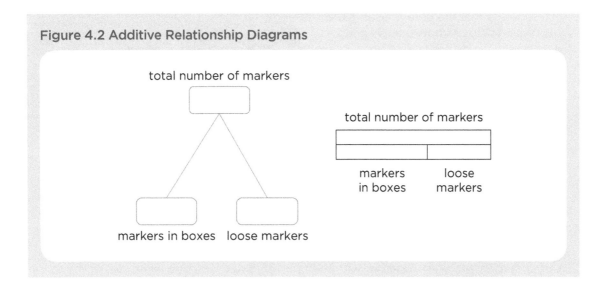

Figure 4.2 Additive Relationship Diagrams

5. Reveal to students that there are 8 boxes of markers. Refer back to the representation on the board. Point to the part of the representation labeled "markers in boxes" and ask, "How many markers are in 8 boxes? How do you know? What expression could we write to represent that?"

   » Write (8 × 10) on the appropriate place in the diagram.

   » Tell students there are 17 loose markers in the collection and add this to the appropriate place in the diagram.

6. Tell students, "We can use parentheses to show that this expression (*indicate the expression* 8 × 10) represents the total number of markers in the boxes. How will that help us figure out how many markers Mitchell has?" Elicit from students that adding that amount to the number of loose markers will give us the total number of markers.

7. Write the expression (8 × 10) + 17 on the board. Have students find the total number of markers and record the total in the diagram. Figure 4.3 shows filled-in diagrams.

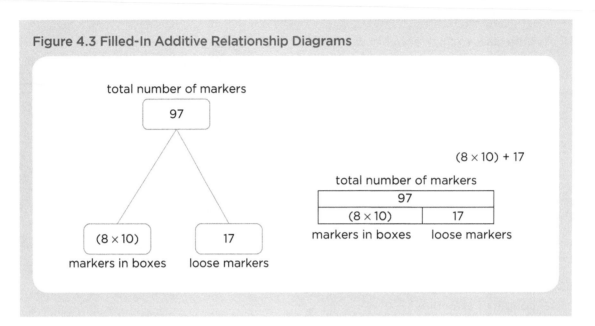

Figure 4.3 Filled-In Additive Relationship Diagrams

total number of markers

97

(8 × 10)   17

markers in boxes   loose markers

(8 × 10) + 17

total number of markers

97	
(8 × 10)	17

markers in boxes   loose markers

8. Tell students that the parentheses in the expression help us know that we need to evaluate 8 × 10 before adding because we want to add *the product of* 8 × 10.

! PRODUCTIVE STRUGGLE

Revisit students' estimates. Ask students to consider if it would make sense to just add 8 and 17. Is 25 a reasonable answer for the total number of markers?

FACILITATE

1. Organize students into pairs or small groups. Give each group a different Counting Marker Collections card and a blank version of the diagram you used to model the initial problem.

   » Say, "Each group is going to get a different card. You will work with your partner to figure out how each part of the story will be represented on the diagram. You will need to label your diagram and write an expression."

2. Direct students to work together with their partners to determine what part of the story is represented by each part of the diagram. Ask students to label the diagram using words from the story (total number of markers, boxed markers, etc.).

3. When each group has labeled their diagram, provide quantities for their problem. Ask them to add those quantities to the diagram and then write an expression that could be used to answer the question.

4. **Interview/Show Me.** Conduct interviews with each small group. Ask students to show and explain how each part of their expression connects to the story and to their diagram.

Note: Consider using the Observation and Interview (small group) tools for monitoring and recording task responses (see Appendix B).

CLOSE: MAKE THE MATH VISIBLE

1. Use an organizing structure such as *One Stay, Two Stray* to mix up the groups. Have the student who stayed explain how their expression represents the answer to their problem.

2. Bring the class together to look at the various expressions and corresponding diagrams. Ask students to share what they notice about how parentheses are used in each expression to represent one quantity from the story.

   » Stories A–C: The expression in parentheses represents the number of markers in boxes.

   » Story D: The expression in parentheses represents the number of markers Jessica has.

   » Story E: The expression in parentheses represents the number of markers Ibrahim has now (after losing some).

   » Story F: The expression in parentheses represents the number of markers Islah gives to River.

3. Focus students' attention on Story F. Ask students how they would evaluate the expression if it didn't have parentheses:

   » $17 - (8 + 5)$ vs. $17 - 8 + 5$

   » In the second expression (without parentheses), we would subtract a smaller amount from the 17. In the context of the story, this would be as if Islah gave River only 8 markers and Islah gets 5 new markers.

4. **Exit Task.** Have students find the value for each of the following expressions and respond to the prompt:

   $$(4 + 8) - 3 \qquad\qquad 10 + (2 \times 4)$$

   Prompt: What do parentheses mean in an expression?

TASK 2: COUNTING MARKER COLLECTION CARDS

online resources ➘ To download printable resources for this task, visit **resources.corwin.com/ ClassroomReadyMath/4–5**

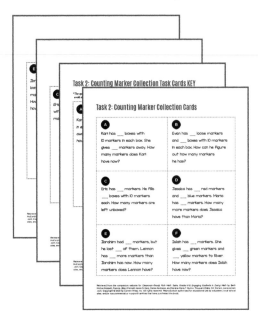

POST-TASK NOTES: REFLECTION & NEXT STEPS

Task 3
Teachers Go Shopping

Represent multiplicative comparison situations

TASK

Teachers Go Shopping

The 4th-grade teachers are ordering materials for classrooms. They want to order three times as many markers as they ordered last year. Last year, they ordered 250 markers. How many markers should they order this year?

TASK PREPARATION

- Have some markers available for students to use as needed to represent smaller cases.

- Consider how you will partner students for the task work.

  » During the Launch, have students share with a partner or small group before allowing ideas to be shared with the whole class. Think about how you will arrange students for this part. Will they come up to the carpet? How will they know who their discussion partner(s) will be?

  » During the Facilitate phase of the task, students could be organized into small heterogeneous groups (2–3).

> **ALTERNATE LEARNING ENVIRONMENT**
>
> When facilitating this task with students at home, consider altering the context to include a typical at-home activity such as picking up toys or gathering sticks from the yard. Show students a small collection and challenge them to collect three times as many.

LAUNCH

1. Share only the first part of the story with students: *The 4th-grade teachers are ordering materials for classrooms. They want to order three times as many markers as they ordered last year.* Ask students:

   » What is happening in this story?

   » Can you picture this story in your head? What do you see?

   » Will the teachers have more markers last year or this year? How do you know?

Mathematics Standards

- Interpret a multiplication equation as a comparison—e.g., interpret $35 = 5 \times 7$ as a statement that 35 is 5 times as many as 7 and 7 times as many as 5. Represent verbal statements of multiplicative comparisons as multiplication equations.

- Multiply or divide to solve word problems involving multiplicative comparison, e.g., by using drawings and equations with a symbol for the unknown number to represent the problem, distinguishing multiplicative comparison from additive comparison.

Mathematical Practices

- Make sense of problems and persevere in solving them.

- Reason abstractly and quantitatively.

Vocabulary

- times as many
- times as much
- comparison

Materials

- markers

2. Listen for and record statements the students make about the relationships in the story. For example:

   » They will have more markers this year.

   » They didn't have as many markers last year.

   » The teachers will get three times as many markers this year as last year.

3. Before sharing the actual number of markers ordered last year, ask students to model some smaller sample cases.

   » Say, "Suppose the teachers only ordered 1 marker last year."

   » **Show Me**. Draw a picture or use counters to show me how many they will order this year.

4. Display student representations and have the class generate equations to match. Facilitate a discussion highlighting the relationships in the problem.

> ### 👓 STRENGTHS SPOTTING
> Encouraging students to represent their solutions in different ways provides teachers an opportunity to notice and leverage representations that are strengths for each student.

FACILITATE

1. Present the full task (see page 57) to the students.

2. Organize the students into pairs or small groups to solve the problem. Ask groups to use a comparison drawing and write an equation to represent the situation.

3. **Observe.** Pay attention to the relationships between the drawings and equations students generate. Students should be able to explain how their representations connect to the story context.

4. Encourage students to refer back to the relationship statements that were recorded on the board to check that their representations make sense.

5. **Interview.** We said that they should have more markers this year. How does your model show that?

Note: Consider using the observation, interview (small group), and Show Me tools for monitoring and recording task responses (see Appendix B).

6. Ask students to tell you how their representations would change and how they would stay the same if the teachers had ordered a different number of markers last year.

7. Consider partnering students who have used different representations. Ask them to identify how their representations are the same and how they are different. How does each representation show the *three times as much* relationship?

8. **Hinge Question**. How is *three times as much* different from *three more*?

CLOSE: MAKE THE MATH VISIBLE

1. Bring the class together to discuss the solution to the task. Display student representations and equations. Encourage students to make connections between and among representations, equations, and the story. Some possible representations are shown in Figure 4.4.

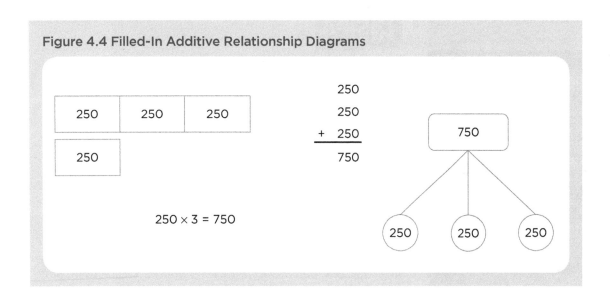

Figure 4.4 Filled-In Additive Relationship Diagrams

It may be necessary to group sets within representations to highlight the "three times as many" relationship.

» How is the *three times as much* relationship represented?

» Where is the number of markers the teachers ordered *last year* represented?

» Where is the number of markers the teachers will order *this year* represented?

2. Revisit the relationship statements students made at the beginning of the task and discuss how their models and equations show those relationships.

» **Exit Task.** Eric has 20 stickers. Jessica has 80 stickers.

» Describe the relationship between the number of stickers that Eric and Jessica each have.

» How is a *times as much* relationship represented?

POST-TASK NOTES: REFLECTION & NEXT STEPS

Mathematics Standard

- Use parentheses, brackets, or braces in numerical expressions, and evaluate expressions with these symbols.

Mathematical Practices

- Reason abstractly and quantitatively.
- Look for and make use of structure.

Materials

- student marker boards/ whiteboards
- Numberless Word Problem task cards
- collection of photos
- photo album (if needed)
- square color tiles

Vocabulary

- expression
- parentheses

Task 4
Karla's Photo Album

Write expressions with parentheses to represent a situation in which multiplication or division is the second step

TASK

Karla's Photo Album

Karla has 49 photos from the school fair and 23 photos from field day. She decides to put all the photos in an album. She puts 6 photos on each page of the album. How many pages will she use?

TASK PREPARATION

- Have a physical collection of photos from magazines (color tiles could be used to represent photos) to show students a representation of the situation. Have the tiles piled in two groups (49 in one and 23 in the other). Students should not be able to readily see the combined total or groups of 6 photos.

- Print and prepare task cards. Have these readily accessible to students.

- Consider how you will partner students for the task work.

  » During the Launch, have students share with a partner or small group before allowing ideas to be shared with the whole class. Think about how you will arrange students for this part. Will they come up to the carpet? How will they know who their discussion partner(s) will be?

  » During the Facilitate phase of the task, students could be organized into small heterogeneous groups (2–3).

LAUNCH

1. Share the task with students and show them the two piles of photos. It may be helpful to show students an example of a photo album so they understand how the photos are meant to be organized (Figure 4.5).

2. Ask students to estimate the total number of album pages needed. Record estimations on the board. Teachers may wish to give students sticky notes to use for this purpose so that students can easily adjust their estimates as they work through the task.

Figure 4.5 Task 4 Sample Image

Source: bgwalker/iStock.com

» **Observe.** Pay attention to how students justify their estimates—are they noticing, for example, that *the two piles together have more than 60 photos, so there should be more than 10 pages*?

» Ask, "How can we find out how many pages Karla will need?"

» Students may suggest counting out groups of 6 photos. Sketch a diagram on the board to represent this idea. Use a representation for equal groups division that will be familiar to your students. See Figure 4.6.

PRODUCTIVE STRUGGLE

This is not a formal "round then compute to estimate" opportunity. Here, we are asking students to think about reasonableness.

Figure 4.6 Group Counting Diagram

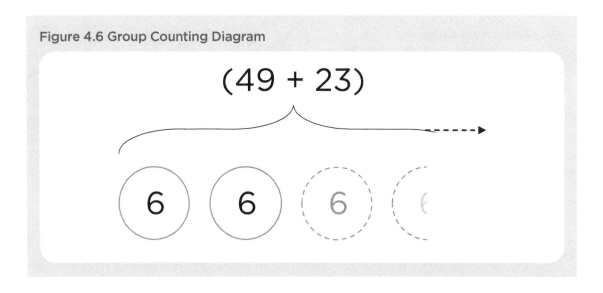

3. Tell students, "We can use parentheses to show that this expression (*indicate the expression* 49 + 23) represents the total number of photos." Ask, "How will that help us figure out how many pages Karla needs?"

4. Write the expression (49 + 23) ÷ 6 on the board. Have students find the number of pages needed and compare it with their estimates (Figure 4.7).

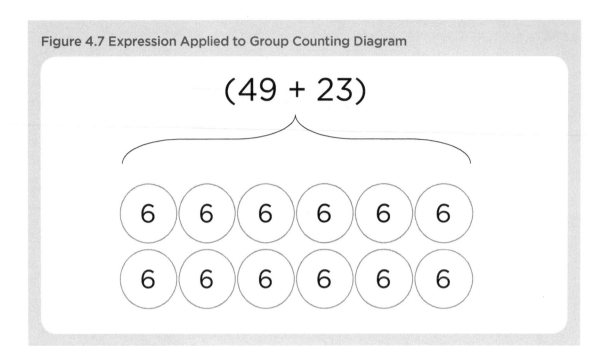

Figure 4.7 Expression Applied to Group Counting Diagram

$$(49 + 23)$$

5. Tell students that the parentheses in the expression help us know that we need to calculate 49 + 23 before dividing because we want to share *the total of 49 + 23* into equal groups of 6.

FACILITATE

1. Organize the students into pairs or small groups. Take a moment to have students share ways they know how to represent multiplication and division situations (area model, number line, etc.).

2. Give each group a different Numberless Word Problem task card. Say, "Each group is going to get a different card. You will work with your partner to figure out how each part of the story will be represented. You will need to label your representation and write an expression."

STRENGTHS SPOTTING

Use a focusing pattern of questioning to bring student strengths to the surface. Listen to students' responses with curiosity and take advantage of opportunities to celebrate strengths in students' ideas by explicitly calling attention to the strength.

3. Direct students to work together with their partners to determine how to represent the story situation. Ask students to label the representation using words from the story.

4. When each group has labeled their representation, provide the missing quantities for their problem. Ask them to add that information to the representation and then write an expression that could be used to answer the question.

5. **Interview/Show Me.** Conduct interviews with each small group. Ask students to show and explain how each part of their expression connects to the story and to their diagram.

Note: Consider using the Interview (small group) and Show Me tools for monitoring and recording task responses (see Appendix B).

CLOSE: MAKE THE MATH VISIBLE

1. Conduct an Open Gallery Walk so students can see the various expressions and corresponding diagrams. Ask students to observe and be prepared to share what they notice about how parentheses are used in each expression to represent one quantity from the story.

2. Focus students' attention on Story A (see Numberless Word Problem Task cards). Ask students how they would evaluate the expression if it didn't have parentheses:

    $5 \times (19 + 23)$ vs. $5 \times 19 + 23$

    » In the second expression (without parentheses), we would represent 5 rows of 19, plus 23 more. In the context of the story, this would represent Kari laying down 19 red tiles in each of 5 rows and then laying 23 yellow tiles (not 23 yellow tiles in each row).

3. **Hinge Question.** What different values could you find for this expression by adding a set of parentheses in different positions?

    $15 \div 3 + 2$

TASK 4: NUMBERLESS WORD PROBLEMS TASK CARDS

online resources ↖ To download printable resources for this task, visit **resources.corwin.com/ClassroomReadyMath/4–5**

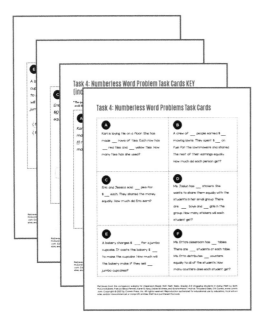

POST-TASK NOTES: REFLECTION & NEXT STEPS

Operations and Algebraic Thinking

Factors and Multiples

TASK 5: GRADE 4: LUNCHTIME LOGISTICS

Solve multistep word problems posed with whole numbers and having whole-number answers using the four operations, including problems in which remainders must be interpreted.

TASK 6: GRADE 5: INK BLOTS

Write simple expressions that record calculations with numbers and interpret numerical expressions without evaluating them.

TASK 7: GRADE 4: RECTANGLE RELAY

Find all factor pairs for a whole number in the range 1–100. Recognize that a whole number is a multiple of each of its factors. Determine whether a given whole number in the range 1–100 is a multiple of a given one-digit number. Determine whether a given whole number in the range 1–100 is prime or composite.

TASK 8: GRADE 4: WHAT'S IN A NUMBER?

Find all factor pairs for a whole number in the range 1–100. Recognize that a whole number is a multiple of each of its factors. Determine whether a given whole number in the range 1–100 is a multiple of a given one-digit number. Determine whether a given whole number in the range 1–100 is prime or composite.

TASK 9: GRADE 4: MASTERING MULTIPLES

Determine whether a given whole number in the range 1–100 is a multiple of a given one-digit number.

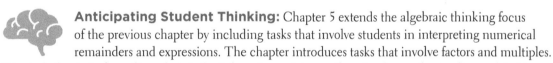

Anticipating Student Thinking: Chapter 5 extends the algebraic thinking focus of the previous chapter by including tasks that involve students in interpreting numerical remainders and expressions. The chapter introduces tasks that involve factors and multiples. The tasks begin to formalize what students have been doing as they develop understandings related to multiplication (factoring) and counting by, for example, 2s, 5s, 10s, and so on (multiples). Also make sure to provide time for students to discuss relatedness and differences between factors of numbers and multiples and other task-related considerations. Your use of observation, interviews, and hinge questions will be an important way to monitor student progress with the important algebra-related concepts in this chapter.

THINK ABOUT IT

Prepare, in advance, the questions you will use with individual or small-group interviews and hinge point questions for the tasks that involve factors and multiples.

Mathematics Standard

- Solve multistep word problems posed with whole numbers and having whole-number answers using the four operations, including problems in which remainders must be interpreted.

Mathematical Practices

- Make sense of problems and persevere in solving them.
- Reason abstractly and quantitatively.
- Construct viable arguments and critique the reasoning of others.

Vocabulary

- quotient
- remainder
- dividend
- divisor
- justify
- expression

Materials

- Lunchtime Logistics student page, one per group
- chart paper
- markers
- Interpreting Remainders student page
- Base Ten Block student page

Task 5
Lunchtime Logistics

Reason about remainders

TASK

Lunchtime Logistics

Mrs. Chu is an assistant principal at a local elementary school. She is trying to figure out the number of tables she will need to seat students in the cafeteria during lunch. She knows that nine students can sit comfortably at one table.

Grade	Number of Students	Number of Tables Needed
K	59	
1	138	
2	75	
3	152	
4	65	
5	64	

1. How many children will need to sit at a table that isn't full?

2. How many tables are needed for each grade? Fill in the chart.

TASK PREPARATION

- Assign students to work in groups of 4. Plan for heterogeneous groups.

LAUNCH

1. Present part of the task:

> Mrs. Chu is an assistant principal at a local elementary school. She is trying to figure out the number of tables she will need to seat students in the cafeteria during lunch. She knows that nine students can sit comfortably at one table.
>
> | Grade | Number of Students | Number of Tables Needed |
> |---|---|---|
> | K | 59 | |
>
> How many tables will be completely filled?

2. Utilize *See-Think-Wonder*. Ask students, "What do you *see* and *think* you know so far?"

3. Record student ideas.

4. Ask students, "What questions or wonders do you have?"

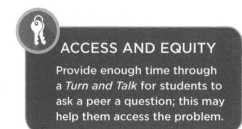

ACCESS AND EQUITY

Provide enough time through a *Turn and Talk* for students to ask a peer a question; this may help them access the problem.

FACILITATE

1. Assign students to their groups. Distribute materials. Give groups time to explore how to find a solution to the question. Monitor students who may need support with dividing a 2-digit dividend by a 1-digit divisor.

2. Then ask for and list possible solutions (some groups may arrive at an answer of 6, while others might give an answer of 7).

3. Ask, "Who would like to justify their group's solution?" After the student explains the expression they used to solve the problem (59 ÷ 9), pause and ask, "Why did many of you also choose 59 as your dividend and 9 as your divisor?"

4. Ensure that there is agreement that the quotient for 59 ÷ 9 is 6, with a remainder of 5 students. Then ask, "While 7 is a reasonable quotient, why does it not precisely answer the question?"

5. Discuss with students the "treatment" of the remaining students in this scenario by using questioning to elicit students' ideas:

   » If the question is, "How many tables will be completely filled?" the solution would be 6. However, there would be children who would not have a seat. What do we do with the children who do not have a seat?

   » If the question is, "How many tables are needed?" then we would include the remainder, and the solution would be 7 tables, because we need to account for the 5 extra kindergartners who need a table. *Note: Some students may argue that only 6 tables are needed because as we are considering kindergartners, they may be able to fit 5 extra students in 6 tables. Accept this student reasoning AND indicate that students must provide this written justification in their work.*

   » If the question is, "If as many tables as possible are filled with equal groups of 9 students, how many students will still need a table?" then the solution would be the remainder, which is 5 students.

6. Assign specific groups to calculate the number of tables needed for a particular grade (e.g., Group 1 works on Grade 1, . . .). Have all groups work on the last question.

CLOSE: MAKE THE MATH VISIBLE

1. Monitor group work and select and sequence how you will post student work on chart paper based on the division strategies they employ.

2. After group work is posted on the walls of the classroom in a particular sequence, call on groups to explain their solutions. Invite questions from other groups.

3. Focus on student thinking and reasoning about the remainder. For example, when solving for the number of tables needed in third grade, highlight the following as shown in Figure 5.1.

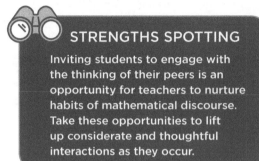

STRENGTHS SPOTTING

Inviting students to engage with the thinking of their peers is an opportunity for teachers to nurture habits of mathematical discourse. Take these opportunities to lift up considerate and thoughtful interactions as they occur.

Figure 5.1 Highlighted Third-Grade Student Thinking

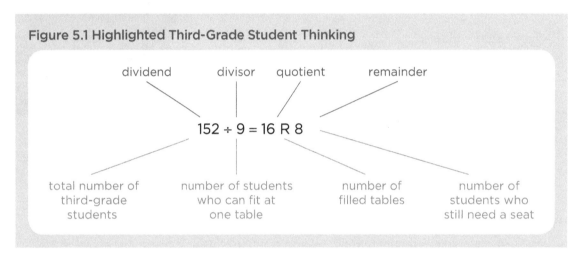

4. **Hinge Question.** What is the maximum number of tables Mrs. Chu will need for any one grade?

TASK 5: INTERPRETING REMAINDERS STUDENT PAGE

To download printable resources for this task, visit **resources.corwin.com/ ClassroomReadyMath/4–5**

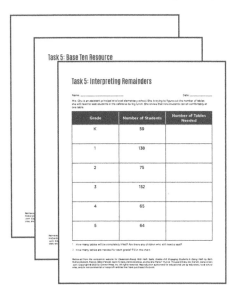

POST-TASK NOTES: REFLECTION & NEXT STEPS

Task 6
Ink Blots

Reason about how two or more expressions compare in value

TASK

Ink Blots

Mrs. Kay wrote some expressions on index cards for her math class. The next day, she noticed that some ink had spilled on the index cards. She showed the stained cards (Figure 5.2) to her class, and the students noticed that they could still put the cards in order from least to greatest. How could they do it? *The first number on all five cards is the same.*

Figure 5.2 "Stained" Cards

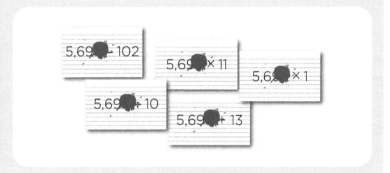

5,69█ – 102

5,69█ × 11

5,69█ × 1

5,69█ ÷ 10

5,69█ + 13

Ink blot source: fongfong2/iStock.com; Index card source: freesvg.org

TASK PREPARATION

- Group students into heterogeneous pairs or groups of three. Each group will get a set of the five expression cards to put in order from least to greatest.

ALTERNATE LEARNING ENVIRONMENT

An interactive version of this activity is available on Desmos for teachers facilitating this task through distance learning (https://bit.ly/31AwIPC).

- Students will also need space to lay out and rearrange their cards as they think through the task.

LAUNCH

1. Tell students the story and show them one of the "stained" cards (Figure 5.3). *Do not reveal the whole set.*

Figure 5.3 One "Stained" Card

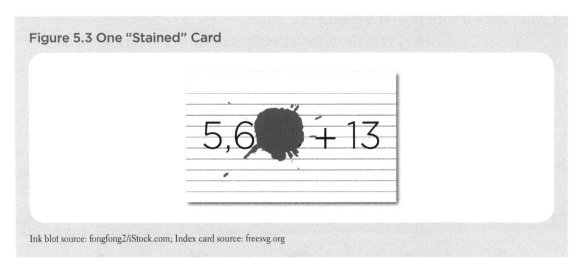

Ink blot source: fongfong2/iStock.com; Index card source: freesvg.org

2. Ask, "What can we know about the value of this expression even though there is a stain covering part of it? How do you know?"

3. Encourage students to engage in a *Pair-to-Pair Share* first; then have students share their ideas with the class. Encourage students to justify their thinking. Listen for reasoning that demonstrates understanding of the values and operations visible on the card. For example . . .

   » "It has to be more than 5,600 because the first number has 5 thousands and 6 hundreds, and it's even more than that because of the plus 13."

FACILITATE

1. Organize the students into pairs or small groups and give each group a set of expression cards.

2. Direct students to work together to put the expressions in order from least to greatest. As students work together, visit each group to:

   » **Observe.** Listen to students' discussions as they determine where to place each card. Their arguments will provide evidence of their understandings about the meaning of the operations on the cards.

   » **Interview.** Ask the following:

      » Which of these expressions has the least value? Why?

      » Which has the greatest value? How do you know?

      » How did you decide that this expression has a greater value than this one (*indicate two cards the students have ordered*)?

> **!** **PRODUCTIVE STRUGGLE**
>
> In order for students to have opportunities to make sense of and critique the reasoning of others, teachers must resist the urge to intercede too soon. Allow students to order the cards in ways that make sense to them. Use questioning to uncover conceptions (and misconceptions) about the values on each card.

Note: Consider using the Observation and Interview (small group) tools for monitoring and recording task responses (see Appendix B).

3. Consider partnering groups that finish early. Have partnered groups share their ordered sets and discuss their thinking.

4. **Hinge Question.** What is an answer that you know for sure would be *between* these two cards (*indicate two cards students have ordered*)?

CLOSE: MAKE THE MATH VISIBLE

1. Conduct an Open Gallery Walk or display all ordered sets in a place where the whole class can see them all.

2. Bring the class together to discuss the task. Ask students to share strategies you wish to highlight (from the observations and interviews).

3. Revisit the original task (Figure 5.4) and ask students to leverage the strategies discussed to quickly order that set of expressions.

Figure 5.4 "Stained" Cards

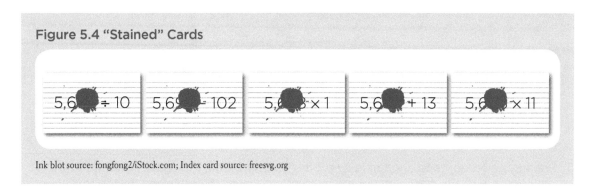

Ink blot source: fongfong2/iStock.com; Index card source: freesvg.org

---

Some examples of student reasoning may include . . .

» *Reasoning about the first two expressions:* Dividing 5,600 into 10 equal groups would make less than 1,000 in each group. Subtracting 102 from 5,600 would still leave more than 5,000.

» *Reasoning about the 2nd and 4th expressions:* Subtracting more than 100 would make the answer less than 5,600. If I add 13 to a number that is already at least 5,600 it has to be greater than that amount.

» *Reasoning about the 3rd and 5th expressions:* One group of 5,600 has to be less than 11 groups of 5,600!

4. **Exit Task.** Write an expression that you know for sure would have a value *between* two of the cards in this list. Explain your thinking.

TASK 6: INK BLOT EXPRESSION CARDS

To download printable resources for this task, visit **resources.corwin.com/ ClassroomReadyMath/4–5**

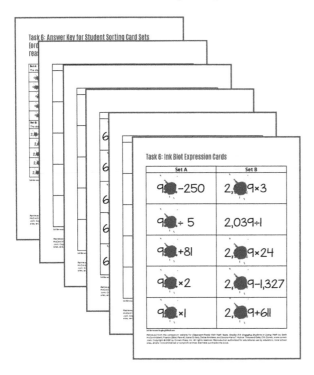

POST-TASK NOTES: REFLECTION & NEXT STEPS

Mathematics Standard

- Find all factor pairs for a whole number in the range 1–100. Recognize that a whole number is a multiple of each of its factors. Determine whether a given whole number in the range 1–100 is a multiple of a given one-digit number. Determine whether a given whole number in the range 1–100 is prime or composite.

Mathematical Practice

- Look for and make use of structure.

Vocabulary

- factor
- multiple
- commutative property of multiplication
- area
- prime
- composite

Materials

- centimeter grid paper
- centimeter cubes (base 10 unit cubes) or color tiles
- markers
- scissors
- tape or glue
- plain paper for posters (chart paper, large sticky notes, etc.)

Task 7
Rectangle Relay

Understand why the number 1 is neither prime nor composite

TASK

Rectangle Relay

Create a poster showing area models representing all possible rectangles for a given area from 1 square unit (1 u^2) to 100 square units (100 u^2). Analyze patterns in the resulting collections of rectangles.

TASK PREPARATION

- Prepare enough sets of materials for each pair of students. Determine in advance how you will assign areas to student pairs so that each pair has about the same number of rectangles to make (e.g., the group with *Area = 4 u^2* will have fewer rectangles to make than the group with *Area = 36 u^2*).

- It may be helpful to pre-cut rectangles with *Area = 16 u^2* out of centimeter grid paper for the sample poster, but *do not add them to the poster in advance* (see Launch, Step 2).

LAUNCH

1. Introduce the task to students. Tell them, "Today we are going to explore all the different rectangles we can build with the same area."

2. Ask, "How many rectangles could be made using 16 square units? What dimensions might the rectangle have?"

   » Have students *Turn and Talk* with their partner. How many rectangles do you estimate we might find?

   » Ask students to share possible dimensions and record their dimensions on the grid paper listing the equation (e.g., 4×4). As each set of factors is named, add the corresponding rectangle(s) to a prepared poster.

> ## ! PRODUCTIVE STRUGGLE
>
> Allow student thinking to guide the construction of the poster—do not pre-make it. Provide collections of 16 unit cubes or color tiles for students to arrange into rectangles. Use a document camera to show student arrangements and connect them to the grid paper representation of each rectangle.

3. Ask students, "How is a 2 × 8 rectangle the same or different from an 8 × 2 rectangle?" Listen for ideas such as:

   » They are "going different directions."

   » One has 2 rows and one has 8 rows.

   » They both have 16 squares in all.

4. Tell students that for today's activity, we will consider the rectangles like 2 × 8 and 8 × 2 to be different because one is oriented at a 90° rotation from the other. This is a great opportunity to review the Commutative Property of Multiplication. Ask, "If we represent 2 × 8 with a rectangle that has 2 rows of 8, what would the rectangle look like for 8 × 2?" and "Why is there only one rectangle for 4 × 4? Why do you think people call 16 a square number?"

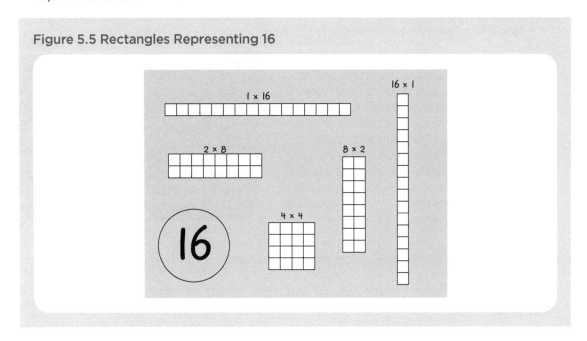

Figure 5.5 Rectangles Representing 16

5. Once the poster is complete (see Figure 5.5), ask, "Look back at our predictions. Did we find as many rectangles as we thought we might? How do we know when we have shown all the possible rectangles with an area of 16 square units?"

FACILITATE

1. Group students into heterogeneous pairs.

2. Assign area posters to each group. Be sure several pairs start off with some prime numbers, but consider keeping a few of the areas with 3 to 4 factor pairs back for early finishers to complete as time allows.

3. Have students post each completed poster on the class marker board or some other common location in the classroom.

4. **Interview.** As students work, conduct interviews with each pair.

   » How many rectangles do you estimate you will have for this area? Why?

   » Did you find an even number of rectangles or an odd number of rectangles? Why do you think that happened?

   » What are you noticing about the shape of the different rectangles on your poster?

» Are you noticing any patterns in the rectangles you see on the posters people are hanging up?

» Write an expression to describe the area of this rectangle. Which factor represents the rows? Which factor represents the columns?

Note: Consider using the Interview (small group) tool for monitoring and recording task responses (see Appendix B).

CLOSE: MAKE THE MATH VISIBLE

1. After enough of a collection of posters is displayed on the board (including the poster for 1 u^2 several prime numbers, several square numbers, and several composite numbers), bring the whole class together.

2. Facilitate a Notice and Wonder about the posters.

3. Record student observations on the board. After recording several student observations, rearrange several of the posters to make two groups: posters with exactly two rectangles (prime numbers) and posters with more than two rectangles (composite numbers) as shown in Figure 5.6. *Do not label the groups. Pull down the poster for 1 u^2 and a few other posters (some primes and some composites) to save for classification at a later time.*

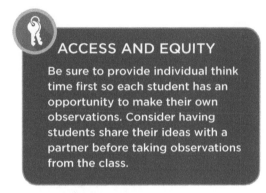

ACCESS AND EQUITY

Be sure to provide individual think time first so each student has an opportunity to make their own observations. Consider having students share their ideas with a partner before taking observations from the class.

Figure 5.6 Posters of Prime and Composite Numbers

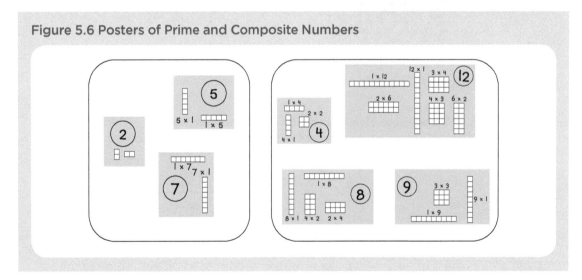

4. Ask students, "Look at these two groups. What rule do you think I used to group the posters?"

5. Show another poster (*not* 1). Ask students to predict where the poster belongs. Place the poster in the correct group and ask students to reflect on their predictions. "Has your thinking changed? Tell your neighbor what you think the rule is now."

6. Once the class has agreed that one group is posters with two rectangles and the other has more than two, direct their attention to the first group.

» Ask, "What do you notice about the two rectangles on each of these posters?" (They are all 1 × *n* and *n* × 1 rectangles.)

» Label this group "Prime Numbers" and tell students the definition and write it on the board: "When a number has *exactly two factors*, 1 and itself, mathematicians call it a prime number."

7. Next, direct students' attention to the second group of posters. Ask students, *"Turn and Talk* with your neighbor. How do you know that these numbers are *not* prime numbers?"

   » Ask, "What do you notice about the number of rectangles on each of these posters?" (There are more than two rectangles.)

   » Label this group "Composite Numbers"; tell students the definition and write it on the board: "When a number has *more than two factors* mathematicians call it a composite number."

8. One at a time, show students each of the posters that haven't yet been placed in a group (save the poster 1 for last). Ask, "Is ___ a prime number or a composite number?" Place each poster as the class agrees on its classification.

   » Have students practice the definitions using the sentence frame: "___ is a *prime/ composite* number because ___. (For example, *"15 is a composite number because it has more than two factors."*)

9. Finally, show students the poster for 1 and have students *Pair-to-Pair Share:* "What do you notice about this poster? Does it fit in either of our groups?"

   » Listen in on student discussions. Ask students with different ideas to share them with the class. Some students may think 1 can go in the prime number group because it has two factors (even though they are the same). Other students may say there should be a new group for "fewer than two factors."

   » Facilitate a discussion with the class. After students have an opportunity to discuss their thinking, tell them that the number 1 is neither prime nor composite. Ask, "What is special about this number that makes it different from prime numbers and composite numbers?" (There is only one rectangle—1 has exactly one factor.)

10. **Hinge Question.** The number 2 is prime because it has exactly two factors: 1 and 2. Are there any other even numbers that are prime? Explain.

POST-TASK NOTES: REFLECTION & NEXT STEPS

_____

_____

_____

_____

_____

Mathematics Standard

- Find all factor pairs for a whole number in the range 1–100. Recognize that a whole number is a multiple of each of its factors. Determine whether a given whole number in the range 1–100 is a multiple of a given one-digit number. Determine whether a given whole number in the range 1–100 is prime or composite.

Mathematical Practices

- Look for and make use of structure.
- Construct viable arguments and critique the reasoning of others.

Vocabulary

- factor
- multiple

Materials

- factor/multiple Venn diagram page (If desired, these can be laminated so students can write on them with dry-erase markers.)
- number cards. *n* values could be written right on the Venn pages in lieu of printing these cards)
- calculators, one per student

Task 8
What's in a Number?

Understand that every number is both a factor and a multiple of itself

TASK

What's in a Number?

Students will generate factors and multiples of a given number and sort them using a Venn diagram.

TASK PREPARATION

- Organize students into heterogeneous pairs.
- Prepare one Venn diagram page and one number card for each pair.

LAUNCH

1. Show students the Venn diagram for *n* = 100 without labeling the circles. Write a few numbers in the left and right side of the Venn but cover them with sticky notes before students see them (Figure 5.7).

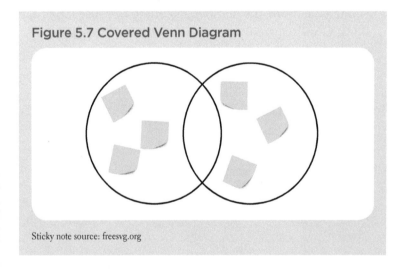

Figure 5.7 Covered Venn Diagram

Sticky note source: freesvg.org

2. One by one, reveal the numbers in the diagram. After each number is revealed, ask students to make predictions about the labels for each circle. Give them opportunities to *Pair-to-Pair Share* before taking ideas from the class.

3. Allow students to suggest additional numbers to write in the diagram. As they suggest additional numbers, write them where they belong in the diagram (some will fall outside the circles). See Figure 5.8.

Figure 5.8 Filled Venn Diagram

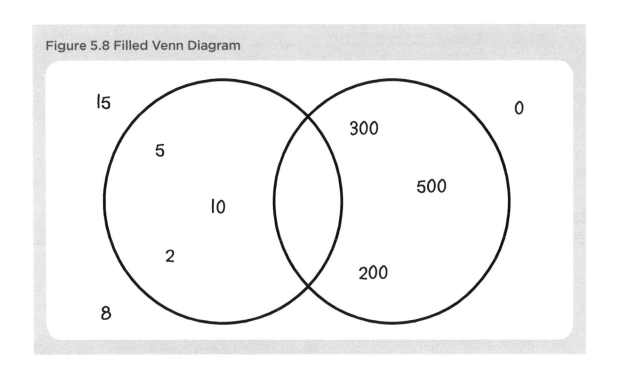

PRODUCTIVE STRUGGLE

Students may figure out the rule for the right circle more quickly than the left. Allow students to grapple with the missing rule(s) for a few minutes. If you notice students are starting to make random guesses, reveal the missing rule(s) and move on.

4. Once the rules have been revealed, give students the opportunity to share additional factors and multiples. Encourage them to write these up on the poster themselves. Figure 5.9 shows a filled-in Venn diagram with rules revealed.

Figure 5.9 Expanded Venn Diagram

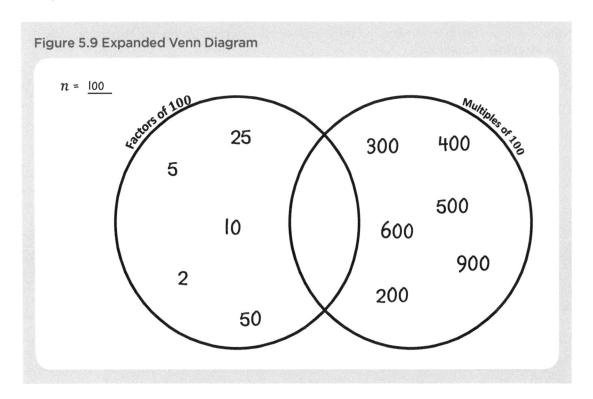

5. After placing a few examples of factors and multiples, tell students they will work with partners to make posters like this for different values of n.

FACILITATE

1. Organize the students into pairs or small groups and give each group a number card, a Venn diagram page, and calculators.

2. Direct students to work together to generate as many factors and multiples of their number as they can in the time allowed.

3. **Interview.** As students work, visit each pair to ask how they are finding factors and multiples. Select one of the numbers ($\neq n$) students have already placed in the diagram. Ask how they know the number can be placed only in that specific place on the diagram. For example, "How do you know that 4 can only be in the 'Factors of n' part of the Venn. Why can't it go in the 'Multiples of n' part?"

ACCESS AND EQUITY

The purpose of this activity is for students to be able to notice how a number n relates to both its factors and its multiples. This activity is not meant to be computation practice. The use of calculators will ensure that each and every student can engage in the task, regardless of their computational proficiency with multiplication and division.

4. **Hinge Question.** Where would n fit your diagram? Why?

Note: Consider using the Interview (small group) tool for monitoring and recording task responses (see Appendix B).

CLOSE: MAKE THE MATH VISIBLE

1. Display all the Venn diagrams in a location in the room where everyone can see them (document camera if available).

2. Bring the class together to discuss the task.

3. Facilitate a "Notice and Wonder" about the student work. Have students do a *Pair-to-Pair Share* before taking observations from the class. Some examples of student "notices" might include . . .

   » The numbers in the leftmost section of the diagram are all less than n.

   » The numbers in the rightmost section of the diagram are all greater than n.

   » We can skip count by n to find more multiples.

   » We can always add more multiples to a poster, but there are a limited number of factors.

4. Call students' attention to the placement of *n* in each diagram.

» If some pairs have already placed their *n* number in the center part of the diagram: Direct students to look at the posters with a number in the center part of the diagram. Ask, "What do you notice about the numbers in the center of a diagram? Is there a number that could fit in the center of your diagram? Why?"

» If no pairs have placed their *n* number in the Venn: Ask students, "Think about your *n* number. Where would that go in your diagram? Why?"

» If some pairs have placed their *n* number in the diagram but in different spots: Say, "I see that some students have added their *n* number in their diagram (*circle or highlight these*). Some groups think it goes in the left part of the Venn diagram, but others think it goes in the right part or in the center. Talk with your partner. In which place do you think your *n* number would fit on your diagram? Can it go in more than one place? Why?"

5. Through questioning, elicit the justification that *n* can be considered both a "Factor of *n*" and also a "Multiple of *n*" because *n* • 1 = *n*. Have every pair add their *n* number to their own diagram in the center overlap.

6. **Hinge Question.** Can any other number fit in the center part of your diagram? Explain.

TASK 8: STUDENT NUMBER CARDS

To download printable resources for this task, visit **resources.corwin.com/ ClassroomReadyMath/4–5**

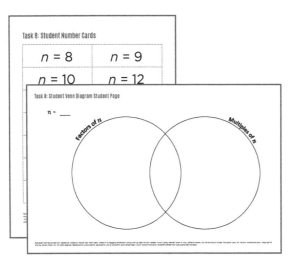

POST-TASK NOTES: REFLECTION & NEXT STEPS

Mathematics Standard

- Determine whether a given whole number in the range 1–100 is a multiple of a given one-digit number.

Mathematical Practice

- Look for and make use of structure.

Vocabulary

- multiple
- array

Materials

- color tiles, wooden cubes, or connecting cubes
- 1-inch grid paper
- markers
- number cards, one per group

Task 9
Mastering Multiples

Develop a conceptual understanding of multiples

TASK

Mastering Multiples

Students will build rectangular arrays for a given whole number and determine whether a number *n* is a multiple of that number.

TASK PREPARATION

- Organize students into heterogeneous groups of four.

- Prepare grid paper, markers, color tiles, wooden cubes, or connecting cubes and one number card (from companion website) for each group.

LAUNCH

1. Organize the students into groups of 4.

2. Display the following question on the board and ask students to *Think-Pair-Share*.
   Is 18 a multiple of 4?

3. Ask, "Are there other mathematics words that you think about when you hear the word *multiple*?" (*Students may share the words* multiply, product, *and* factors).

4. Clarify with students that when we multiply 4 by another whole number, the product is called a *multiple* of 4. So 8 is a multiple of 4 because $8 = 2 \times 4$.

5. Share with students that they will be making arrays (*starting with a* $1 \times 4 \ldots 8 \times 4$) to identify the multiples of 4 (see Figure 5.10). They can draw these arrays on grid paper or use color tiles, wooden cubes, or connecting cubes.

FACILITATE

1. Distribute the materials to the groups.

2. As an entire class, have students share the multiples of 4 they created (with different tools).

3. Have students compare their models and ask, "What relationships do you notice?" For example, students may notice that they can make the next multiple by adding another row of 4, noting that the multiples of 4 can be determined by skip counting by 4.

Figure 5.10 A Model Showing Multiples of 4

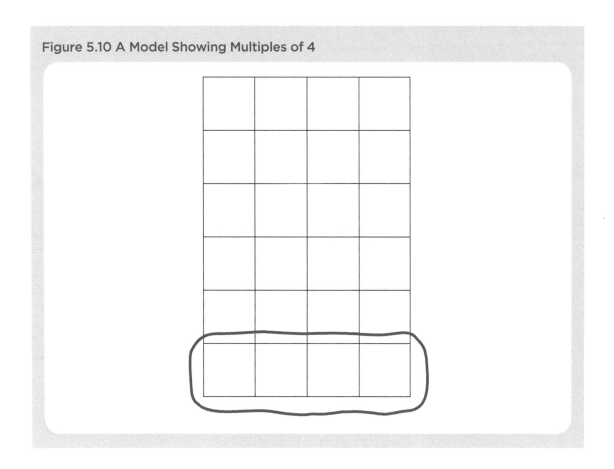

4. Start listing the multiples of 4 on the board as 4: 4, 8, 12, 16. Ask, "Aside from 4, 8, 12, and 16, what other numbers can be multiples of 4?

5. Then ask, "How could you tell if a number is or is not a multiple of 4? Can 18 be a multiple of 4?"

6. Distribute one number card for each group and ask students to build as many arrays as they can find for their given number.

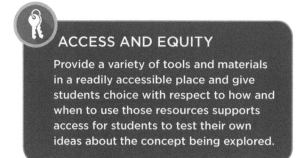

ACCESS AND EQUITY

Provide a variety of tools and materials in a readily accessible place and give students choice with respect to how and when to use those resources supports access for students to test their own ideas about the concept being explored.

7. **Observe.** Monitor group work, noting the tools groups choose to use (after creating a few arrays with concrete materials, some groups may choose to use grid paper or just make a list of the remaining multiples, having generalized the idea of multiples as $1 \times n$, $2 \times n$, etc.) and the strategies they employ.

Note: Consider using the Observation tool for monitoring and recording task responses (see Appendix B).

8. **Hinge Question.** Is 16 a multiple of 3? How do you know?

CLOSE: MAKE THE MATH VISIBLE

1. Explain to students that they will be doing a Gallery Walk to observe each group's solution to their particular number card.

2. Have students share and compare their solution pathways.

3. Ask, "How can we find the multiples of a number?"

4. Emphasize the following:

   » We can find the multiple of a number by finding the product of that number and a whole number. The rectangular arrays in Figure 5.11 show showing the multiples of 4: 4, 8, 12, 16, 20, and 24.

Figure 5.11 Rectangles Showing Multiples

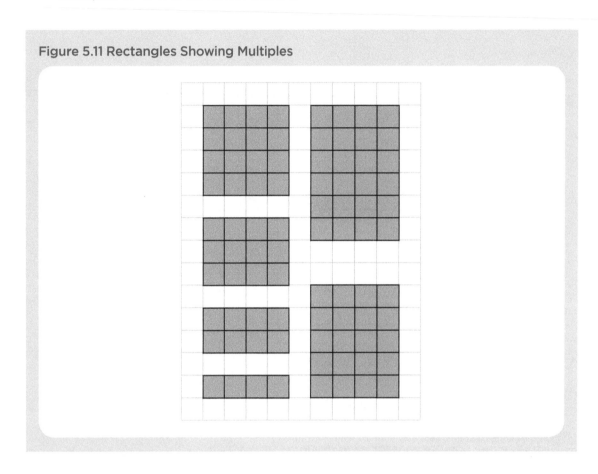

   » To determine whether a number, *n*, is a multiple of a given number (such as 6), ask yourself, "Is there a whole number I can multiply by 6 to get the product of *n*?" or "Could I make a rectangular array with a side length 6 to get an area of *n*?"

ALTERNATE LEARNING ENVIRONMENT

The NCTM Activity "The Product Game" (https://www.nctm.org/Classroom-Resources/Illuminations/Interactives/Product-Game/) could be used for additional practice with distance learners.

TASK 9: NUMBER CARDS

To download printable resources for this task, visit **resources.corwin.com/ ClassroomReadyMath/4–5**

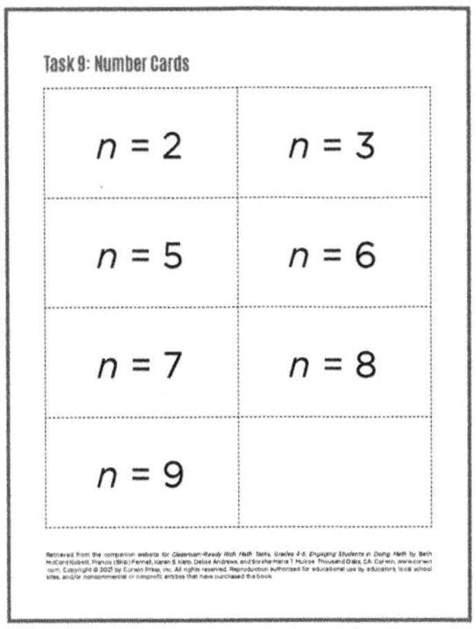

Task 9: Number Cards

$n = 2$	$n = 3$
$n = 5$	$n = 6$
$n = 7$	$n = 8$
$n = 9$	

POST-TASK NOTES: REFLECTION & NEXT STEPS

_____

_____

_____

_____

_____

_____

_____

_____

_____

Operations and Algebraic Thinking

Patterns and Relationships

GETTING STARTED

TASK 10: GRADE 4: DAISY CHAIN

Generate a number or shape pattern that follows a given rule. Identify apparent features of the pattern that were not explicit in the rule itself.

TASK 11: GRADE 5: RYAN AND RACHEL'S DEBATE

Generate two numerical patterns using two given rules. Identify apparent relationships between corresponding terms. Form ordered pairs consisting of corresponding terms from the two patterns, and graph the ordered pairs on a coordinate plane.

TASK 12: GRADE 5: THE SEQUENCE GAME

Generate two numerical patterns using two given rules. Identify apparent relationships between corresponding terms. Form ordered pairs consisting of corresponding terms from the two patterns, and graph the ordered pairs on a coordinate plane.

TASK 13: GRADE 4: CURIOUS COUNTING

Generate a number or shape pattern that follows a given rule. Identify apparent features of the pattern that were not explicit in the rule itself.

Anticipating Student Thinking: The algebraic thinking tasks in this chapter focus on patterns. The two 4th-grade tasks engage students in analyzing and generating patterns. The 5th-grade tasks focus on exploring numerical patterns and graphing ordered pairs to represent the similarities and differences of the patterns. As you plan for implementing these tasks, make sure to provide time for student exploration and discussion of the patterns within the tasks. Use of the observation and Show Me formative assessment techniques to monitor student progress should guide the pace of the implementation of the tasks. Each of the chapter's tasks should provide your students with the type of productive struggle important for students as they actually do mathematics and continue to connect their work with numbers and geometry to algebra.

THINK ABOUT IT

As you observe your students engaging in pattern-based tasks, interview them about what they are seeing and possible next steps in generating a pattern. Start with a strength—a portion of the task that you know represents a starting point for that student as they analyze a pattern and consider extending it.

Mathematics Standard

- Generate a number or shape pattern that follows a given rule. Identify apparent features of the pattern that were not explicit in the rule itself.

Mathematical Practices

- Make sense of problems and persevere in solving them.
- Look for and express regularity in repeated reasoning.

Vocabulary

- shape pattern
- number pattern
- growing pattern
- function table

Materials

- pattern blocks—the hexagon blocks (ensure there are enough hexagons; you will need at least 20 for each pair)
- Daisy Chain Patterns student page

Task 10
Daisy Chain

Connect visual and numerical representations of growing patterns

TASK

Daisy Chain

Draw the 4th picture in the pattern (Figure 6.1).

How many hexagons will you need to make the 8th picture in the pattern?

Figure 6.1 Daisy Chain Shape Pattern

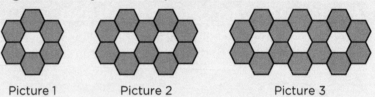

Picture 1   Picture 2   Picture 3

TASK PREPARATION

- Organize students into heterogeneous pairs.
- Prepare copies of the Daisy Chain Pattern student page.

ALTERNATE LEARNING ENVIRONMENT

To facilitate this task online, use a free digital manipulative like the Pattern Shapes app from the Math Learning Center (https://apps.mathlearningcenter.org/pattern-shapes/).

LAUNCH

1. Display the Figure 6.1 image on the board.

2. Activate student thinking by implementing the *See-Think-Wonder* routine. Ask, "What do you see? What are you thinking about? What do you wonder?"

3. Focus the class discussion on how students see the pattern growing.

FACILITATE

1. Group students in pairs and distribute pattern blocks.

2. **Observe.** Monitor pairs as they discuss how to make the 4th picture in the pattern.

3. **Interview.**

   » What do you notice is happening from one picture or pattern block model to the next?

   » How can we describe what is happening numerically? How can we describe the growth?

   » How did you know how many hexagons to use for Picture 4?

   » If there were a picture 0, how many hexagons would be in the picture?

> **! PRODUCTIVE STRUGGLE**
>
> Provide enough time for students to use hexagons to either make or draw the 4th or 5th term in the pattern as a way to understand what is happening numerically.

4. **Observe.** As you monitor student work, take note of pairs who continue to draw hexagons for the 5th picture, 6th, . . . ; students who may have created an organized list or table; and students who wrote equations.

Note: Consider using the Observation and Interview (small group) tools for monitoring and recording task responses (see Appendix B).

5. **Hinge Question.** How can you describe the number pattern for each time a hexagon is added?

CLOSE: MAKE THE MATH VISIBLE

1. Sequence student sharing based on your observations of student work.

2. Highlight three points in this task by eliciting student work and ideas:

   » We can connect a shape pattern to a numerical pattern.

Figure 6.2 Daisy Chain Shape Pattern Showing Growth

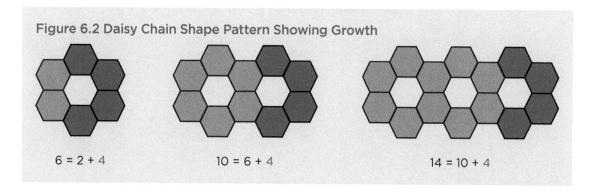

6 = 2 + 4   10 = 6 + 4   14 = 10 + 4

   » We can describe how the pattern grows (+ 4).

   » Some students, having noted that it takes 18 hexagons to create picture 4, may have incorrectly doubled 18 to figure out the number of hexagons needed for picture 8, arriving at a solution of 36. It may be helpful to show how many hexagons would be needed for picture 0, noted by 2 gray hexagons in Figure 6.2. We would need 34 hexagons to create picture 8 because we are starting with 2 hexagons, not 4.

TASK 10: DAISY CHAIN PATTERNS STUDENT PAGE

 To download printable resources for this task, visit **resources.corwin.com/ ClassroomReadyMath/4–5**

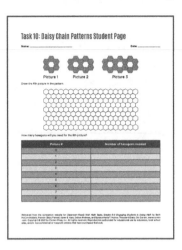

POST-TASK NOTES: REFLECTION & NEXT STEPS

Task 11
Ryan and Rachel's Debate

Visualize the difference between adding n and multiplying by n

TASK

Ryan and Rachel's Debate

Ryan and Rachel were exploring number patterns. They were looking at the rule $y = x + 2$ and the rule $y = x \times 2$. They organized their patterns in tables, and then they graphed both rules on a coordinate grid. Ryan graphed his points in gray, and Rachel graphed her points in blue. Figure 6.3 shows their work.

Figure 6.3 Ryan and Rachel's graphs

Rule: $y = x + 2$	
x	y
0	2
1	3
2	4
3	5

Rule: $y = x \times 2$	
x	y
0	0
1	2
2	4
3	6

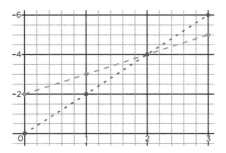

Ryan made a conjecture that adding 2 was not much different from multiplying by 2 because the *y* value was increasing with both kinds of rules. Rachel says multiplying by 2 is different from adding 2 because the *y* values changed more. Ryan and Rachel are both a little unsure, so they need your help to continue their exploration.

ACCESS AND EQUITY

The use of a technology-based tool like Desmos will enable students to quickly generate appropriately scaled graphs in order to engage in the reasoning and sense-making central to this task.

Mathematics Standard

- Generate two numerical patterns using two given rules. Identify apparent relationships between corresponding terms. Form ordered pairs consisting of corresponding terms from the two patterns, and graph the ordered pairs on a coordinate plane.

Mathematical Practices

- Construct viable arguments and critique the reasoning of others.
- Look for and make use of structure.

Vocabulary

- conjecture
- rule
- ordered pair
- coordinate plane
- graph
- point
- function table
- input
- output

Materials

- sticky notes
- T-chart (on poster paper or on the board)
- student devices with access to https://www.desmos.com/calculator
- Rule Cards
- Function Table pages

TASK PREPARATION

- Organize students into heterogeneous groups of 3 or 4. Provide each group with a device and access to Desmos or another digital graphing tool.

- Prepare student rule cards. Be sure that only one group gets the card labeled J ($n = 1$), half of the remaining groups get whole number cards (A–I), and the rest get fraction cards (K–P).

- Consider how you will share student graphs with the rest of the class. Can they be displayed on the class projector? Can they export graphs and share them to a class website? Can they print the graphs out?

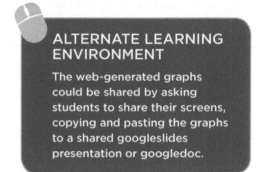

ALTERNATE LEARNING ENVIRONMENT

The web-generated graphs could be shared by asking students to share their screens, copying and pasting the graphs to a shared googleslides presentation or googledoc.

LAUNCH

1. Bring the whole class together for a quick discussion around the task.

2. Display only the image from the task at first. Facilitate a quick *See, Think, and Wonder*. Have students *Pair-to-Pair Share*; then elicit and record ideas from the whole class.

3. **Show Me**.

   » Point to a row in one of the tables: "Show me where this part of the pattern is represented on the graph."

   » Point to a point on the graph: "Show me where this point is represented in one of the tables."

   » Indicate the point (2,4) on the graph: This point looks like it is both on the blue line and on the gray line! What does this mean?"

4. After students have made connections between the tables and the graph, show them the entire task.

5. Ask students to *Turn-and-Learn* what their partner is thinking about Ryan's conjecture. Then give each student a sticky note and have them write a justification to add to a class T-chart like the one shown in Figure 6.4.

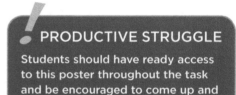

PRODUCTIVE STRUGGLE

Students should have ready access to this poster throughout the task and be encouraged to come up and edit or move their sticky note as their thinking develops.

Figure 6.4 Class T-Chart

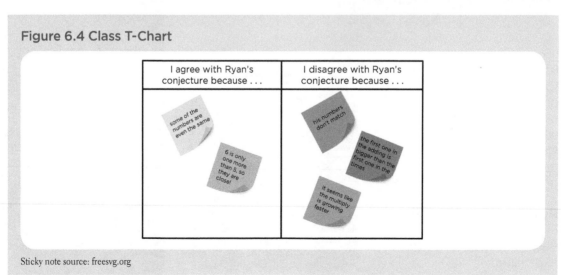

Sticky note source: freesvg.org

FACILITATE

1. Tell students they will have an opportunity to explore some more rules like the ones Ryan and Rachel were exploring. Say, "Together as a class, we will try to help Ryan and Rachel be able to justify their thinking and revise their conjectures if needed."

2. Organize the students into small groups. Each group should have a computer or other tool for generating graphs (see materials), a rule card, and one function table handout. Be sure that only one group has the card labeled J (add 1, multiply by 1).

   » Say, "Each group is going to get a different set of rules—one with addition and one with multiplication. You will work with your group to complete a table for each of your rules. Then you will graph the ordered pairs you generate."

   » Direct all groups to graph their points from the addition rules in red and their points from the multiplication rules in blue (as indicated on their rule cards). This will help facilitate the whole-group discussion at the conclusion of the task.

3. **Interview/Show Me.** Conduct interviews with each small group. Ask the following:

   » How are you finding the *y* values for your tables?

   » What are you noticing about the *y* values for the addition rule compared to the *y* values for the multiplication rule?

   » **Show me** which points on your graph represent your addition rule. Which ones represent your multiplication rule? How do you know?

4. As groups finish with each set of rules, let them know how you want them to share their graphs with the rest of the class.

5. Consider partnering early finishers with another small group to compare and discuss their graphs.

CLOSE: MAKE THE MATH VISIBLE

1. Bring the class together and revisit the T-chart made during the Launch phase of the task. Encourage students to share how their thinking may have changed or been refined during the exploration.

2. Select and Sequence students to share their results based on your interviews with the small groups. Encourage students to use the graphs and tables they and other groups have made to justify their thinking.

3. As students look at the various graphs each group has made, the following ideas should be highlighted:

   » When the number we are adding to *x* or multiplying by *x* is greater than 1, a value generated by the multiplication rule will increase more quickly than a value generated by the addition rule.

   » In the graph that shows *x* + 1 and *x* • 1, the lines are parallel and increase at the same rate.

4. Ask students to think about ways they can justify why these observations are true. Revisit the initial task and ask, "What is another way we can explain why the graph for *y* = *x* • 2 increases more quickly than the graph for *y* = *x* + 2?"

STRENGTHS SPOTTING

When students articulate how their thinking has changed or grown, focus on the strengths they share by naming the strength. For example, perhaps they tried multiple solution pathways. When students understand how they used their strengths to revise learning or build new learning, they are more likely to exhibit this behavior again.

» Students might use manipulatives or drawings to show specific cases to justify their thinking. For example, a student might show 5 × 2 = 5 + 5, which is adding more to 5 than 5 + 2.

5. **Hinge Question.** Ask, "What conjectures might we make about how our graphs would look if we used subtraction or division rules?"

TASK 11: RULE CARDS FOR $Y = X + N$ AND $Y = X \times N$

To download printable resources for this task, visit **resources.corwin.com/ ClassroomReadyMath/4–5**

POST-TASK NOTES: REFLECTION & NEXT STEPS

Task 12
The Sequence Game

Identify relationships between terms in numerical patterns

TASK

The Sequence Game

Kay and Jerry were playing a game making number sequences. They decided to start both of their sequences with the number 10. Then Kay used the rule "add 5" to build her sequence and Jerry used the rule "add 8" to build his sequence. Kay noticed a relationship between the two lists. She said that the next number in Jerry's sequence would be 15 more than the next number in Kay's sequence.

Kay's sequence: 10, 15, 20, 25, 30
(rule: add 5)

Jerry's sequence: 10, 18, 26, 34, 42
(rule: add 8)

Do you agree with Kay? What pattern do you think she noticed?

TASK PREPARATION

- Organize students into heterogeneous pairs. Each pair should have a student page, a calculator, and a number cube. If desired, you could have students use Google's random number generator (https://www.google.com/search?q=random+number) or a similar site to choose the starting number for the game.

ACCESS AND EQUITY

This activity is not meant to be computation practice. The use of calculators will ensure that each and every student has the opportunity to explore and discover patterns in the number sequences, regardless of their computational proficiency.

Mathematics Standard

- Generate two numerical patterns using two given rules. Identify apparent relationships between corresponding terms. Form ordered pairs consisting of corresponding terms from the two patterns, and graph the ordered pairs on a coordinate plane.

Mathematical Practices

- Make sense of problems and persevere in solving them.
- Look for and make use of structure.

Vocabulary

- sequence
- term

Materials

- The Sequence Game (addition) student page, at least one copy per pair (also a subtraction page)
- number cube
- calculators
- online access (for Google random number generator)
- document camera

LAUNCH

1. Show students the two sequences from the task, but do not include the rules.

> Kay's sequence: 10, 15, 20, 25, 30
>
> Jerry's sequence: 10, 18, 26, 34, 42

2. Facilitate a Notice and Wonder. Encourage students to *Turn and Learn* with a partner and then ask several students to share their partner's ideas with the class. Record student notices on the board. Student notices might include some of the following:

   » The numbers in Kay's sequence are all multiples of 5.

   » The numbers in Jerry's sequence are increasing by 8.

   » Both sequences start with 10.

   » Jerry's sequence is growing faster than Kay's sequence.

3. Share the full task with students. Take a moment to make connections to the notices recorded on the board, then ask students to work with their partners to check out Kay's prediction about the next term in the two sequences.

4. Ask students to *Turn and Talk* about what they think Kay noticed. Ask, "How did Kay know that the next terms would have a difference of 15? Do you think the same kinds of patterns might show up if you used different starting numbers or different rules?"

FACILITATE

1. Distribute game boards, number cubes, and calculators to each pair of students. Explain that they will get to play the Sequence Game with different starting numbers so we can see what happens.

2. As students play the game, circulate through the room conducting interviews. Ask the following:

   » What is the difference between your _____ terms (pick a term both students have filled in)? Is that the same difference for all of your terms so far?

   » Do you have a prediction about the difference between your _____ terms (the first term that is incomplete for both)? What makes you think that?

3. **Observe.** As pairs complete their pages, have them meet with a second pair and do a *Pair-to-Pair Interview* about their sequences and any patterns they noticed.

Note: Consider using the Observation and Interview (small group) tools for monitoring and recording task responses (see Appendix B).

 STRENGTHS SPOTTING

Providing opportunities for students to make conjectures and then collaborate with peers as they try to prove or disprove them fosters development of strengths in communication and reasoning—two critical components of the adaptive reasoning strand of Mathematical Proficiency. (*Adding It Up*, NRC, 2001)

4. If time allows, give the pairs new game boards. Encourage them to replay the game using the same rules but a new starting number to see what happens to the patterns they noticed.

CLOSE: MAKE THE MATH VISIBLE

1. Once each pair has completed at least one round of the game and a *Pair-to-Pair Interview* with another team, bring the class together for a discussion about the task.

2. Use a document camera to show several student game boards. Sequence this sharing based on your observations and interviews during the Facilitate phase of the task.

3. Revisit the Launch discussion. Ask, "How were some of the patterns we noticed the same or different from the pattern Kay noticed when she and Jerry played the game?" Through questioning and use of student examples, elicit the following ideas:

   » The differences between corresponding terms will make a sequence.

   » The rule for the new sequences will be to add the difference between the addends from the two rules (e.g., if Player One's rule was "add 3" and Player Two's rule was "add 7" the rule for the sequence of differences will be "add 4").

   » As long as the two rules stay the same, changing the starting number will not change the differences between corresponding terms.

4. **Exit Task.** Have students play the Sequence Game with a subtraction rule (see attached student page).

TASK 12: STUDENT PAGE SEQUENCE GAME

 To download printable resources for this task, visit **resources.corwin.com/ClassroomReadyMath/4–5**

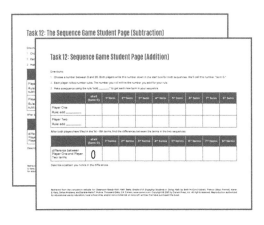

POST-TASK NOTES: REFLECTION & NEXT STEPS

Task 13

Curious Counting

Explore numbers sequence

TASK

Curious Counting

Makai read and reread the sequence of numbers below and then said, "I think I see how the numbers are connected! Cool!"

2, 1, 3, 4, 7, 11, 18, 29, . . .

Describe the pattern Makai noticed. Find the 10th number in this sequence.

TASK PREPARATION:

- Organize students into heterogeneous pairs.

- Prepare copies of the task's student page.

- Decide how you will project the Number Talk and task (through a document camera, slide, or chart paper).

LAUNCH

1. Conduct a discussion based on the following sequence of numbers:

2, 10, 50, 250, . . .

Mathematics Standard

- Generate a number or shape pattern that follows a given rule. Identify apparent features of the pattern that were not explicit in the rule itself.

Mathematical Practices

- Make sense of problems and persevere in solving them.

- Look for and express regularity in repeated reasoning.

Vocabulary

- sequence
- term

Materials

- Curious Counting student page, one for each pair of students

- connecting cubes (optional)

2. Ask, "What do you notice about the pattern?" Ask students to show you when they are ready to describe something they notice about the number sequence.

3. Have students *Turn and Talk* to discuss what they notice.

4. Invite students to share ideas with the whole group and record their thoughts on the board.

5. Ask, "How might we figure out how to find the next term in the sequence?"

6. Have students share ideas.

ACCESS AND EQUITY

Consider using hand signals to indicate where students are in their thinking: for example, "I'm still thinking about the task" (one finger up); "I'm ready to share my answer" (two fingers up). This can help prevent eager students from interrupting a peer's opportunity to consider the question.

FACILITATE

1. Organize students into heterogeneous pairs, display the task on the board, and distribute the student page.

2. Encourage students to carefully review the number sequence from the first number to the eighth and vice versa and share what they are noticing.

3. **Show Me.** As students work, visit each pair and ask whether they are observing any patterns in the series of numbers. Ask them to show you which numbers they are considering to continue the pattern. Have them show you through equations, number sequences, or words how the numbers are related.

PRODUCTIVE STRUGGLE

Students who may be focused on pairs of numbers may exhibit some frustration while trying to notice a pattern. Encourage students to carefully examine different pairs of numbers in the sequence.

4. Provide enough time to visit each pair and provide encouraging feedback to students who may be stuck.

CLOSE: MAKE THE MATH VISIBLE

1. Group two sets of student pairs in a *Pair-to-Pair Share* to discuss what they noticed about the sequence. Listen to their explanations. (*They may share that they first noticed the last three numbers in the sequence 11, 18, and 29 and realized that 11 + 18 = 29. Then, they looked at 7, 11, and 18 and realized it followed the same pattern.*)

2. Based on monitoring pair discussions, select students to share their explanation about the connections Makai noticed. You may sequence the sharing based on students who described the number relationships using words first, then equations.

3. Support student understanding by examining 3 numbers at a time:

2, 1, 3	2 + 1 = 3
1, 3, 4	1 + 3 = 4
3, 4, 7	3 + 4 = 7
4, 7, 11	4 + 7 = 11
7, 11, 18	7 + 11 = 18
11, 18, 29	11 + 18 = 29

4. **Hinge Question.** What would be the 9th number in the sequence?

2, 1, 3, 4, 7, 11, 18, 29, . . .

TASK 13: CURIOUS COUNTING STUDENT PAGE

 To download printable resources for this task, visit **resources.corwin.com/ ClassroomReadyMath/4–5**

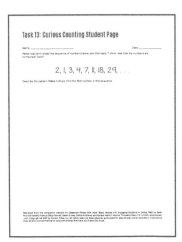

POST-TASK NOTES: REFLECTION & NEXT STEPS

Number and Operations in Base Ten

It's All About Place Value

TASK 14: GRADE 4: HOW MANY TIMES GREATER?

Recognize that in a multidigit whole number, a digit in one place represents 10 times what it represents in the place to its right.

TASK 15: GRADE 5: PENNIES, PATTERNS, AND PLACE VALUE

Recognize that in a multidigit number, a digit in one place represents 10 times as much as it represents in the place to its right and $\frac{1}{10}$ of what it represents in the place to its left.

TASK 16: GRADE 4: GETTING CLOSER!

Use place value understanding to round multidigit whole numbers to any place.

TASK 17: GRADE 4: WOULD YOU RATHER HAVE?

Read and write multidigit whole numbers using base-ten numerals, number names, and expanded form. Compare two multidigit numbers based on meanings of the digits in each place, using >, =, and < symbols to record the results of comparisons.

TASK 18: GRADE 5: A POWERFUL POINT

Explain patterns in the number of zeros of the product when multiplying a number by powers of 10 and explain patterns in the placement of the decimal point when a decimal is multiplied or divided by a power of 10. Use whole-number exponents to denote powers of 10.

TASK 19: GRADE 5: WHO WINS SILVER AND BRONZE?

Read, write, and compare decimals to thousandths.

TASK 20: GRADE 5: 5 OR 6?

Use place value understanding to round decimals to any place.

Anticipating Student Thinking: The seven tasks in this chapter focus on important understandings and applications related to place value. Reading, writing, and comparing whole numbers and decimals provides the foundational building blocks for working with operations involving such numbers. As you plan to implement the task-lessons in this chapter consider how you will provide your students with access to place value models (virtual or manipulative) as they engage in the tasks. Because students have been working with whole number place value concepts for several years, you may anticipate providing more time for student engagement and discussion relative to the tasks that involve patterns in the placement of decimal points, using exponents, and comparing and rounding decimals.

THINK ABOUT IT

Make sure to provide the necessary wait time for students as they work through particular elements of a task that truly engages them in productive struggle.

Task 14
How Many Times Greater?

Visualize the value and relationships of digits in adjoining place values

TASK

How Many Times Greater?

Figure 7.1 Base Ten Blocks

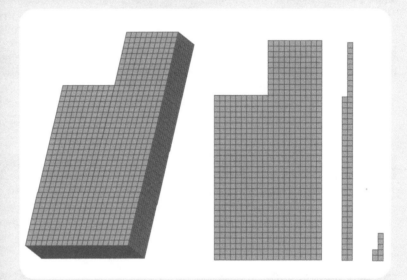

Alexa observed the representations in Figure 7.1 and stated, "*I can see that 700 is ten times as much as 70.*" Dimitri's group used base ten blocks to create the same pattern and he said, "*I think 7,000 is one hundred times as much as 70.*" Can both observations be correct? Why or why not? Explain your thinking.

TASK PREPARATION

- Prepare enough sets of materials for each group of students. Determine in advance how you will group students based on their strengths and what you may know about their understanding of place value.

LAUNCH

1. On the board, write:

   375   **8,752**

2. Have students *Turn and Talk* to discuss the relationship between the digit 5 in 375 and in 8,752 (noting place and value of the digit 5 in each of the numbers).

3. Invite students to make other comparisons between the value of digits in 375 and 8,752. Students may notice that when comparing the digit 5 in both numbers, 50 is ten times 5, or when comparing the digit 7 in both numbers, 700 is ten times as much as 70.

4. Introduce the task to students. Ask students to describe what they *See, Think, and Wonder*. Record these observations on chart paper or the board.

FACILITATE

1. Group students heterogeneously in triads or quads.

2. Listen for students who discuss what the digits mean in both numbers and how they are related.

3. Encourage students to describe the differences they observe in using the materials, on the place value chart or in symbolic form. (There are 7 *thousands* blocks, then 7 *hundreds* blocks, . . . ; $7,000 \div 10 = 700$, $700 \div 10 = 70$ . . . or $7 \times 10 = 70$, $70 \times 10 = 700$ . . .).

4. Connect the patterns students describe to the phrase "times as much." Say, "Another way mathematicians describe the relationship between the numbers 7,000, 700, 70, and 7 in the number sequence is to say that 70 is ten times as much as 7. Ask, "What other comparisons can you make using the phrase "times as much?"

> **PRODUCTIVE STRUGGLE**
>
> Provide enough time for students to discuss and make connections between their ideas about place value. Noticing this relationship provides a powerful opportunity to promote conceptual understanding.

5. Ask, "How could we use multiplication to describe the relationship between 700 and 7,000 (7,000 is 10 times 700)?

6. **Interview.** As students work, conduct interviews with each group.

   » How can you show me that 70 is 10 times as much as 7?

   » How can you describe the relationship between 7,000 and 70?

   » How many times greater is 7,000 than 7?

Note: Consider using the Interview (small group) tool for monitoring and recording task responses (see Appendix B).

CLOSE: MAKE THE MATH VISIBLE

1. Based on your interviews, select one student from each group to share their thinking.

2. Sequence the order of students who share based on their choice of strategy (concrete to semi-concrete to abstract, or CSA)—base ten blocks, use of place value chart, equations.

3. Using the picture in the task, highlight the connections between

   » The strategies utilized, and

   » The number sequence: 7,000, 700, 70, and 7, and the value of each digit as ten times the value of the digit to its right. See Figure 7.2.

Figure 7.2 Showing Thinking With Base Ten Blocks

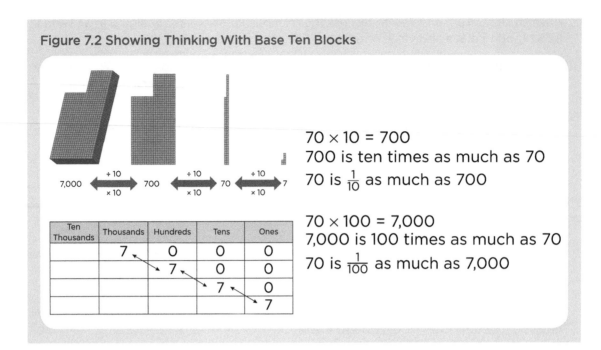

$70 \times 10 = 700$
700 is ten times as much as 70
70 is $\frac{1}{10}$ as much as 700

$70 \times 100 = 7,000$
7,000 is 100 times as much as 70
70 is $\frac{1}{100}$ as much as 7,000

POST-TASK NOTES: REFLECTION & NEXT STEPS

Task 15

Pennies, Patterns, and Place Value

Describe patterns found in the place value system

TASK

Pennies, Patterns, and Place Value

Jordan's elementary school is raising money for a local food bank. They are calling their collection Pennies and Dimes for Food. Each grade is collecting spare change in pennies and dimes. After two weeks, each grade has collected the following:

Grade	Change Collected	Total Value
1	965 dimes	
1	3,642 pennies	
2	865 dimes	
2	238 pennies	
3	3,642 dimes	
3	144 pennies	

Image sources: Penny: MisterVector/iStock.com; Dime: KavalenkavaVolha/iStock.com;

1. Help Jordan calculate the total value of pennies and of dimes collected for the food bank in Grades 1 through 3 by completing the table.

2. Calculate the total amount collected by Grade 2 (pennies and dimes), and then describe any patterns you notice.

3. Describe how Jordan can explain the difference in value between the number of pennies collected by Grade 1 and the number of dimes collected by Grade 3?

Mathematics Standard

- Recognize that in a multidigit number, a digit in one place represents 10 times as much as it represents in the place to its right and $\frac{1}{10}$ of what it represents in the place to its left.

Mathematical Practices

- Make sense of problems and persevere in solving them.
- Reason abstractly and quantitatively.

Vocabulary

- place value
- value
- pattern
- digit
- one-tenth as much, one-hundredth as much, ten times as much, etc.

Materials

- Pennies, Patterns, and Place Values student page, one copy for each pair or triad
- plastic coin manipulatives (pennies, dimes)
- place value chart

TASK PREPARATION

- Organize your class into heterogeneous groups of 2 to 3.

- Make copies of the student page.

LAUNCH

1. Project the image shown in Figure 7.3 on the board. Invite students to gather as a group in the front of the room.

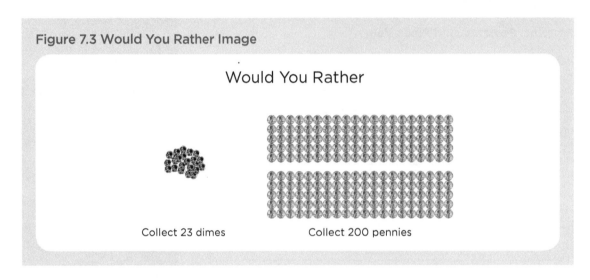

Figure 7.3 Would You Rather Image

> ## Would You Rather
>
> Collect 23 dimes   Collect 200 pennies

2. Ask, "Would you rather collect 23 dimes, or 200 pennies? Why?" Record student ideas.

3. Ask, "What comparisons can we make between the value of one penny, one dime, and one dollar?" (Students may say a penny is worth 1 cent so we need 100 pennies to equal a dollar, the value of one dime is 10 cents so we need 10 dimes to equal one dollar, or it takes 10 pennies to equal one dime.)

4. Write $1.00, 0.10, 0.01 on a place value chart.

5. Ask, "What fraction of one dollar is one penny, one dime?" (A penny is one-hundredth of a dollar; a dime is one-tenth of a dollar.) How do you know?

6. Ask, "If a penny is one-hundredth of a dollar, how many times as much is 1 dollar compared to one penny?" What equations could you write to show the relationship?

7. Have students *Turn and Talk* to discuss how using the place value chart can help us make comparisons between pennies, dimes, and dollars.

8. **Hinge Question.** What fraction of a dime is one penny?

FACILITATE

1. Display the task and review the information in the table and the assigned questions.

2. Assign student pairs or triads and distribute the student page.

3. Say, "If we know that a dime is one-tenth of a dollar, how can we use this knowledge to find the value in dollars of 965 dimes (with the answer in dollars)?

4. Provide enough time for pairs/triads to calculate the total value of pennies and of dimes collected by each grade.

5. Circulate around the room and observe student work.

6. **Show Me.**

   » How did you calculate how much 865 dimes is worth in dollars?

   » How did you calculate how much 238 pennies is worth in dollars? How can you prove this?

CLOSE: MAKE THE MATH VISIBLE

1. Gather students back together as a whole group.

2. After reviewing the total value of dimes and pennies collected for each grade, select particular students (based on Show Me) to describe the patterns they noticed in the total amount collected for Grade 2.

3. Invite students to construct models to show the relationships they noticed:

   » 8 cents is $\frac{1}{10}$ as many pennies as 80 cents,

   » 80 cents is $\frac{1}{10}$ as many dimes as $8.00, etc.

4. Have students explain the difference in value between 3,642 pennies and 3,642 dimes. Ask:

   » How is the 6 in $36.42 related to the 6 in $364.20?

   » How is the 3 in $364.20 related to the 3 in $36.42?

   » What comparison can you make between the 4 in $36.42 and the 4 in $364.20?

TASK 15: PENNIES, PATTERNS, AND PLACE VALUE STUDENT PAGE

 To download printable resources for this task, visit **resources.corwin.com/ ClassroomReadyMath/4–5**

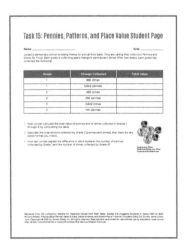

POST-TASK NOTES: REFLECTION & NEXT STEPS

_____

_____

_____

_____

_____

_____

_____

_____

_____

_____

_____

_____

_____

Task 16
Getting Closer!

Use rounding to reason about the relative size of numbers

TASK

Getting Closer!

The class is organized into teams with one team of student leaders. The team of student leaders will pick a mystery number. As the student leaders give clues about the mystery number, students in the class will make and record educated guesses about the number.

1. A team of three student leaders picks a mystery number between 0 and 1,000 that *is not* a multiple of 10. The student leaders should write this number down and show it to the teacher but not to the class.

2. The student leaders begin by telling the class if the mystery number is closer to 0 or closer to 1,000.

3. Using the clue, the rest of the student teams record their initial guesses based on the clue on the Student Record Keeping page.

4. The student leaders call on each student team in a random order.

5. Each team can either make a guess for the exact mystery number OR ask the student leaders one question using the sentence frame: "Is the mystery number closer to _____ or _____?"

6. As the student leaders answer each group's question, the teams adjust their guess and record the adjusted guess on the Student Record Keeping page.

7. Repeat until a team correctly guesses the mystery number.

TASK PREPARATION

- Organize students in teams of two or three. Consider which group will be the student leaders' team first and plan how teams will take turns.

- It may be helpful to post choices student teams make during their turn: guess the mystery number OR ask a question using the sentence frame: "Is the mystery number closer to _____ or _____?"

Mathematics Standard

- Use place value understanding to round multidigit whole numbers to any place.

Mathematical Practice

- Attend to precision.

Vocabulary

- multiple
- educated guess

Materials

- Getting Closer Student Record Keeping Page, one copy per team

LAUNCH

1. Bring the class together to introduce the activity.

2. Tell students that today they are going to play a game where they will try to make an educated guess to figure out a mystery number.

3. Begin an abbreviated "sample" round with students. Tell them you are thinking of a mystery number. Say, "The mystery number is less than 1,000 and is *not* a multiple of ten."

4. Ask, "What do you know about the mystery number so far? What are some possible values it *could* be? What are some values that *couldn't* be the mystery number? How do you know?" Record the possible values on the board.

5. Tell students, "The mystery number is closer to 1,000 than 0."

6. Ask, "Now what do you know about the mystery number? Which of the numbers we guessed before (indicate list on the board) could still be the mystery number? Which ones couldn't be the mystery number? Why?"

7. Ask the class to think of a question they could ask about the mystery number using the sentence frame, "Is the mystery number closer to _____ or _____?" Answer the question. Then repeat the questions listed in step 6.

FACILITATE

1. Once the class understands the general rules for the activity, choose the first team to be student leaders and have them write down a mystery number and secretly show you. They will begin by telling the class if their number is closer to 0 or 1,000.

2. Allow time for the rest of the class to make an educated guess as a team in the first space on the Student Record Keeping page.

3. By turns, allow each team to ask a question using the sentence frame (or guess if they think they know the number).

4. **Observe.** As students refine their guesses about the mystery number, pay attention to strategies they are developing. Notice how students are reasoning about range. For example, if the number is closer to 500 than 600, do students presume it must be greater than 500? Or do they still consider values less than 500 to be possible? Repeat the questions from Launch step 6 with individual teams.

> **! PRODUCTIVE STRUGGLE**
>
> Teams should be given the opportunity to choose their own values to complete the sentence frame, even if they choose values that will not give additional information about the value of the mystery number. Through trial and error, students will begin to recognize which number ranges will be most useful in a way that supports their own agency as young mathematicians.

CLOSE: MAKE THE MATH VISIBLE

1. Repeat the activity several times with new student leaders as time allows.

2. Bring the class back together. Based on your observations/interviews, ask students to share strategies they developed during the activity.

3. **Hinge Question**. "Did your strategy change as the activity went on? What did you do differently?"

> **STRENGTHS SPOTTING**
>
> Students with strengths in adaptive reasoning (NRC, 2001) will demonstrate comfort with reflecting on the success of their approach and enjoy the opportunity to describe how they shifted strategies while solving the task.

4. Highlight student teams who began to "funnel" the possible values by narrowing the range (e.g., if at first the number was closer to 1,000 than 0, then the next logical question would be, "is the mystery number closer to 500 or 1,000" and so on. Sketch an open number line on the board to show how students might use this strategy to slowly narrow the possible range of guesses. Figure 7.4 shows an example.

Figure 7.4 Number Line Showing Possible Guesses

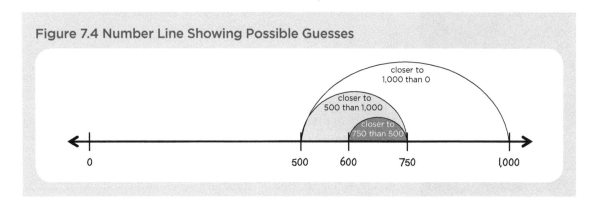

5. Ask students to discuss how they were able to eliminate certain values during each turn. Through questioning, call students' attention to how knowing that a number is "closer to" one value than another means knowing that the number is greater than or less than the point on the number line that is halfway between the two values.

TASK 16: GETTING CLOSER STUDENT RECORD KEEPING PAGE

 To download printable resources for this task, visit **resources.corwin.com/ClassroomReadyMath/4–5**

POST-TASK NOTES: REFLECTION & NEXT STEPS

Mathematics Standard

- Read and write multidigit whole numbers using base ten numerals, number names, and expanded form. Compare two multidigit numbers based on meanings of the digits in each place, using >, =, and < symbols to record the results of comparisons.

Mathematical Practices

- Reason abstractly and quantitatively.
- Attend to precision.

Vocabulary

- place value

Materials

- Game Cards (prepare both Set 1 & Set 2, but keep them separate)
- marker board and marker
- base ten materials from companion website

Task 17
Would You Rather Have?

Consider the importance of place value

TASK

Would You Rather?

Rules: The teacher competes with the class. A record of team scores is kept on a public T-chart. In each round, the teacher draws a card and asks the class, "Would you rather have ___ or ___?" as indicated on the card. The choice the class makes will be added to the class score and the other possible choice that was not selected is added to the teacher's score.

The catch: In this game, only the teacher knows the *place value* of the numbers in play.

Example: The teacher draws the card shown in Figure 7.5 and asks the question. The class chooses 9. The teacher adds 5 tens (50) to the teacher score and 9 ones (9) to the class score.

Figure 7.5 Would You Rather Card and T-Chart

Question	Teacher	Class
Would you rather have **5** or **9**?	50	9
Scores		
5 tens or **9 ones**		

TASK PREPARATION

- Print and prepare game cards.

- This is designed to be a whole-class activity, but teachers will want to plan for a structure that will allow for equitable participation. Consider: Who will make the final choice for the class? Will this role rotate from student to student? How will the decision be made? Will the class vote?

- Teachers may want to designate scorekeepers to manage the T-chart. Consider two scorekeepers to save time; one will add up the teacher's score, and the other will keep track of the class score.

LAUNCH

1. Tell students that today they will be playing a new game where they will get to compete with the teacher to get the highest score.

2. Share the game directions with students (don't give away the catch!):

   » In this game, I will draw a card that has two different scores on it. I will ask you (the class) which score you want. Whichever score you pick will be added to the class score, and the one you don't choose gets added to the teacher score.

3. Begin playing with Set 1.

FACILITATE

1. Record scores and encourage students to reflect:

   » Is that the score you expected? Why or why not?

   » Who is winning right now?

   » Will these results change how you will answer for the next card?

2. **Observe.** Listen carefully for students to make conjectures or notice relationships. Record them on the board. For example, students may say things like:

   » It doesn't matter which number we pick because the place values might be different.

   » We want you to tell us the place value first!

   » The only way it matters which number is greater is if they have the same place value.

3. As the class comes to the conclusion that they don't really have enough information to consistently choose the best score, offer to play a different version of the game. Ask, "Because you are thinking this game isn't fair, do you want to play a different version? In the other version, you will get to choose the place value first!"

> **! PRODUCTIVE STRUGGLE**
>
> Record every observation made without providing evaluative feedback. This is an opportunity for students to grapple with the unpredictable results of the game and test the strategies suggested by their peers.

4. Repeat the game with Set 2.

5. As students make each choice, ask, "Why did you choose __?"

6. Record scores and encourage students to reflect:

   » Is that the score you expected? Why or why not?

   » Who is winning right now?

   » Will these results change how you answer for the next card?

7. **Observe.** Again, record students' notices on the board. This time they may say things like:

   » As long as the place values are different, we can always select the higher score.

   » When the place values are the same, we want to know the digits!

Note: Consider using the Observation tool for monitoring and recording the student notices (see Appendix B).

CLOSE: MAKE THE MATH VISIBLE

1. After playing both versions of the game, bring the class together to reflect on the strategies they used in each version.

2. Ask, "How did you know which score was greater in each round?

3. **Hinge Question.** What information was most important?

4. Ask students to give specific examples to support their claims about the importance of place value. For example, they might say:

   » A 2 in the tens place is worth less than a 2 in the millions place.

   » Even though 9 > 5, 9 tens (90) is still less than 5 hundreds (500) because 1 hundred = 10 tens.

STRENGTHS SPOTTING

Recognize students' communication strengths when they support their ideas with mathematical details. Some students can demonstrate this strength by explaining others' ideas and asking explicit questions.

TASK 17: GAME CARDS

 To download printable resources for this task, visit **resources.corwin.com/ ClassroomReadyMath/4–5**

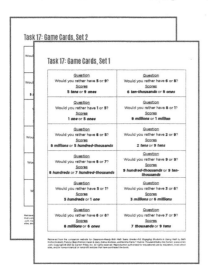

POST-TASK NOTES: REFLECTION & NEXT STEPS

A Powerful Point

Reason about the placement of the decimal point when dividing by ten

Mathematics Standard

- Explain patterns in the number of zeros of the product when multiplying a number by powers of 10, and explain patterns in the placement of the decimal point when a decimal is multiplied or divided by a power of 10. Use whole-number exponents to denote powers of 10.

Mathematical Practices

- Attend to precision.
- Look for and express regularity in repeated reasoning.

Vocabulary

- decimal point
- equivalent
- powers of ten
- dividend

Materials

- calculators
- A Powerful Point student page, one per group
- Base Ten Materials
- money manipulatives

TASK

A Powerful Point

Sana and Aysha were working on their division homework. They got different answers for problem number three. Read their reasoning (Figure 7.6). Can you figure out why their answers are different? Which answer is correct? Why?

Figure 7.6 Sana's and Aysha's Work

Sana

3. $0.45 \div 10$

$$10 \overline{) 0.45} \quad 4.5$$

I learned this trick for dividing with decimals. You can count zeros and move the decimals that many spots! The answer is 4.5.

Aysha

3. $0.45 \div 10$

$$\frac{0.45}{10} = \frac{0.45 \times 100}{10 \times 100} = \frac{45}{1,000} = 0.045$$

I wrote the division in fraction form and found an equivalent fraction. The answer is 45 thousandths.

TASK PREPARATION

- Prepare a large copy of the task or plan for a way to project it so the whole class can see.

- Plan to organize students into heterogeneous groups of 3 or 4. Consider how you will structure the group work to ensure that each student participates and can articulate the group's thinking.

LAUNCH

1. Display the image only from the task. Provide time for students to Notice and Wonder about the student work shown.

2. Record student notices and wonders on the board or some other public space.

> **! PRODUCTIVE STRUGGLE**
>
> It is important that student notices/wonders are accepted without judgment. Consider your physical reaction as well as your words: Do you raise your eyebrows or smile/frown when receiving students' ideas? To create a space where productive struggle can flourish, students must not be conditioned to seek only the "correct" ideas but rather be shown that each of their ideas is worth considering.

FACILITATE

1. Present the full task.

2. Group students into heterogeneous groups of 3 or 4.

3. Each group should have a copy of the image, a calculator, paper or marker boards, and ready access to manipulatives like base ten blocks and money manipulatives.

4. Direct students to come to a consensus with their small group about whether Sana or Aysha has the correct quotient.

5. **Show Me.** As groups work, ask students to demonstrate their thinking—why they think one student is correct/incorrect. Students should be encouraged to use equations, draw representations, model with manipulatives, etc. to present their case. Student reasoning might include . . .

   » Model 0.45 with base ten blocks. Consider the "thousands cube" to represent 1 whole, so flat-shaped pieces that were formerly "hundreds" represent tenths and rod-shaped pieces (formerly "tens") represent hundredths. Model the sharing of 0.45 with the materials into ten groups of equal size. Each of the ten groups will end up with "unit cubes" which represent thousandths (0.045).

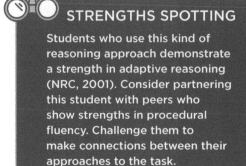

STRENGTHS SPOTTING

Students who use this kind of reasoning approach demonstrate a strength in adaptive reasoning (NRC, 2001). Consider partnering this student with peers who show strengths in procedural fluency. Challenge them to make connections between their approaches to the task.

   » Use patterns to show that dividing any number by 10 results in a quotient that is $\frac{1}{10}$ the size of the dividend (original number). Thus, Sana's answer of 4.5 is not reasonable because 4.5 is greater than 0.45.

   » Draw a number line and represent 0.45 partitioned into 10 equal parts (Figure 7.7).

Figure 7.7 Number Line Showing 0.45 in 10 Equal Parts

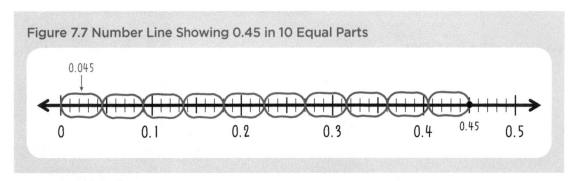

   » Represent 0.45 with money manipulatives and model sharing the money into 10 equal groups. Each group can get 4 pennies, then $\frac{1}{10}$ of the remaining 5 pennies (this means each group would have more than 4¢ but less than 5¢).

6. **Hinge Question.** Think about the work of the student (Sana or Aysha) you say is correct. Will that method work to divide any number by ten?

CLOSE: MAKE THE MATH VISIBLE

1. When most groups have come to a consensus, bring the class back together.

2. Give each group a small sticky note or sticker dot and have them put it next to the work their group thinks to be correct.

3. Let the class consider the results of the informal poll. Do they all agree? If not, why not?

4. Have one of the groups show how they proved that Aysha found the right product. If necessary, teachers may need to affirm for students that although we do not consider it to be a common fraction, a fraction can be written with a decimal in it.

5. Facilitate a discussion about the relationship between the value of 0.45 and the value of 0.045. Ask students to notice what happened to the *digits* in the number. (The same digits are in the same order in both numbers, but the digits in the quotient have shifted one place value to the right in relation to the decimal point; they are each $\frac{1}{10}$ the value of the digits in the dividend.)

6. Ask students, "How can you use what you know about the quotient to explain the error in Sana's work?" Encourage students to notice that Sana *did* shift the digits in her quotient one place value; the error was that she shifted the digits to the *left*, which meant that the digits in her quotient were 10 times greater than the value of the digits in the dividend. Sana actually multiplied by 10 instead of dividing by 10.

7. **Exit Task.** Write feedback for Sana. Be sure to note a strength in Sana's work, then explain to Sana how she could use fractions to think about the division. Show her another example using $30.5 \div 100$.

TASK 18: A POWERFUL POINT STUDENT PAGE

 To download printable resources for this task, visit **resources.corwin.com/ ClassroomReadyMath/4–5**

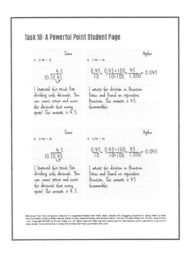

POST-TASK NOTES: REFLECTION & NEXT STEPS

Mathematics Standard

- Read, write, and compare decimals through thousandths.

Mathematical Practices

- Reason abstractly and quantitatively.
- Attend to precision.

Vocabulary

- decimals
- hundredths
- thousandths

Materials

- Silver and Bronze student page, one for each student
- sticky notes
- base ten blocks (optional)
- blank hundreds grid (optional)

Task 19
Who Wins Silver and Bronze?

Compare decimals through the hundredths place

TASK

Who Wins Silver and Bronze?

At the most recent Olympic Games, the results for the Women's 100 Meter Butterfly in swimming were:

	Canada	56.46 seconds
	China	56.76 seconds
	Japan	56.86 seconds
	Sweden	55.48 seconds
	USA	56.63 seconds

Source: flagpedia.net

Carlos says, "I know that Sweden wins the gold medal because they had the fastest time, but I'm not sure who wins the silver and bronze medals because the difference in time between the rest of the swimmers is less than one second!"

Help Carlos determine who wins the rest of the medals by locating each swimmer's time on the number line and labeling the country they represent. Convince him that you have accurately identified the correct winners by making comparisons between their times.

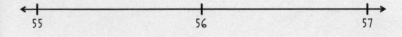

TASK PREPARATION

- Think about how to organize students into heterogeneous pairs.

- Consider similar contexts students may be familiar with from their own funds of knowledge (such as a PACER, FitnessGram, or other aerobic fitness tests implemented in physical education classes).

LAUNCH

1. Project the image in Figure 7.8 and facilitate a Notice and Wonder (anticipate student questions such as how long 100 meters is, what "butterfly" means in the context of swimming, etc.).

Figure 7.8 Women's 100M Butterfly Image

Source: IOC © Copyright 2020.

2. Have students *Turn and Talk* to discuss:

   » What does the timer on the lower right-hand corner of the screen signify (how much time has passed since the start of the race)?

   » What does the WR and green line on the screen mean (how fast swimmers are going compared to the world record for the event)?

   » How is the winner determined (fastest time)?

   » Who do you think will win the race and what might the winning time be? Have pairs record their predictions on sticky notes.

ACCESS AND EQUITY

Frame for students that the Olympic Games is an international event and that countries from around the world participate. Explain that they will be watching a video clip of the 2016 Olympic Games in Rio (play only the first 30 seconds of the video before the discussion): https://bit.ly/31ASJO8

STRENGTHS SPOTTING

Highlight student pairs that are working well together by discussing their ideas and collaborating on decisions about the placement of the decimals on the number line.

FACILITATE

1. Organize students in heterogeneous pairs.

2. Distribute the student page and review the task with students. Call on several students to read the times for each country.

3. Circulate around the room and monitor pair work: Notice how students locate and label times on the number line.

4. After some time, pause pair work and ask,

   » "What did you notice about the number line you were given?" (The tick marks go only to the whole number.)

   » "Because the times you were given are up to the hundredths place, how did you and your partner visualize how to mark the times on the number line? (Students may share that they located the center point in between two whole numbers and marked it, so 55.48 would be located to the left of 55.5.)

5. **Interview.**

   » Approximately how many seconds was the difference in time between Sweden and Canada? What expression (using comparison symbols) can you write to make this comparison?

   » How did you determine that the Canadian swimmer was faster than the US swimmer? What expression can you write to compare these two numbers?

Note: Consider using Interview (individual or small group) tool for recording the student responses (see Appendix B).

CLOSE: MAKE THE MATH VISIBLE

1. Bring the class together for a discussion about the task.

2. Use a document camera to show the work of several students (based on your observations and interview).

3. Through questioning, elicit the following ideas by asking questions first and eliciting students' ideas before stating or telling:

   » We can more accurately plot decimal numbers in the hundredths place on a number line with tick marks to the whole number by finding the midpoint in between two tick marks as a benchmark and deciding whether the given number is less than or greater than the midpoint number.

   » Because in swimming, the swimmer with the fastest time is the winner, we know that the gold medal winner's time is the least (leftmost) number on the given number line (the distance from zero), and the silver and bronze winners are the second and third closest decimal numbers plotted from the zero of the number line. Thus, we can make comparisons on a number line (see Figure 7.9).

   » We can also determine who wins the silver and bronze medals by comparing the digits in the tenths place and we can use comparison symbols to compare two decimal numbers.

4. Reveal who wins the silver and bronze medals by playing the rest of the video for students.

5. **Exit Task.** In the preliminary heat 3 of the 100 meter women's butterfly, there was a tie between two 4th-place swimmers who both swam a time of 59.45. Plot this time on the number line. How do you think the judges can break the tie?

Figure 7.9 Number Line

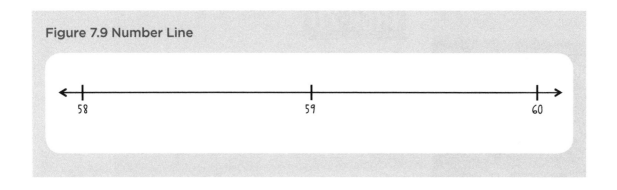

TASK 19: SILVER AND BRONZE STUDENT PAGE

 To download printable resources for this task, visit **resources.corwin.com/ ClassroomReadyMath/4–5**

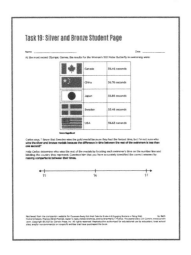

POST-TASK NOTES: REFLECTION & NEXT STEPS

Mathematics Standard

- Use place value understanding to round decimals to any place.

Mathematical Practices

- Construct viable arguments and critique the reasoning of others.
- Model with mathematics.

Vocabulary

- sum
- estimate

Materials

- base ten blocks
- marker boards or paper

Task 20
5 or 6?

Round with decimal numbers

TASK

5 or 6?

Aaliyah and Becky wanted to estimate the sum of 5.18 + 0.82. They agreed that it would make sense to round both numbers to the nearest whole number, but they disagreed about what the result would be. Aaliyah says that rounding both numbers to the nearest whole number would give the estimated sum 5 + 1 = 6. Becky says that Aaliyah is rounding incorrectly. She says, "There's an 8 in the first number. When a number is more than 5 you should round up! We should use 6 + 1 = 7, so the estimated sum is 7."

What whole number is nearest to 5.18? Which student's estimate is nearest to the actual sum of 5.18 + 0.82? Use base ten blocks to support your thinking.

TASK PREPARATION

- Consider how you will help students connect the representation of base ten blocks to decimal fractions. Will you consider the flat square to be 1 whole, or will you use the large cube as 1 whole? An advantage of using the flat square as 1 whole is the ability for students to sketch their models. An advantage of using the large cube as 1 whole is the ability to include exploration of thousandths with the physical representations. Investigate how such tools are used in 4th and 6th grades in your school district to determine which representation for 1 whole will best connect to prior instruction and support subsequent instruction.

ALTERNATE LEARNING ENVIRONMENT

To facilitate this task online, consider using digital base ten manipulatives such as the Math Learning Center's Number Pieces app (https://apps .mathlearningcenter.org/ number-pieces/).

LAUNCH

1. Bring the class together and share the task.

2. Have students *Turn-and-Talk* with a partner. Ask, "What do you think Becky means when she says, "When the number is more than 5 you should round up"?

3. Remind students that both Aaliyah and Becky have estimates that are pretty close to the actual sum. We are trying to determine which estimate is closest to the actual sum, so we want to have a common understanding of how to round to the nearest whole number.

FACILITATE

1. Organize students into pairs.

2. Ask each pair to represent 5.18 using base ten blocks.

3. **Show Me.** "Show me how you can use this model to help Aaliyah and Becky convince themselves that 5.18 is closer to 5 or 6."

4. **Interview.**

   » How important is the number of hundredths for your argument?

   » Is there any number of hundredths that would change which whole number you would round to? Explain.

Note: Consider using the Show Me and Interview (small group) tools for monitoring and recording task responses (see Appendix B).

CLOSE: MAKE THE MATH VISIBLE

1. When each group is ready to communicate a justification for which whole number is nearest to 5.18, direct students to *Pair-to-Pair Share*.

2. Bring the class together and have students discuss the different arguments that surfaced in the group. Possible arguments to listen for:

   » Students may build 5 and 6 and show that 5.18 is $\frac{18}{100}$ away from 5 but $\frac{82}{100}$ away from 6, so 5.18 would round to 5.

   » Students may show that 0.18 is less than half of 1 whole by layering 0.18 on top of 1 whole.

 STRENGTHS SPOTTING

   » Students may show that the 8 in 5.18 represents less than $\frac{1}{10}$ and reason that 5.18 is less than 5.2. Because 5.2 rounds to 5, 5.18 must also round to 5.

3. **Exit Task.** Change one digit in the number 5.18 so that Becky's estimate of 6 + 1 = 7 will be closer to the actual sum than Aaliyah's estimate of 5 + 1 = 6.

POST-TASK NOTES: REFLECTION & NEXT STEPS

Number and Operations in Base Ten

Operations

TASK 21: GRADE 4: EXPLORING EVEN NUMBERS

Multiply a whole number of up to four digits by a one-digit whole number, and multiply two two-digit numbers, using strategies based on place value and the properties of operations. Illustrate and explain the calculation by using equations, rectangular arrays, and/or area models.

TASK 22: GRADE 5: THE BROKEN CALCULATOR

Add, subtract, multiply, and divide decimals to hundredths, using concrete models or drawings and strategies based on place value, properties of operations, and/or the relationship between addition and subtraction; relate the strategy to a written method and explain the reasoning used.

TASK 23: GRADE 5: QUICK QUOTIENTS

Find whole-number quotients of whole numbers with up to four-digit dividends and two-digit divisors, using strategies based on place value, the properties of operations, and/or the relationship between multiplication and division. Illustrate and explain the calculation by using equations, rectangular arrays, and/or area models.

TASK 24: GRADE 4: MAYA'S ADVICE

Fluently add and subtract multidigit whole numbers using the standard algorithm.

TASK 25: GRADE 5: WHAT'S THE CONNECTION?

Fluently multiply multidigit whole numbers using the standard algorithm.

Anticipating Student Thinking: The tasks in this chapter are all about operations. These tasks focus on understandings and proficiency related to operations involving whole numbers (Tasks 21, 23, 24, and 25) and decimals (Task 22). As your students engage in the chapter tasks, plan to engage them in validating the reasonableness of their responses. Some of the tasks directly involve estimation, but all student work in *doing-math tasks* involving whole number and decimal operations should include time for reflection on the reasonableness of strategies used and solutions discovered. As you plan for implementing the tasks, also recognize the importance of starting with the strengths of your students. Such starting points will, of course, vary, but moving forward from strengths represents each student's beginning of their personal journey toward developing understanding and fluency. And both are essential.

THINK ABOUT IT

Students should have access to visual and/or manipulative models for the chapter tasks. Online manipulative tools may also be considered. Consider how you will engage students individually or in small groups as they solve the tasks, using visual, manipulative, or online models as well as symbols. This will be particularly important for students completing the task activities remotely.

Mathematics Standard

- Multiply a whole number of up to four digits by a one-digit whole number, and multiply two two-digit numbers, using strategies based on place value and the properties of operations. Illustrate and explain the calculation by using equations, rectangular arrays, and/or area models.

Mathematical Practices

- Construct viable arguments and critique the reasoning of others.
- Reason abstractly and quantitatively.

Vocabulary

- digit
- factors
- product
- array
- area model
- partial products
- conjecture
- counterexample
- condition

Materials

- Exploring Even Numbers student page
- marker boards
- dry-erase markers
- chart paper
- markers
- base ten blocks

Task 21

Exploring Even Numbers

Practice multiplying multidigit numbers

TASK

Exploring Even Numbers

Figure 8.1 Talia's Work

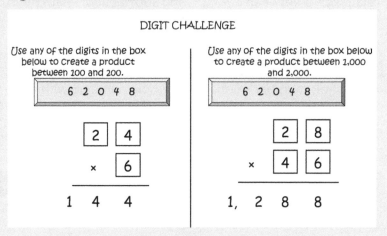

After working on the *Digit Challenge* with her partner, Ted, Talia noticed that it is impossible to get an odd product with the digits given. She made a conjecture that multiplying two even numbers would always result in a product that is an even number (see Figure 8.1). Ted said, "I'm not sure yet, I want to investigate with more examples to see if what you said is always true."

Create your own multiplication examples to help Ted figure out whether Talia's conjecture is true. Try a 4-digit by 1-digit or a 2-digit by 2-digit example to see if you get the same or a different result.

TASK PREPARATION

- Organize your class into small groups of 3 or 4. Consider how you will group students heterogeneously, based on your knowledge about their flexibility and fluency with multiplying numbers.
- Make copies of student page.

LAUNCH

1. Distribute marker boards and dry-erase markers to the entire class.

2. Project the image shown in Figure 8.2 on the board.

Figure 8.2 Digit Challenge

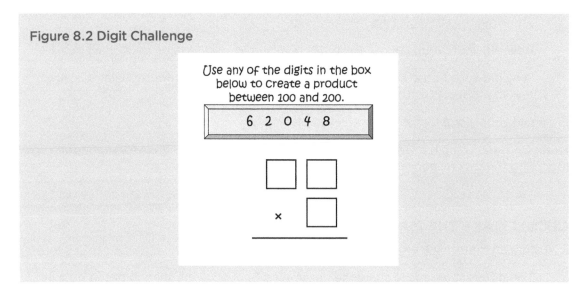

3. Tell students that they will be working independently to find as many combinations of the given digits that meet the condition: to create a product between 100 and 200.

4. Have students share the combinations they developed and verify whether their peer's product is between 100 and 200. Record their factors and product on the board.

5. Provide time for students to carefully review what you have recorded.

   » What do you notice about the combinations we generated as a class? (Students will likely notice that all of the factors and products recorded are even numbers.) If necessary, you may need to connect back to the fact that the digits given are all even numbers.

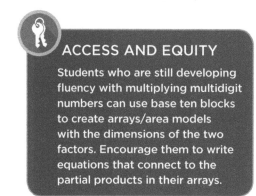

ACCESS AND EQUITY

Students who are still developing fluency with multiplying multidigit numbers can use base ten blocks to create arrays/area models with the dimensions of the two factors. Encourage them to write equations that connect to the partial products in their arrays.

FACILITATE

1. Organize students into small heterogeneous groups and distribute all materials.

2. Read the task with students, then refer them back to the ideas you recorded on the board (number 4 in launch).

3. Ask, "Can you think of an example of two even factors to demonstrate Talia's conjecture is true? Can you think of a counterexample, an example of two even factors to prove Talia's conjecture is false?"

4. Explain to students that they can develop as many examples and counterexamples as time allows. Encourage them to show their calculations and representations (arrays) for how they arrived at their product. Direct them to come to a consensus about whether or not they agree with Talia's conjecture.

PRODUCTIVE STRUGGLE

Based on your observations in the launch, encourage students who are still developing fluency with multiplying multidigit numbers to start by generating 1-digit × 1-digit examples to explore Talia's conjecture, and then have them work up to 2-digit × 1-digit and 3-digit × 1-digit examples.

5. **Observe** students as they collaborate on generating examples and counterexamples with the strategies they are comfortable using. Listen to the group discussions on deciding whether Talia's conjecture is true.

6. **Interview.**

   » Show me the strategies your group used.

   » How did your group choose the types of examples you have on your chart paper?

   » Why did you choose an area model to calculate the product for this example, and partial products (written method only) for this one?

   » Did your group find any counterexamples?

Note: Consider using the Observation and Interview (small group) tools for monitoring and recording the task responses above (see Appendix B).

CLOSE: MAKE THE MATH VISIBLE

1. Gather students back together as a whole group.

2. Call on different groups to share their examples. Sequence the sharing based on your group observations.

3. Ask, "Were the results the same or different whether your example was 1-digit × 1-digit, 2-digit × 1-digit, 4-digit × 1 digit, or 2-digit × 2-digit? How can we prove this visually?" Figure 8.3 shows how results might be shown.

Figure 8.3 Showing Results Visually

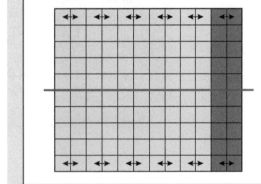

24 groups of 5

$24 \times 5 = (2 \times 12) \times 5 = 2 \times (12 \times 5)$

so there are 2 groups of 12×5

24 groups of n

$24 \times n = (2 \times 12) \times n = 2 \times (12 \times n)$

so there are 2 groups of $12n$

4. Focus students' attention on the fact that if there is one even factor, then blocks can be paired off with nothing left over, resulting in a product that is even. It doesn't matter how large or small the factors are.

   » Did any group find a counterexample to disprove Talia's conjecture?

   » **Hinge Question.** Why do you agree or disagree with Talia's conjecture? What conclusions can we make?

 STRENGTHS SPOTTING

Highlight students who enjoy finding counterexamples and disproving ideas, which is a strength that is not often recognized or supported. These students want to make sense of the mathematics they are learning and feel encouraged when they are supported.

TASK 21: EXPLORING EVEN NUMBERS STUDENT PAGE

 To download printable resources for this task, visit **resources.corwin.com/ClassroomReadyMath/4-5**

Task 21: Exploring Even Numbers Student Page

Name: _____ Date: _____

Tala's Work

DIGIT CHALLENGE

Use one of the digits in the box below to create a product between 100 and 200.

6 2 0 4 8

```
  2   4
×     6
---------
1 4 4
```

Use one of the digits in the box below to create a product between 1,000 and 2,000.

6 2 0 4 8

```
  2   8
×   4   6
---------
1, 2 8 8
```

After working on the *Digit Challenge* with her partner Ted, Tala noticed that it is impossible to get an odd product with the digits given. She made a conjecture that multiplying two even numbers would always result in a product that is an even number. Ted said, "I'm not sure yet. I want to investigate with more examples to see if what you said is always true."

Create your own multiplication examples to help Ted figure out whether Tala's conjecture is true. Try a 4-digit × 1-digit or a 2-digit × 2-digit example to see if you get the same or a different result.

POST-TASK NOTES: REFLECTION & NEXT STEPS

Mathematics Standard

- Add, subtract, multiply, and divide decimals to hundredths, using concrete models or drawings and strategies based on place value, properties of operations, and/or the relationship between addition and subtraction; relate the strategy to a written method and explain the reasoning used.

Mathematical Practices

- Use appropriate tools strategically.
- Look for and express regularity in repeated reasoning.

Vocabulary

- decimal
- estimation
- rounding
- approximation
- product
- quotient
- reasoning

Materials

- The Broken Calculator student page
- calculators or devices with a calculator app

Task 22
The Broken Calculator

Estimate to reason about decimal placement

TASK

The Broken Calculator

Edla is using a calculator to do some calculations for a project at home, but the decimal point key on the calculator is broken (see Figure 8.4). Edla says she can still use this calculator to find any product or quotient even if she doesn't use the decimal point. For example, if Edla wants to find the product of 34×5.1, she punches in 34×51 and finds the product equals 1734.

Figure 8.4 Broken Calculator

Source: in8finity/iStock.com

Edla says, "That's easy! I know that 34×5.1 is definitely greater than 17.34 but the answer has to be less than 1,000, so the actual product has to be 173.4!"

Will Edla's estimation strategy always work? Explain.

TASK PREPARATION

- If possible, find an old calculator that doesn't work properly or a computer keyboard that might be missing a key or two so students can see an example of what might be happening to Edla in this situation.

ACCESS AND EQUITY

In the Launch phase of the task, you will show students a calculator. Consider how you can do this to best provide each and every student with a clear view of the tool. Will you bring the whole class to the carpet and allow them to pass calculators around? Will you use a document camera to show the calculator on the projector? Or a whiteboard calculator app?

ALTERNATE LEARNING ENVIRONMENT

Students can use the broken calculator application on googleplay to simulate this experience (https://bit .ly/2DbXVPe).

- Prepare copies of the student page (one per student pair).

- Consider how you will partner students for the task work during the Facilitate phase of the task. Students should be organized into heterogeneous pairs. Pairs should share a calculator and student page.

LAUNCH

1. Bring the class together and show them a calculator or calculator app on a whiteboard (or an adding machine).

2. Facilitate: *See, Think, and Wonder.*

3. Ask

   » Do you know what this device or app is?

   » Have you ever used one before?

   » How does it work?

   » What are some ways you might use this tool?

   » Have you ever tried to use a tool like this and it didn't work?

4. Present the first part of the task to students: Edla is using a calculator to do some calculations for a project at home, but the decimal point key on the calculator is broken. Edla says she can still use this calculator to find any product or quotient even if she doesn't use the decimal point. For example, if Edla wants to find the product of 34×5.1, she enters 34×51 in the calculator and finds the product equals 1734. (See Figure 8.4.)

5. Ask these questions:

   » What is going on in this situation?

   » How do you think Edla feels about this situation?

   » What should Edla do?

6. If students have conjectures at this point, record them on the board or on chart paper.

FACILITATE

1. Organize students into heterogeneous pairs.

2. Share the rest of the task with the class.

3. Encourage students to *Turn and Talk* about Edla's strategy, then provide time for the class to *Pair-to-Pair Share.*

4. **Observe.** Listen in on the conversations. Take note of how students make their case to agree or disagree with Edla's approach. These arguments can be revisited during the Close phase of the task as an opportunity for students to refine and revise their thinking.

Note: Consider using the Observation tool for recording the responses (see Appendix B).

5. Give each pair a calculator and the student page.

6. Read through the directions together with students. Emphasize that even though they are using calculators that aren't broken, they can test Edla's reasoning by pretending the decimal point keys are broken to do the initial calculations.

7. **Interview.** As students work, make sure to visit every pair.

   » What are you noticing?

   » Why do you think that might be happening?

   » How could you test your conjecture to see if it works every time?

   » **Hinge Question.** Do you still agree/disagree with Edla's strategy? Why?

8. Challenge early finishers to see if they can come up with counterexamples for Edla's strategy.

ACCESS AND EQUITY

As you ask questions, listen with curiosity! Challenge the tendency to listen for errors or look for opportunities to correct thinking. Listening with curiosity means listening **to** each student with the goal of really seeing the task from their point of view. Such a perspective can often open your eyes to strong reasoning and important mathematical ideas which may not be evidenced in traditional ways.

CLOSE: MAKE THE MATH VISIBLE

1. Bring the class together to discuss their findings.

2. Based on observations and interviews, sequence student pairs to share their notices from the task.

   » If a student has proposed the rule (with or without understanding it), consider having them share first just to get it on the table.

   » Next, have student partners who noticed instances when the rule no longer works share those examples.

   » Take the opportunity to remind students that rules sometimes no longer work, so it is important to be able to rely on mathematical reasoning to recognize when a result is unreasonable. For example, when students enter #6 on the student page (70.8×2.5) into the "broken" calculator, they will get the result 17,700 and could easily apply the rule. But if they use a working

STRENGTHS SPOTTING

Students with a strong sense of mathematical agency will be wise consumers of mathematical ideas. Help students recognize the power in asking, "Does this make sense? Can it be proven?"

calculator, entering in 70.8×2.5 will give the result 177. If a student is relying solely on applying the algorithmic rule of counting decimal places here, they will likely believe the calculator *is* broken and the answer should be 1.77. Emphasize the importance of understanding *why* the rule works in order to be able to use the tools effectively.

3. Highlight the difference between Edla's broad approximations and more traditional "round then estimate" approaches to estimating the product. Ask:

   » Edla said, "I know 34×5.1 is definitely greater than 17.34." How does she know that? *(Multiplying 34 by a number greater than 1 will result in a product greater than 34.)* Why does that matter? *(This means placing the decimal anywhere to the left of the 3 will result in a value too small to be the actual product.)*

» Edla said 34 × 5.1 has to be less than 1,000. How does she know that? *(Possible reasoning: 1,000 = 100 × 10—because the first factor is less than 100 and the second factor is less than 10, the product has to be less than 1,000.)* Why does that matter? *(This means placing the decimal anywhere to the right of the 4 will result in a value too great to be the actual product.)*

TASK 22: BROKEN CALCULATOR STUDENT PAGE

online resources

To download printable resources for this task, visit **resources.corwin.com/ ClassroomReadyMath/4–5**

POST-TASK NOTES: REFLECTION & NEXT STEPS

Mathematics Standard

- Find whole-number quotients of whole numbers with up to four-digit dividends and two-digit divisors, using strategies based on place value, the properties of operations, and/or the relationship between multiplication and division. Illustrate and explain the calculation by using equations, rectangular arrays, and/or area models.

Mathematical Practices

- Look for and make use of structure.
- Attend to precision.

Vocabulary

- estimate
- missing factor
- quotient
- inverse
- divisor
- dividend
- related equations

Materials

- Student Place Value Cards

Task 23
Quick Quotients

Introduce two- to four-digit quotients

TASK

Quick Quotients

Leora says she has discovered a way to quickly find quotients. She thinks it is easier to multiply than to divide, so her strategy uses multiplication and estimation to find quotients. Listen to how Leora finds the quotient of $7{,}016 \div 5$ (see Figure 8.5).

Figure 8.5: Leora's Thoughts

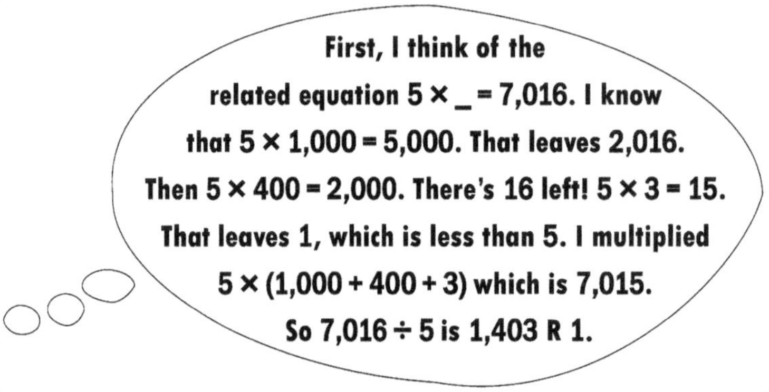

> **First, I think of the related equation $5 \times \_ = 7{,}016$. I know that $5 \times 1{,}000 = 5{,}000$. That leaves 2,016. Then $5 \times 400 = 2{,}000$. There's 16 left! $5 \times 3 = 15$. That leaves 1, which is less than 5. I multiplied $5 \times (1{,}000 + 400 + 3)$ which is 7,015. So $7{,}016 \div 5$ is 1,403 R 1.**

How do you think Leora would find the quotient of $1{,}430 \div 2$?

TASK PREPARATION

- Plan for heterogeneous groups of 3 or 4.

- Although students will be organized into small groups and encouraged to make collaborative decisions, consider giving each student a complete set of Student Place Value Cards so that individual students can manipulate the numbers as they think about the task.

- Prepare sets of Student Place Value Cards. These should be cut apart and organized into sets in baggies before the task begins. Consider printing on card stock and laminating for continued use.

- Have a variety of division expressions ready to give to small groups. Consider using division expressions pulled from curriculum materials used by your school's 5th-grade team.

LAUNCH

1. Facilitate a *See, Think, and Wonder.* Display the following expressions (Figure 8.7).

Figure 8.7 Expressions for See, Think, and Wonder

$$2 \times (600 + 10 + 1)$$
$$4 \times (1,000 + 200 + 30 + 2)$$
$$5 \times (2,000 + 100)$$

2. Record student wonders on the board.

3. **Observe**. Listen for evidence of students' prior knowledge about expressions like these. In particular, listen for:

   » Evidence of students' knowledge about the meaning of parentheses in expressions

   » Evidence of students' knowledge about place value relationships

   » Evidence of students' knowledge of numbers written in expanded form

   Note: Consider using the Observation tool for monitoring and recording the responses noted above (see Appendix B).

4. Take a few moments to answer some key wonders that come up. Possible wonders to discuss:

   » Why is the number in the parentheses written in expanded form?

   » What is the value of the expressions?

   Note that each expression can be simplified quickly using mental math. To facilitate the conversation, do not have students do any paper/pencil computation at this time.

   » Which expression has the greatest/least value?

FACILITATE

1. Display the first part of the task (see Figure 8.6).

Figure 8.6 Leora's Theory

Leora says she has discovered a way to quickly find quotients. She thinks it is easier to multiply than to divide, so her strategy uses multiplication and estimation to find quotients. Listen to how Leora finds the quotient of $7,016 \div 5$.

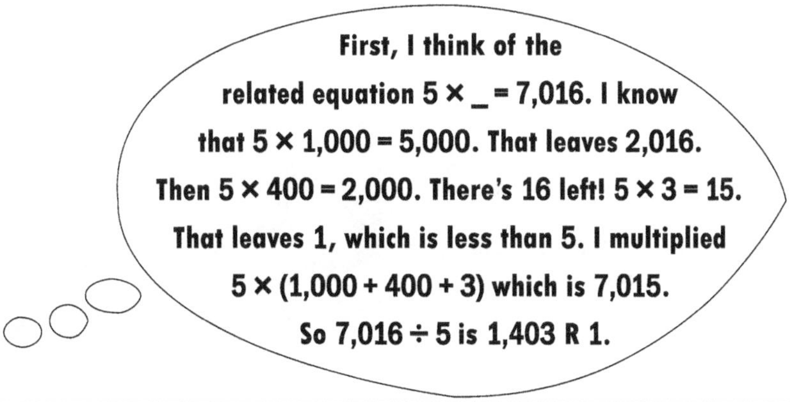

First, I think of the related equation $5 \times \_ = 7,016$. I know that $5 \times 1,000 = 5,000$. That leaves 2,016. Then $5 \times 400 = 2,000$. There's 16 left! $5 \times 3 = 15$. That leaves 1, which is less than 5. I multiplied $5 \times (1,000 + 400 + 3)$ which is 7,015. So $7,016 \div 5$ is 1,403 R 1.

2. Have students *Turn and Talk* with a partner to make sense of Leora's strategy.

3. After students have time to chat, use a set of Student Place Value Cards to show the factors she used to construct the quotient (students can place the cards on top of each other, right justified). See Figure 8.7.

Figure 8.7 Using Student Place Value Cards to Construct the Quotient

| 1,000 | 400 | 3 |

4. Ask, "How did Leora use these three factors to find the quotient? Could you use Leora's strategy to solve a new division problem? What are some things you noticed about Leora's strategy?"

5. Record student notices on the board.

6. Display the last part of the task. Then organize students into small groups and distribute Student Place Value Cards.

7. Encourage groups to work collaboratively to identify the steps Leora would take to find the quotient of 1,430 ÷ 2, representing the factors used with the Student Place Value Cards.

8. **Interview.** Visit each group to conduct interviews as they work.

   » How did you decide to use the (name a card) card? What partial product did you find with this factor?

   » Why didn't you use any thousand cards?

   » Do you expect this problem to have a remainder? Why or Why not?

   Note: Consider using the Interview (small group) tool for recording the task responses above (see Appendix B).

9. Challenge early finishers to use Leora's strategy on a more complex division problem.

ACCESS AND EQUITY

The use of place value cards to keep track of the partial quotients will support those students who may find it challenging to hold all the numbers and values in their heads at the same time. Using the cards instead of asking students to keep a written record will also encourage standard notation as they can be directed to use no more than one card from each place value position.

CLOSE: MAKE THE MATH VISIBLE

STRENGTHS SPOTTING

1. When every group has found the quotient 1,430 ÷ 2 = 700 + 10 + 5, bring the class together to discuss their work.

2. Highlight the following ideas by asking questions, eliciting students' ideas, and then using those ideas to create meaning before stating or telling:

Students who are willing to take risks should be celebrated. Estimating *before* computing (not just to check an answer) can help students notice and begin to prevent computational errors. Encourage students to ask, "What kind of a result do I expect to get?"

   » Estimation can be used to know that the greatest digit in this quotient has to be in the hundreds place. No number of 1,000s can be multiplied by 2 without exceeding the dividend.

» Once the greatest place value is known, estimation can be used to determine the multiple of that power of 10 (if the greatest place is hundreds, estimation can be used to decide how many hundreds).

» All the factors used can be added together to find the quotient. Demonstrate by laying the cards on top of each other with the 100s on the bottom, then the tens, and finally the ones on top, right justified.

» Leora's strategy can be used to find a quotient without using the division algorithm! That's because division and multiplication are related; they are inverse operations. Instead of subtracting groups, Leora's strategy is more like an "adding up" approach.

3. **Hinge Question.** Will Leora's strategy work for every division problem? What if the divisor has two digits? Three? Explain.

TASK 23: PLACE VALUE CARDS STUDENT PAGE

 To download printable resources for this task, visit **resources.corwin.com/ ClassroomReadyMath/4–5**

Task 23: Student Place Value Cards

1	10	100	1,000
2	20	200	2,000
3	30	300	3,000
4	40	400	4,000
5	50	500	5,000
6	60	600	6,000
7	70	700	7,000
8	80	800	8,000
9	90	900	9,000

POST-TASK NOTES: REFLECTION & NEXT STEPS

Mathematics Standard

- Fluently add and subtract multidigit whole numbers using the standard algorithm.

Mathematical Practices

- Reason abstractly and quantitatively.
- Attend to precision.

Vocabulary

- regroup
- sum
- difference

Materials

- Maya's Advice student page, one for each pair or group
- base ten blocks for each pair or group of 4
- chart paper
- markers

Task 24
Maya's Advice

Reasoning about the standard algorithm for subtraction

TASK

Maya's Advice

Greg is working on a problem in class (see Figure 8.8). He turns to Maya and says, "I'm stuck. I know that for this problem I need to regroup because there are only 4 ones and I need to subtract 8 ones, but there aren't any tens to regroup."

Figure 8.8 Greg's Work

$$\begin{array}{r} 6\cancel{0}4 \\ -\ 268 \\ \hline \end{array}$$

What should Maya say or do to help Greg? Work with your partner to help Maya advise Greg.

TASK PREPARATION

- Provide base ten blocks for each pair of students. Plan to have at least 6 hundreds, 10 tens, and 15 unit blocks for each pair. Depending on the number of base ten blocks available, you may also consider organizing the students into heterogeneous groups of 4.

ALTERNATE LEARNING ENVIRONMENT

When facilitating this task via distance learning, teachers or families may wish to use digital base ten blocks such as the Number Pieces app (https://apps.mathlearningcenter.org/number-pieces/) by the Math Learning Center.

LAUNCH

1. Write the following addition problem horizontally on the board:

635 + 367

2. Facilitate a Number Talk and have students show you with hand signals ("I'm still thinking about the prompt," "I'm ready to share my answer") when they are ready with a solution or if they have more than one way to solve the problem.

3. Call on 3 or 4 students to share possible sums and record these on the board. Ask, "Who would like to defend one of these solutions?"

4. Be prepared to record student strategies (some students may have decomposed both addends, then added hundreds to hundreds, tens to tens, . . . ; other students may have decomposed 367 to add on to 635; etc.).

5. Ask, "Based on the strategies shared by your classmates, are we convinced that one of the sums we recorded is the correct answer? Is 1,002 the agreed-on sum? Why are there no tens in the sum when there were tens in both addends?"

ACCESS AND EQUITY

Listen carefully to student explanations so that you are able to accurately represent their thinking on the board. As student thinking is made visible, other students may ask clarifying questions, revise their own thinking, or affirm and agree with their peers' ideas. Be careful about privileging particular ideas over others. Students will notice those ideas that you focus on first.

FACILITATE

1. Project the image from the task to the entire class as you read the scenario.

2. **Observe** as the students *Turn and Talk* to discuss a reasonable estimate for Greg's problem: the difference between 604 and 268. Record these estimates on the board.

3. Conduct a *Pair-Share* and ask students to discuss their initial thoughts about how Maya can help Greg.

4. Organize students in pairs or groups of 4. Have base ten blocks readily accessible for pairs or quads should they need them and distribute the rest of the materials.

5. Explain to students that they will use chart paper to show their work and response to the task.

6. Ensure that you have provided enough time to visit each pair or group in your class. Observe their discussions and note how they apply their understanding of place value to develop their advice for Maya.

PRODUCTIVE STRUGGLE

Asking students to provide advice to Greg from Maya's point of view may be challenging for some students. Encourage them to move forward by providing feedback about how they can organize their thinking, clarify ideas through the use of tools or pictures, and refine their explanations using precise vocabulary.

Note: Consider using the Observation tool for monitoring and recording the responses above (see Appendix B).

7. **Interview.**

   » "Because there aren't any tens to regroup, what does Maya have to think about next?" Note: Some students may decide to regroup 1 hundred into 100 ones. Be prepared to support students in explaining why we need to ungroup 1 hundred to 10 tens using base ten blocks.

   » "How did using base ten blocks help you with explaining how to regroup? How did drawing the problem help you with explaining how to regroup in the hundreds place?"

   » "What does this 10 above the 0 mean? **Show me** where that is represented?"

CLOSE: MAKE THE MATH VISIBLE

1. Gather students back together to discuss the task.

2. Call on specific pairs/groups to share their work, using the document camera if they want to demonstrate with base ten blocks (sequence the sharing based on your interviews).

3. Invite students to ask questions about their peers' work.

4. Through questioning rather than stating, elicit the following ideas:

> » Greg needs to regroup 1 hundred from 600. This is why the 6 in 6 hundred is replaced with a 5 to represent the 500 that remains after the 1 hundred was regrouped.

> » The 1 hundred from the hundreds place is then regrouped in the tens place. This is why there are now 10 tens instead of 0 tens.

> » Now that there are 10 tens, 1 ten can be regrouped to the ones' place. This is why there are 14 ones instead of 4 and 9 tens instead of 10 tens.

> » The difference between 604 and 268 equals 336.

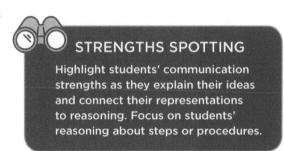

STRENGTHS SPOTTING

Highlight students' communication strengths as they explain their ideas and connect their representations to reasoning. Focus on students' reasoning about steps or procedures.

TASK 24: MAYA'S ADVICE STUDENT PAGE

 To download printable resources for this task, visit **resources.corwin.com/ ClassroomReadyMath/4–5**

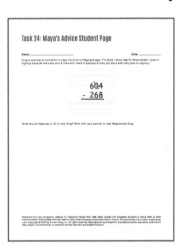

POST-TASK NOTES: REFLECTION & NEXT STEPS

Task 25
What's the Connection?

Reason about place value methods for multidigit multiplication

TASK

What's the Connection?

Mrs. Lloyde asked her 5th-grade class to study the examples she posted on the board carefully and to share their observations.

Figure 8.9 Mrs. Lloyde's Students' Work

Priya said, "I can definitely see how my strategy and Adrian's strategy are similar, but I have no idea what Nico did and how he got the same product as us." Help Nico explain how his method for multiplying is similar to Priya and Adrian's strategy. Then, try using Nico's way to solve 342×6.

Mathematics Standard

- Fluently multiply multidigit whole numbers using the standard algorithm.

Mathematical Practices

- Look for and express regularity in repeated reasoning.
- Attend to precision.

Vocabulary

- distributive property
- partial product

Materials

- What's the Connection student page, one for each pair

TASK PREPARATION

- Plan to make large copies of each of the student examples in Figure 8.9.

- Think about how you will heterogeneously group students in pairs to promote productive discussions about the three strategies used in the task.

LAUNCH

1. Post Priya and Adrian's strategy on the board (large copy).

2. Organize students into heterogeneous pairs, and then have them *Turn and Talk* to compare both strategies.

3. Ask for a volunteer to explain Adrian's strategy. Call on another student to explain Priya's strategy.

4. Ask:

    » What connections are you making between Priya's strategy and Adrian's strategy?

    » Where and how do you see the distributive property applied?

    » What does the 35 represent? What does the 420 represent?

    » How are the strategies of Priya and Adrian different? The same?

ACCESS AND EQUITY

By starting with Adrian's strategy, which is supported by a drawing that students can connect to numerical work, students can better access reasoning about place value methods for multidigit multiplication.

FACILITATE

1. Post Nico's work on the board and ask students to carefully study his method compared with Priya and Adrian's strategies.

2. Facilitate a *Pair-to-Pair Share*. Observe student pairs as they discuss their thoughts about Nico's strategy and compare this with Priya and Adrian's strategies.

3. Distribute and review the task with students.

4. **Show Me.**

PRODUCTIVE STRUGGLE

Provide enough time for students to examine Nico's method and to be able to go back and forth between reviewing his method and Priya and Adrian's strategies. In this way, you are supporting their ability to repeatedly reason about multidigit multiplication.

    » How the 3 above the 6 tens in 265 in Nico's strategy (see Figure 8.9) connects with Adrian's drawing

    » Where 420 in Priya's strategy is captured in Nico's strategy

    » Where the partial product 1,400 is recorded in Nico's strategy

Note: Consider using the Show Me tool for monitoring and recording the responses above (see Appendix B).

CLOSE: MAKE THE MATH VISIBLE

1. Gather students back together to discuss the task.

2. Call on specific students (based on their Show Me responses) to explain how Nico's strategy is similar to Priya and Adrian's strategies.

3. Invite a pair of students to explain how they used Nico's strategy to solve 342 × 6.

4. Using the work of Adrian and Priya, highlight the following:

   » In Adrian's strategy, the products of base ten units are shown as part of a rectangular region (for example, 7 ones × 5 ones = 35 ones = 35).

   » In Priya's strategy, the products of base ten units are shown along with the thinking but without a drawing (for example, the expression 7 × 5 is shown next to the partial product 35).

5. Then point out that Nico's strategy is a shorter version of both Priya and Adrian's strategies. The products of base ten units are shown, but the digits representing new units are written above 265. For example, the 3 in the partial product 35 is recorded above the 6 tens in 265 because it represents a new unit (tens, not ones). Adrian, Priya, and Nico's strategies each result in a product of 1,855.

6. Using Nico's strategy to solve 342 × 6, the 1 in the partial product 12 is recorded above the 4 tens in 342 because it represents a new unit (tens, not ones). This 1 ten is added to the partial product 240, for a sum of 250. Likewise, the 2 in 250 is recorded above the 3 in 342 because it represents a new unit (hundreds, not tens). The product of 342 × 6 equals 2,052.

TASK 25: WHAT'S THE CONNECTION STUDENT PAGE

online resources To download printable resources for this task, visit **resources.corwin.com/ ClassroomReadyMath/4–5**

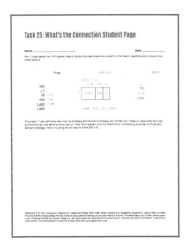

POST-TASK NOTES: REFLECTION & NEXT STEPS

CHAPTER

9

Number and Operations—Fractions

Equivalence, Comparing, and More

TASK 26: GRADE 4: RAIN DELAY

Compare two fractions with different numerators and different denominators. Recognize that comparisons are valid only when the two fractions refer to the same whole. Record the results of comparisons with symbols >, =, or <, and justify the conclusions.

TASK 27: GRADE 5: GREATER OR LESS THAN N?

Interpret multiplication as scaling (resizing), by:

a. Comparing the size of a product to the size of one factor on the basis of the size of the other factor, without performing the indicated multiplication.

b. Explaining why multiplying a given number by a fraction greater than 1 results in a product greater than the given number. Also explaining why multiplying a given number by a fraction less than 1 results in a product smaller than the given number.

Add, subtract, multiply, and divide decimals to hundredths.

TASK 28: GRADE 4: ARTISTIC ARRANGEMENTS

Explain why a fraction $\frac{a}{b}$ is equivalent to a fraction $\frac{(n \times a)}{(n \times b)}$ by using visual fraction models,

with attention to how the number and size of the parts differ even though the two fractions themselves are the same size. Use this principle to recognize and generate equivalent fractions.

TASK 29: GRADE 5: FITNESS FUNDRAISER

Solve real world problems involving division of unit fractions by non-zero whole numbers and division of whole numbers by unit fractions.

Anticipating Student Thinking: Fractions and related work with decimals are very important topics at the 4th- and 5th-grade levels. This chapter's tasks, particularly Tasks 27 and 29 provide important prerequisite mathematical experiences for middle school mathematics. These tasks emphasize student reasoning as students build procedural knowledge. Resist the temptation to tell students the steps in the procedures for multiplying fractions and decimals while students are developing their understanding of the meaning of the operations. Students who are challenged by these topics may need more time to prepare to share their reasoning and justify their explanations. Provide a variety of fraction manipulatives for students to use and ensure that students are creating visual models to accompany explanations. Consider strategic pairing or grouping of students to ensure that students are able to comfortably share their ideas.

THINK ABOUT IT

How will you group students during the task lessons to increase discourse opportunities between and among students as they engage with visual representations?

Mathematics Standard

- Compare two fractions with different numerators and different denominators. Recognize that comparisons are valid only when the two fractions refer to the same whole. Record the results of comparisons with symbols >, =, or <, and justify the conclusions.

Mathematical Practices

- Make sense of problems and persevere in solving them.
- Reason abstractly and quantitatively.

Vocabulary

- compare
- numerator
- denominator
- greater than
- less than
- equal

Materials

- fraction materials such as fraction tiles, Cuisenaire rods, fraction towers
- Rain Delay student page, one copy for each pair
- student copies of blank number lines
- Organizer to Anticipate Student Thinking

Task 26
Rain Delay

Compare fractions with unlike denominators

TASK

Rain Delay

Maria's field hockey team was running laps around the track until it started raining. So far,

- Maria has run $\frac{7}{8}$ of a mile.
- Lea has run $\frac{1}{4}$ of a mile.
- Addy has run $\frac{3}{6}$ of a mile.
- Sam has run $\frac{2}{3}$ of a mile.
- Kristen has run $\frac{4}{10}$ of a mile.
- Jada has run $\frac{4}{12}$ of a mile.

The coach announced that any field hockey player who ran a half mile or less needs to run laps again indoors. Who needs to run again? Defend your answer.

TASK PREPARATION

- Organize students into heterogeneous pairs.
- Gather all materials in a central location and ensure there is sufficient space for groups to access them.
- Review the task and record anticipated strategies in the anticipation organizer.

LAUNCH

1. Display the following on the board: $\frac{3}{8} \bigcirc \frac{8}{12}$
2. Ask students to compare the fractions. Use *Think-Pair-Share*.
3. Call on students to share their thinking (some students may use benchmarks and

STRENGTHS SPOTTING

As students share, have those who used different representations demonstrate their thinking. Take note of the particular representation a student uses and listen for how they make connections between the fraction model and other representations. Highlight students' unique thinking.

reason that while both fractions are close to one-half, $\frac{8}{12} > \frac{3}{8}$ because $\frac{3}{8}$ is less than $\frac{1}{2}$ and $\frac{8}{12}$ is greater than $\frac{1}{2}$).

FACILITATE

1. Organize students into pairs and distribute all materials.

2. Project the task on the board and review the situation with students.

3. Ask, "What is going on in the Rain Delay problem? How can you use what you know about comparing fractions to think about this situation?"

4. Provide time for pairs to work through the problem.

5. Pause pair work for a moment and ask, "So far, who do you know definitely does not need to run again? How do you know this? Why does Kristen need to run again, but not Sam? Why does Lea need to run again but not Maria?"

6. Have students continue working and observe the strategies they employ.

7. **Observe.** Use the organizer to anticipate student thinking to record student names and information you want to lift up in the whole-class discussion next to those who

   » Use manipulatives or sketches to create equivalent fractions before comparing

   » Use a number line to compare fractions

   » Mentally compare fractions to $\frac{1}{2}$ and write expressions using benchmark fractions and comparison symbols

   » Use equations to create like denominators

8. Decide on the sequence in which you want to call on students. Also include any questions you want to ask of students or that you want to connect to another student's strategy.

> ### ACCESS AND EQUITY
>
> Allowing students to self-select strategies and tools may provide access for students who have unique approaches to the problem. Purposeful questioning and sequencing during the lesson close will facilitate connections between and among students' thinking.

CLOSE: MAKE THE MATH VISIBLE

1. Facilitate student sharing based on the sequence you determined. Figure 9.1 shows how the math can be made visible on number lines.

2. Ask questions that connect students' use of fraction tiles or Cuisenaire rods to compare fractions with students who used a number line.

   » What do you notice about the representations that we used?

   » Which representation makes the most sense to you? Why?

3. Emphasize the following using student work and through questioning:

   » Maria and Sam do not need to run again because $\frac{7}{8}$ and $\frac{4}{6}$ are both greater than $\frac{1}{2}$.

   » Addy needs to run again because $\frac{3}{6} = \frac{1}{2}$.

   » Lea needs to run again because $\frac{1}{4} < \frac{1}{2}$, and it takes two fourths to equal one-half.

» Kristen needs to run again because $\frac{4}{10}$ is $\frac{1}{10}$ less than $\frac{1}{2}$.

» Jada needs to run again because $\frac{4}{12} < \frac{1}{2}$, since $\frac{6}{12} = \frac{1}{2}$, four-twelfths is two-twelfths less than one-half.

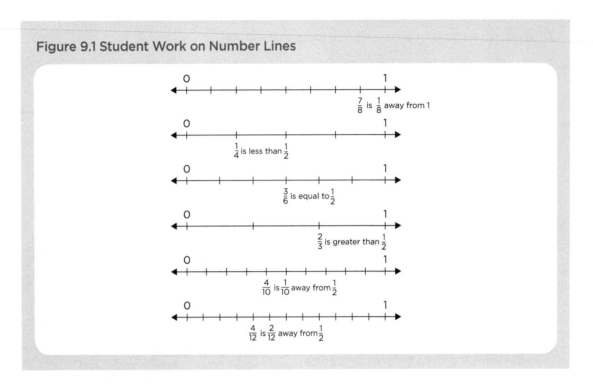

Figure 9.1 Student Work on Number Lines

$\frac{7}{8}$ is $\frac{1}{8}$ away from 1

$\frac{1}{4}$ is less than $\frac{1}{2}$

$\frac{3}{6}$ is equal to $\frac{1}{2}$

$\frac{2}{3}$ is greater than $\frac{1}{2}$

$\frac{4}{10}$ is $\frac{1}{10}$ away from $\frac{1}{2}$

$\frac{4}{12}$ is $\frac{2}{12}$ away from $\frac{1}{2}$

TASK 26: RAIN DELAY STUDENT PAGE

online resources ▷ To download printable resources for this task, visit **resources.corwin.com/ClassroomReadyMath/4–5**

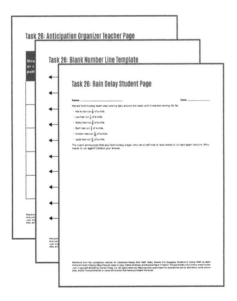

POST-TASK NOTES: REFLECTION & NEXT STEPS

Task 27
Greater or Less Than *n*?

Compare the size of a product to the size of one factor

TASK

Greater or Less Than *n*?

Use what you know about multiplication to sort your expression cards into two groups. Can you tell which expression cards have a product greater than *n* and which ones have a product less than *n*? Be ready to justify your thinking!

TASK PREPARATION

- Consider how to organize your class into heterogeneous groups of three or four students. Plan for an even number of groups so that each small group can partner with another group during the task.

- Print and cut apart one set of Product Expression cards.

- Print sorting mats (one per small group).

- Plan for a way to display all the expression cards in order from least to greatest later in the task (on marker board, large table, etc.).

LAUNCH

1. Write on the board:
   _____ < 20 < _____

2. Ask students to *Turn and Talk*: "What numbers might go in the blanks?"

3. Give several students the opportunity to come up and write a product in one of the blanks. Challenge the class to critique their reasoning. Use this opportunity to explicitly practice ways students have learned to agree and disagree with peers in a respectful manner.

STRENGTHS SPOTTING

Students may share an expression that has already been discussed. Instead of dismissing an idea, leverage the opportunity to help students use what they know by encouraging students to identify and defend another expression that would follow the same reasoning.

Mathematics Standards

- Interpret multiplication as scaling (resizing), by

  a. Comparing the size of a product to the size of one factor on the basis of the size of the other factor, without performing the indicated multiplication.

  b. Explaining why multiplying a given number by a fraction greater than 1 results in a product greater than the given number. Also explaining why multiplying a given number by a fraction less than 1 results in a product smaller than the given number.

- Add, subtract, multiply, and divide decimals to hundredths.

Mathematical Practices

- Reason abstractly and quantitatively.

- Construct viable arguments and critique the reasoning of others.

Vocabulary

- factor
- product

Materials

- Sorting Mat student page, one for each group
- Product Expression Cards student page, one for each group
- magnets/removable, restickable glue sticks, etc. (If needed to display expression cards)

4. Show students the sorting mat. Tell them that $n > 0$. Ask them to volunteer some possible values for n.

FACILITATE

1. Organize students into small groups and distribute the 30 expression cards among the groups. Give each group a sorting mat.

2. Present the task to students. Explain that in order to place an expression card on the mat the entire group must agree on and be able to justify the placement. If the group cannot agree, they should set the card aside and move on to another card.

3. **Interview.** As students work, circulate to each group, observing their work:

   » What is your justification for placing this expression here?

   » What is a context you could use to support your reasoning?

   » How could you represent this expression with a math drawing? How would that support your reasoning?

   » Which of these expressions (indicating two cards on the same side of the mat) has the greatest/least value? How do you know?

   Note: Consider using the Interview (small group) tool for monitoring and recording responses to the questions above (see Appendix B).

4. After each group has placed the majority of their expression cards on the mat, pair up the groups.

5. Have the two groups work together to organize all their expression cards from least value to greatest value.

CLOSE: MAKE THE MATH VISIBLE

1. When paired groups have ordered at least half their cards, bring the whole class together at the board (or around a large table) where everyone will be able to see cards as they are displayed.

2. Ask the group that has card J (n) to place their card at about the center of the board. Label the far left side of the board "least value" and the far right side of the board "greatest value."

3. Next, ask another group to choose one of their cards and place it on the board on the appropriate side of card J (greater than or less than). As one student in the group places the card, ask another group member to justify the group's reason for placing it in that spot.

4. Ask another group to add a card that fits on the opposite side of *n* from the previous card. Again, as one student in the group places the card, ask another group member to justify the placement.

5. As time allows, have students continue to add expression cards to the ordered list on the board.

6. After several cards have been placed in the public ordered list (some on each side of *n*), ask students to *Turn and Talk*. Ask, "What do all of the expressions that are less than *n* have in common? What do the expressions greater than *n* have in common?"

7. **Hinge Question.** Would you change where any of these expressions are placed if I told you that *n* is a fraction less than 1? Explain.

TASK 27: SORTING MAT STUDENT PAGES

online resources ⌕ To download printable resources for this task, visit **resources.corwin.com/ ClassroomReadyMath/4–5**

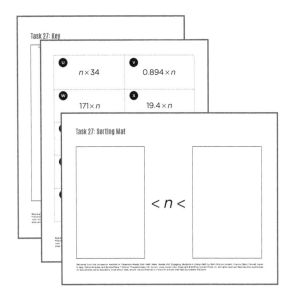

POST-TASK NOTES: REFLECTION & NEXT STEPS

Task 28
Artistic Arrangements

Represent equivalent fractions

TASK

Artistic Arrangements

Mr. Pica's 4th-grade art class is learning about the use of positive and negative space. Their assignment is to cover $\frac{3}{4}$ of the area of the square shown in Figure 9.2, using it as their positive space. They need to leave the rest of the area blank for their negative space.

Complete Mr. Pica's assignment using your choice of colors. You may add additional lines inside the square to suit your design. You must explain how the positive space in your artwork is equivalent to $\frac{3}{4}$ using words, pictures, and equations.

Figure 9.2 Mr. Pica's Square

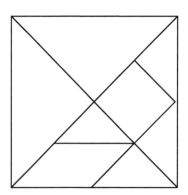

ALTERNATE LEARNING ENVIRONMENT

Families or providers who might be facilitating this task with students at home may consider using space on a sidewalk or in a driveway to duplicate the square design above. Different colored chalk may be used to color $\frac{3}{4}$ of the area of the square.

TASK PREPARATION

- Think about how to organize students into heterogeneous groups of four.
- Prepare copies of the student page.

ALTERNATE LEARNING ENVIRONMENT

This Google Doc version (https://bit.ly/3gFokTh) could be assigned by teachers who might be facilitating this task in a remote learning environment.

LAUNCH

1. Project the image shown in Figure 9.3 and ask, "Which one doesn't belong?" "Why?"

Figure 9.3 Which Square Doesn't Belong?

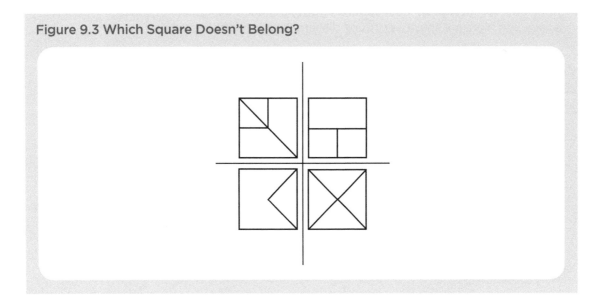

2. Call on several students to share their ideas and justify their thinking. Prompt students to identify fractional parts and to be specific when explaining their reasoning. For example, students may say that ◺ doesn't belong because while $\frac{1}{4}$ can be shown in the areas of the other squares, you can only see partitions of $\frac{1}{8}$ and $\frac{3}{8}$ on this square.

3. Have students repeat/revoice their peers' ideas and invite them to add to or ask questions about another student's ideas.

FACILITATE

1. Display the task and organize the class into groups of four.

2. Distribute the student page, chart paper, crayons, and colored pencils. Students may use chart paper to enlarge the picture.

3. Monitor student work and listen to student discussions as they collaborate on a design that shows $\frac{3}{8}$.

4. **Interview.**

   » "What fraction does this part of your design represent?"

   » "What fraction would describe the amount of negative space in your design? How do you know?"

   » "What equation(s) did you write to prove that your design equals $\frac{3}{4}$ of positive space?"

5. Set aside time so that you can display group work around the room.

CLOSE: MAKE THE MATH VISIBLE

1. Conduct a Something Similar and Something Different Gallery Walk.

2. Have students walk around the room to find peers' work that is similar or different from their group's work. Assign one colored dot to describe work that is similar and assign another color for students to use to signify work that is different.

3. Start the whole class discussion by reviewing work that students noted was similar to their own, then move to work that was noted as different from most groups (perhaps a work that was highly creative).

4. Focus the discussion on justifications about how each design encompasses $\frac{3}{4}$ positive space and highlight these as groups discuss their work or their peers' work.

TASK 28: ARTISTIC ARRANGEMENTS STUDENT PAGE

 To download printable resources for this task, visit **resources.corwin.com/ ClassroomReadyMath/4–5**

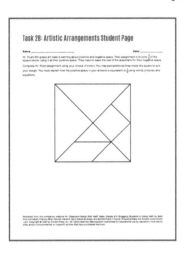

POST-TASK NOTES: REFLECTION & NEXT STEPS

Task 29
Fitness Fundraiser

Divide a whole number by a unit fraction

TASK

Fitness Fundraiser

Lincoln Elementary School held a fundraiser to buy new tablet computers for students. A local business pledged to donate $100 for every lap a student made around the school track (Figure 9.4).

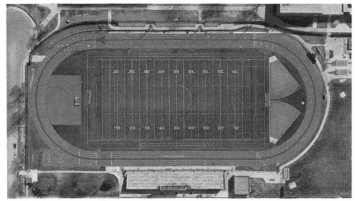

Figure 9.4 A Lap on the Track

Source: Imagery ©2020 Maxar Technologies, U.S. Geological Survey, Map data ©2020 Google

One lap around the track is $\frac{1}{4}$ mile. Every student wore a fitness tracker during the event. After the event was over, the students realized that they had traveled a combined distance of 54 miles. How many laps did the students make?

TASK PREPARATION

- Organize students into heterogeneous groups of two or three students.

- Consider using Google Earth (earth.google.com) in 3D mode to take students on a quick virtual field trip to track at a local high school or other local site familiar to students (Figure 9.5).

LAUNCH

1. If possible, project Google Earth for the class to see. Enter the name of a local high school or other area track that would be familiar to students. Use 3D mode.

Mathematics Standard

- Solve real world problems involving division of unit fractions by non-zero whole numbers and division of whole numbers by unit fractions.

Mathematical Practice

- Make sense of problems and persevere in solving them.

Vocabulary

- unit fraction
- factor
- quotient
- product

Materials

- sticky notes, one per student
- image of a local track, one per group
- student marker boards and dry-erase markers

Grade 5

Figure 9.5 The Track in 3D Mode

Source: Imagery ©2020 Maxar Technologies, U.S. Geological Survey, Map data ©2020 Google

2. Ask students to *Pair-to-Pair Share* things that come to mind when they look at the track.

3. Present the task to students.

4. Ask, "What kind of an answer would you expect to get when you solve this problem? Would you expect there to be *more* than or *fewer* than 54 laps completed by the students? Why?"

5. Have students write their name on a sticky note and indicate their response on a class T-chart. Be sure to let students know that they can move their sticky note at any time if their thinking changes as they work on the task (see Figure 9.6).

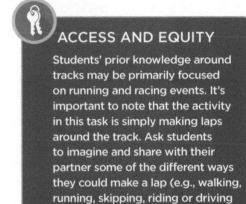

ACCESS AND EQUITY

Students' prior knowledge around tracks may be primarily focused on running and racing events. It's important to note that the activity in this task is simply making laps around the track. Ask students to imagine and share with their partner some of the different ways they could make a lap (e.g., walking, running, skipping, riding or driving a wheelchair, pushing a baby sibling in a stroller, etc.). Encourage each student to see themselves in the context of the task.

Figure 9.6 The Class T-Chart

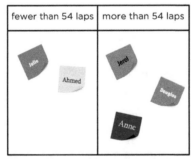

fewer than 54 laps	more than 54 laps
Jallo Ahmed	Jerel Douglas Anne

Sticky note source: freesvg.org

FACILITATE

1. Organize students into heterogeneous groups of two or three. Give each group a copy of the track image (Figure 9.5) for reference and marker boards or paper to record their work.

2. **Show Me.** As students work, circulate from group to group prompting students to demonstrate and explain their thinking. For example,

   » Show me what it looks like to make one lap around the track. What are some ways you could represent that?

   » Show me what this number/equation/drawing represents in the story.

» Show me how you could represent 1 mile in laps.

» When we started, you were thinking that the students must have made (more/fewer) than 54 laps. Is that still your thinking? Why or Why not?

Note: Consider using the Show Me tool for monitoring and recording responses to the Show Me prompts above (see Appendix B).

3. Ask any early finishers to figure out how much money the business will donate based on their pledge.

CLOSE: MAKE THE MATH VISIBLE

1. When most groups have reached a solution and all groups have come to an agreement that there must be more than 54 laps run, bring the class together to discuss the problem.

2. Based on your observations, select and sequence groups to share how they approached the task. Possible approaches to highlight:

   » Some students may draw laps one at a time and count by one-fourths until they reach 54.

   » Some students may recognize that it takes four laps to make one mile, so 54 miles is 54 groups of 4.

PRODUCTIVE STRUGGLE

Some students who recognize that it takes four laps to make one mile might try to find $54 \div 4$ to solve. Take advantage of the opportunity for students to work together to determine which expression (54×4 or $54 \div 4$) matches the context. Because students agree that four laps equals one mile, begin there. Ask the class, "How many laps would it take to equal two miles? Three? Ten?"

3. Using the students' work as a foundation, help students notice how we can write different (but related) equations to represent number of laps:

   » $n \times \frac{1}{4} = 54$

This equation represents the idea that students ran n laps of $\frac{1}{4}$ mile for a total distance of 54 miles.

   » $54 \div \frac{1}{4} = n$

This equation represents the question, "How many $\frac{1}{4}$ mile laps are in 54 miles?"

   » $54 \times 4 = n$

This equation represents the idea that students made 54 groups of 4 laps (because every group of 4 laps will make one mile).

4. Encourage students to discuss the relationships between each of these equations and the story context and the representations they created while working on the task.

5. **Exit Task:** Draw a representation that shows $8 \times \frac{1}{4} = 2$. Explain how your representation could also show $2 \div \frac{1}{4} = 8$ and $2 \times 4 = 8$.

POST-TASK NOTES: REFLECTION & NEXT STEPS

CHAPTER

10

Number and Operations—Fractions

Operations With Fractions

TASK 30: GRADE 4: FRACTION CONUNDRUM

Understand addition and subtraction of fractions as joining and separating parts referring to the same whole.

Decompose a fraction into a sum of fractions with the same denominator in more than one way, recording each decomposition by an equation. Justify decompositions.

TASK 31: GRADE 5: BUILDING SHELVES

Interpret a fraction as division of the numerator by the denominator $\left(\frac{a}{b} = a \div b\right)$. Solve word problems involving division of whole numbers leading to answers in the form of fractions or mixed numbers.

TASK 32: GRADE 4: REVISING A RECIPE

Solve word problems involving addition and subtraction of fractions referring to the same whole and having like denominators.

TASK 33: GRADE 5: LAYING TILE

Apply and extend previous understandings of multiplication to multiply a fraction or whole number by a fraction.

a. Interpret the product $\frac{a}{b} \times q$ as a parts of a partition of q into b equal parts;

equivalently, as the result of a sequence of operations $a \times q \div b$.

b. Find the area of a rectangle with fractional side lengths by tiling it with unit squares of the appropriate unit fraction side lengths, and show that the area is the same as would be found by multiplying the side lengths. Multiply fractional side lengths to find areas of rectangles, and represent fraction products as rectangular areas.

TASK 34: GRADE 5: CONSIDERING CONJECTURES

Interpret multiplication as scaling (resizing), by

a. Comparing the size of a product to the size of one factor on the basis of the size of the other factor, without performing the indicated multiplication.

b. Explaining why multiplying a given number by a fraction greater than 1 results in a product greater than the given number; explaining why multiplying a given number by a fraction < 1 results in a product smaller than the given number; and relating the principle of fraction equivalence $\frac{a}{b} = \frac{(n \times a)}{(n \times b)}$ to the effect of multiplying $\frac{a}{b}$ by 1.

TASK 35: GRADE 5: THE PIZZA PROBLEM

Add and subtract fractions with unlike denominators (including mixed numbers) by replacing given fractions with equivalent fractions in such a way as to produce an equivalent sum or difference of fractions with like denominators.

Anticipating Student Thinking: As noted previously, fractions are a critical area of emphasis and importance at the 4th- and 5th-grade levels. Tasks in this chapter extend the focus on equivalence from the previous chapter and will engage your students in tasks involving fraction operations. The contexts of the chapter tasks involving fraction operations (e.g., recipes, building shelves, laying tile, and of course, pizza) will truly have your students doing mathematics! As you prepare for each task lesson, consider how each of your students will gain access to the task. This will include consideration of grouping: student pairs; small groups; whole class; and use of representative models—such as drawings, number lines, manipulative materials, or online tools. Also consider your use of observation, interviews, and Show Me as formative assessment techniques to monitor both student task engagement and student progress.

THINK ABOUT IT

Ensure that time is provided for students to truly engage in the productive struggle that the chapter tasks provide. This will include opportunities to present and discuss solution strategies.

Task 30
Fraction Conundrum

Analyze the sum of two fractions

TASK

Fraction Conundrum

Claudia's teacher wrote the following problem on the board:

$$\frac{9}{8} + \frac{3}{8}$$

Kelly said, "The sum is $\frac{12}{8}$, you just have to add 3 and 9 because both numbers have a denominator of 8." Claudia was puzzled. She showed Kelly her work and replied, "I decomposed $\frac{9}{8}$ into $\frac{8}{8}$ and $\frac{1}{8}$. I think the sum is $1\frac{4}{8}$." Claudia's work is shown in Figure 10.1.

Figure 10.1 Claudia's Work

Who is correct? Could they both be incorrect? Correct? Justify your thinking.

TASK PREPARATION

- This task requires students to use varied fraction representations to explain their thinking. Ensure that you have access to fraction materials, including fraction tiles, fraction squares or circles, fraction towers, or number lines.

- Organize students into heterogeneous groups of 4. Distribute chart paper, markers, and various fraction manipulatives.

LAUNCH

1. Write the following on the board:

    Represent $\frac{5}{4}$ in multiple ways.

Grade 4

Mathematics Standards

- Understand addition and subtraction of fractions as joining and separating parts referring to the same whole.

- Decompose a fraction into a sum of fractions with the same denominator in more than one way, recording each decomposition by an equation. Justify decompositions.

Mathematical Practices

- Construct viable arguments and critique the reasoning of others.

- Reason abstractly and quantitatively.

Vocabulary

- numerator
- denominator
- compose
- decompose
- sum

Materials

- Fraction Conundrum student page
- chart paper
- markers
- manipulatives students could use to represent whole number sets and fractional amounts (color tiles, counters, fraction strips, fraction circles, dimes, pennies, etc.)
- number lines (you can also use laminated sentence strips)

2. Ask students to think about and then represent $\frac{5}{4}$ in as many ways as they can.

3. **Observe.** As students work, circulate to each group and observe the possible representations that surface including:

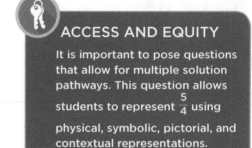

ACCESS AND EQUITY

It is important to pose questions that allow for multiple solution pathways. This question allows students to represent $\frac{5}{4}$ using physical, symbolic, pictorial, and contextual representations.

   » Number line representations, the use of concrete manipulatives, pictures, drawings, or equations that show $\frac{5}{4}$ decomposed in various ways, such as the sum of $\frac{3}{4} + \frac{2}{4}$.

   » Number line representations, the use of concrete manipulatives, drawings, or equations that show $\frac{5}{4}$ composed as the sum of unit fractions: $\frac{1}{4} + \frac{1}{4} + \frac{1}{4} + \frac{1}{4} + \frac{1}{4} = \frac{5}{4}$.

   » Number line representations, the use of concrete manipulatives, drawings, or equations that show $\frac{5}{4}$ as a mixed number.

   Note: Consider using the Observation tool for monitoring and recording the representations used (see Appendix B).

4. Invite students to do a Gallery Walk, asking them to observe other groups' representations.

5. Ask, "What was something similar that you noticed about each other's work? Was there a representation you saw that you hadn't thought about or that you have a question about?"

6. Highlight representations from your observations in Step 3.

FACILITATE

1. Have students return to their groups and distribute the student page.

2. Project the task on the board; read and review the context of the task with students.

3. Remind the groups to use physical or visual representations to justify their thinking.

4. **Show Me.** Ask, "How could you represent Kelly's strategy using (e.g., fraction towers)? How could you represent Claudia's strategy using _____?"

 STRENGTHS SPOTTING

Encourage students who are still developing representational flexibility and fluency by praising their efforts in explaining Kelly and Claudia's strategy through the use of fraction manipulatives or illustrations.

   Note: Consider using the Show Me tool for recording these responses (see Appendix B).

5. Ask, "What did your group determine about Kelly and Claudia's solutions?"

CLOSE: MAKE THE MATH VISIBLE

1. Bring students back together as a whole group.

2. Invite specific groups to share their work using a sequence based on your observations and Show Me responses.

3. Affirm that both representations, Kelly's and Claudia's, are correct.

4. Through both physical and visual representations, highlight the following ideas:

» Kelly's strategy involved composing fractions (Figure 10.2).

Figure 10.2 Kelly's Strategy

$$\frac{9}{8}+\frac{3}{8} = \left(\frac{1}{8}+\frac{1}{8}+\frac{1}{8}+\frac{1}{8}+\frac{1}{8}+\frac{1}{8}+\frac{1}{8}+\frac{1}{8}+\frac{1}{8}\right)+\left(\frac{1}{8}+\frac{1}{8}+\frac{1}{8}\right)$$

$$= \frac{(1+1+1+1+1+1+1+1+1)+(1+1+1)}{8}$$

$$= \frac{9+3}{8}$$

$$= \frac{12}{8}$$

» Claudia's strategy involved decomposing and using the associative property (Figure 10.3).

Figure 10.3 Claudia's Strategy

$$\frac{9}{8}+\frac{3}{8} = \left(\frac{8}{8}+\frac{1}{8}\right)+\frac{3}{8}$$

$$= \frac{8}{8}+\left(\frac{1}{8}+\frac{3}{8}\right)$$

$$= 1+\frac{4}{8}$$

$$= 1\frac{4}{8}$$

» Kelly and Claudia are both correct (Figure 10.4).

Figure 10.4 Comparing Kelly's and Claudia's Strategies

$$\frac{12}{8} \qquad = \qquad 1\frac{4}{8}$$

$$\frac{1}{8}+\frac{1}{8}+\frac{1}{8}+\frac{1}{8}+\frac{1}{8}+\frac{1}{8}+\frac{1}{8}+\frac{1}{8}+\frac{1}{8}+\frac{1}{8}+\frac{1}{8}+\frac{1}{8} \quad = \quad \frac{8}{8} \quad + \quad \frac{4}{8}$$

$$\left(\frac{1}{8}+\frac{1}{8}+\frac{1}{8}+\frac{1}{8}+\frac{1}{8}+\frac{1}{8}+\frac{1}{8}+\frac{1}{8}\right)+\left(\frac{1}{8}+\frac{1}{8}+\frac{1}{8}+\frac{1}{8}\right) = \left(\frac{1}{8}+\frac{1}{8}+\frac{1}{8}+\frac{1}{8}+\frac{1}{8}+\frac{1}{8}+\frac{1}{8}+\frac{1}{8}\right)+\left(\frac{1}{8}+\frac{1}{8}+\frac{1}{8}+\frac{1}{8}\right)$$

TASK 30: FRACTION CONUNDRUM STUDENT PAGE

 To download printable resources for this task, visit **resources.corwin.com/ClassroomReadyMath/4–5**

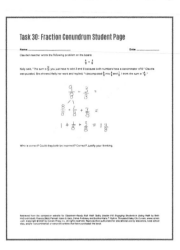

POST-TASK NOTES: REFLECTION & NEXT STEPS

Task 31
Building Shelves

Develop the relationship between division and fractions

TASK

Building Shelves

Haider has a furniture building business. He is building bookcases this week. He wants to use all the boards he has in stock to build bookcases with different numbers of shelves. He wants to figure out how long the shelves can be.

Figure 10.5 Shelves

TASK PREPARATION

- Plan for heterogeneous pairs.

- Print and cut out Building Shelves task cards.

- Prepare paper strips. You will need strips about an inch wide in each of the lengths noted below. Consider using construction paper with a different color for each length.

  » 5 inches

  » 7 inches

  » 8 inches

LAUNCH

1. Present the task to students.

2. Encourage students to *Pair-to-Pair Share* what they know about bookshelves.

3. Ask, "Look at this picture (Figure 10.5). What can you tell about the lengths of the boards in these bookshelves? How are the lengths the same? How are the lengths different?"

4. Record student ideas. Be sure to elicit the idea that each bookshelf is made up of boards that are all the same length, but the taller book-shelf has shorter boards than the three-shelf model.

Mathematics Standard

- Interpret a fraction as division of the numerator by the denominator $\left(\frac{a}{b} = a \div b\right)$. Solve word problems involving division of whole numbers leading to answers in the form of fractions or mixed numbers.

Mathematical Practices

- Look for and make use of structure.

- Use appropriate tools strategically.

Vocabulary

- scale model
- expression

Materials

- Building Shelves student task cards
- paper strips
- scissors
- tape or glue sticks
- poster/chart paper
- markers

FACILITATE

1. Tell students they are going to be exploring Haider's problem using scaled representations for the shelves. They will cut strips of paper to show their solutions.

2. Show students the different lengths of paper strips. Explain that they are using a scale where one inch of paper represents one foot of a board, so a 6-inch strip of paper will represent a 6-foot piece of board.

3. Organize students into pairs and give each pair at least one Building Shelves card to get started.

4. Make sure the paper strips are easily accessible so students may go and get strips as they are needed.

5. **Observe.** As students work on the task, circulate to each group. Make note of the strategies being used to determine shelf length. Possible approaches:

   » Students may quickly determine that division makes sense if the number of shelves is less than the length of the board (for example, making 3 shelves from a 6-foot board).

   » Students may treat the board as one unit and use fractional reasoning (for example, cutting their strip into eighths to represent making 8 shelves).

   » Students may convert the length of the board to inches and then use division to find the lengths of each shelf (for example, 8 ft. = 96 in. so to make 16 shelves from an 8-foot board, students might find the quotient of 96 ÷ 16 and say the shelves would be 6 inches each).

   Note: Consider using the Observation tool for monitoring and recording the strategies noted above (see Appendix B).

6. Ask students to create a small poster to display their solution (see Figure 10.6). The poster should indicate the length of the board and the number of shelves, show the shelves they made, and give the length (in feet) of each shelf.

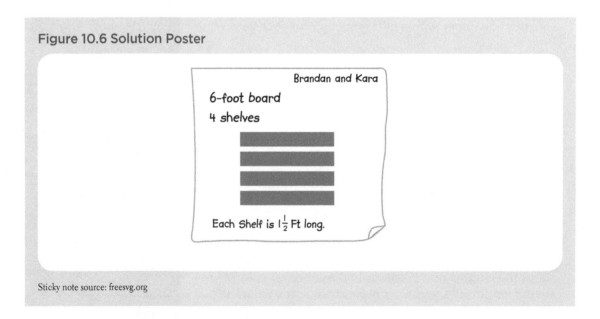

Figure 10.6 Solution Poster

> Brandan and Kara
> 6-foot board
> 4 shelves
>
> Each shelf is $1\frac{1}{2}$ Ft long.

Sticky note source: freesvg.org

7. Because the Building Shelves task cards have different numbers of shelves, students may finish at different rates. Encourage students to grab another card as they finish and see if their same strategy will work with a different set of board lengths and shelf values.

CLOSE: MAKE THE MATH VISIBLE

1. After students have finished working through most of the cards, conduct a Notice and Wonder Gallery Walk.

2. Facilitate a quick discussion around student ideas that surface during the Gallery Walk. Students may say,

   » If the length of the board is greater than the number of shelves, the length of the shelves will be longer than 1 foot.

   » If the length of the board is less than the number of shelves, the length of the shelves will be shorter than 1 foot.

   » If the length of the board matches the number of shelves, the shelves will be exactly 1 foot long.

3. Bring the class together and facilitate a discussion around the data that have been collected. Create a table on the board and begin by adding data for the shelves that are whole number lengths. Leave room to add columns to the right side of the table.

Board Length (ft)	Number of Shelves	Shelf Length (ft)
8	2	4
8	4	2
8	8	1
7	7	1
5	5	1

4. Ask, "What relationships do you notice?"

5. When students notice the multiplicative relationship, add another column to the table and record the division expression.

Board Length (ft)	Number of Shelves	Shelf Length (ft)	Division Expression
8	2	4	8 ÷ 2
8	4	2	8 ÷ 4
8	8	1	8 ÷ 8
7	7	1	7 ÷ 7
5	5	1	5 ÷ 5

6. Add the data for the shelves that are $\frac{1}{2}$ foot long and ask, "If I follow the pattern we noticed, does it make sense to think about this relationship as 5 ÷ 10? How can we explain why that answer would be $\frac{1}{2}$?"

Board Length (ft)	Number of Shelves	Fraction	Division Expression
5	5	1	5 ÷ 5
5	10	$\frac{1}{2}$	5 ÷ 10

7. When students mention that 5 is half of 10, add another column to the right side of the table and record the expression as a fraction. Have students consider what the earlier expressions (e.g., 8 ÷ 2) would be as a fraction.

Board Length (ft)	Number of Shelves	Shelf Length (ft)	Division Expression	Fraction
8	2	4	8 ÷ 2	$\frac{8}{2}$
8	4	2	8 ÷ 4	$\frac{8}{4}$
8	8	1	8 ÷ 8	$\frac{8}{8}$
7	7	1	7 ÷ 7	$\frac{7}{7}$
5	5	1	5 ÷ 5	$\frac{5}{5}$
5	10	$\frac{1}{2}$	5 ÷ 10	$\frac{5}{10}$

8. Use what students discover here to analyze the remaining data. Begin with data for which the shelf length (in feet) cannot be simplified to a whole number (e.g., $\frac{8}{3}$). If students have recorded the length of the shelf in inches, ask the class to tell what that would be in feet and have them simplify the fraction (for example, 10 inches would be $\frac{10}{12}$ ft, which can be simplified to $\frac{5}{6}$ ft).

PRODUCTIVE STRUGGLE

It's okay if students give you mixed number data for the Shelf Length column. Encourage them to analyze the relationships between the mixed number and the division expression/ fraction columns. Be patient and let them grapple with making sense of the number values until they notice the relationship.

9. Use questioning to elicit the big idea that a fraction can be interpreted as *numerator ÷ denominator*.

10. **Hinge Question.** We've just discovered that we can think of a fraction as a division expression. Use what you know to prove that $96 \div 10 = \frac{96}{10}$.

TASK 31: BUILDING SHELVES STUDENT TASK CARDS

To download printable resources for this task, visit **resources.corwin.com/ ClassroomReadyMath/4–5**

POST-TASK NOTES: REFLECTION & NEXT STEPS

Task 32
Revising a Recipe

Solve addition and subtraction of fractions with like denominators

Mathematics Standard

- Solve word problems involving addition and subtraction of fractions referring to the same whole and having like denominators.

Mathematical Practices

- Make sense of problems and persevere in solving them.
- Reason abstractly and quantitatively.

Vocabulary

- converting
- mixed number

Materials

- Revising the Recipe student page, one for each pair
- fraction circles
- fraction strips
- number lines (laminated sentence strips)
- Anticipation Organizer

TASK

Revising a Recipe

Carmen's dad wants to bake a healthier version of his oatmeal chocolate chip cookies (Figure 10.7). These are the recipe adjustments he would like to make:

Figure 10.7 Cookies

Source: pickpik.com

- Decrease the amount of butter by $\frac{1}{3}$ cup,

- Decrease the amount of brown sugar by $\frac{2}{4}$ cup,

- Decrease the amount of flour by $\frac{3}{2}$ cup,

- Increase the amount of oatmeal by $\frac{1}{2}$ cup, and

- Decrease the amount of chocolate chips by $\frac{1}{4}$ cup.

Original Recipe	Adjusted Recipe
$\frac{2}{3}$ cup butter	
$\frac{3}{4}$ cup firmly packed brown sugar	
$\frac{1}{2}$ cup granulated sugar	
2 eggs	
1 teaspoon vanilla	
$2\frac{1}{2}$ cups all-purpose flour	
1 teaspoon baking soda	
1 teaspoon ground cinnamon	
3 cups uncooked oatmeal	
$\frac{1}{2}$ teaspoon salt	
$\frac{3}{4}$ cup chocolate chips	

Complete the table above to help Carmen's dad determine how much of each ingredient he needs.

TASK PREPARATION

- Organize students in heterogeneous pairs to work collaboratively on using physical or visual representations to add and subtract fractions.

- Determine that you have enough fraction circles, strips, and number lines available for each pair of students in your class.

- Use the Anticipation Organizer to plan for how students will respond before implementing the task, record strategies while students are solving the task during the facilitate portion, and note how student pairs will share strategies in the close.

LAUNCH

Figure 10.8 Which Doesn't Belong?

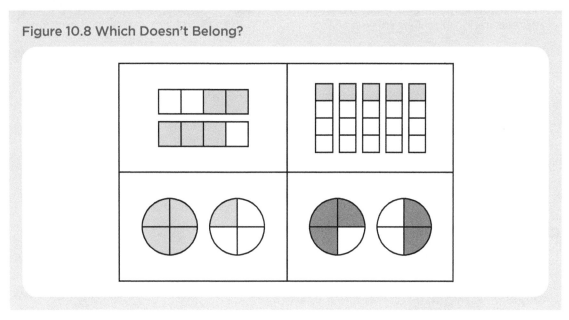

1. Project the Figure 10.8 image on the board and ask, "Which one do you think doesn't belong?"

2. Direct students to *Turn and Talk* to a peer and to share their thinking.

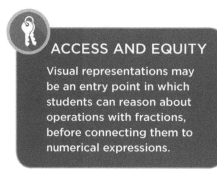

ACCESS AND EQUITY

Visual representations may be an entry point in which students can reason about operations with fractions, before connecting them to numerical expressions.

3. Invite students to share their thinking with the entire group and to defend their choices (some ideas that may emerge include identifying the image on the bottom left because it is the only picture in the selection with an entire whole shaded in or choosing the image on the top right showing $\frac{1}{4} + \frac{1}{4} + \frac{1}{4}$ . . . because it is the only one showing unit fractions . . .).

4. Label each illustration with the thinking that students provide.

5. Reaffirm that each visual model represents an expression whose sum is $\frac{5}{4}$.

FACILITATE

1. Organize students into heterogeneous pairs. Distribute the student page and fraction manipulatives.

2. Project the task on the board and call on several students to read the task.

3. Ensure that you make time to visit each pair of students as they work on the task.

4. **Observe** the strategies students use as they work with fractions with like denominators. Use the Anticipation organizer to anticipate student thinking included with this lesson. Note students who

» Use physical representations such as fraction circles or tiles.

» Sketch pictures or visual representations on a number line.

» Develop equations.

5. Have students meet and share different representations in a *Pair-to-Pair Share*.

> ! **PRODUCTIVE STRUGGLE**
>
> Students who are still developing representational fluency may be challenged with using the number line effectively. Encourage them to use a physical representation first, then connect this with a number line representation.

» For students who used physical representations, ask, "How could you show the same strategy using a number line?"

» For students who used illustrations or a number line, ask, "How could you represent the same strategy symbolically?"

» For students who are fluent with symbolic representations, encourage fluency by asking, "How could you represent your work using pictures, a number line, or fraction tiles?"

CLOSE: MAKE THE MATH VISIBLE

1. Gather students back together to discuss the task.

2. Select pairs of students to share their strategies, sequencing the order from concrete to abstract representations. Think about students who

» Used fraction circles (Figure 10.9) or strips (Figure 10.10) to compute, such as $\frac{2}{3} - \frac{1}{3} = \frac{1}{3}$ to represent the amount of butter or $\frac{3}{4} - \frac{2}{4} = \frac{1}{4}$ to represent the quantity of brown sugar.

» Used illustrations such as number lines (Figure 10.11) to compute. For example, $2\frac{1}{2} - \frac{3}{2} = 1$ to represent the amount of flour.

Figure 10.9 Fraction Circle

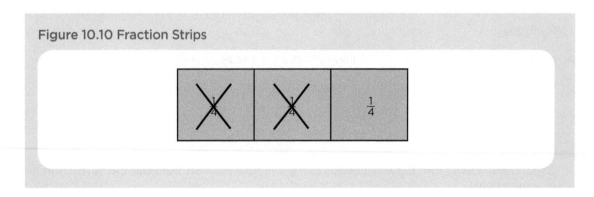

Figure 10.10 Fraction Strips

Figure 10.11 Number Line

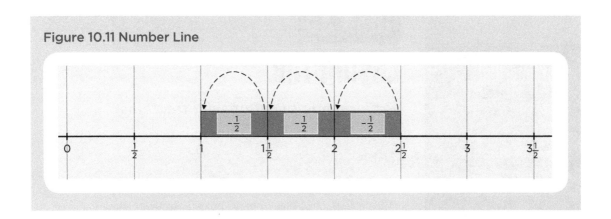

» Used equations such as $3 + \frac{1}{2} = \frac{6}{2} + \frac{1}{2} = \frac{7}{2}$ or $3\frac{1}{2}$ to represent the amount of oatmeal.

Note: A common error occurs when students use a "subtracting up" strategy on a number line. Students may start at $\frac{3}{2}$ or $1\frac{1}{2}$ and add $\frac{1}{2}$ three times, landing on 3 as the difference.

3. **Hinge Question**. What operation was used each time you decreased an amount for the Revised Recipe? The reduction of what ingredient would probably make the Revised Recipe healthier?

4. Affirm the following:

   » Converting a mixed number to a fraction can involve fraction addition.

   » To calculate for $2\frac{1}{2} - \frac{3}{2}$, students may convert $2\frac{1}{2}$ to $\frac{2}{2} + \frac{2}{2} + \frac{1}{2}$ or $\frac{5}{2}$.

   » Subtracting $\frac{3}{2}$ from $\frac{5}{2}$ results in a difference of $\frac{2}{2}$ or 1.

TASK 32: REVISING THE RECIPE STUDENT PAGE

online resources ↖ To download printable resources for this task, visit **resources.corwin.com/ ClassroomReadyMath/4-5**

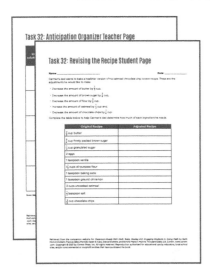

POST-TASK NOTES: REFLECTION & NEXT STEPS

Mathematics Standard(s)

- Apply and extend previous understandings of multiplication to multiply a fraction or whole number by a fraction.

  a. Interpret the product $\left(\frac{a}{b}\right) \times q$ as a parts of a partition of q into b equal parts; equivalently, as the result of a sequence of operations $a \times q \div b$.

  b. Find the area of a rectangle with fractional side lengths by tiling it with unit squares of the appropriate unit fraction side lengths, and show that the area is the same as would be found by multiplying the side lengths. Multiply fractional side lengths to find areas of rectangles, and represent fraction products as rectangular areas.

Mathematical Practices

- Reason abstractly and quantitatively.
- Model with mathematics.

Vocabulary

- area
- expression

Materials

- Laying Tile student page, one copy per group

Task 33
Laying Tile

Explore multiplication with fractions

TASK

Laying Tile

Della's family was installing new tile on their floor (see Figure 10.12).

Figure 10.12 Tiles

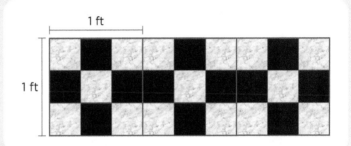

After they had put down a few tiles, Della said, "I wonder what fractional part of the area we've covered so far is black!" Everyone had a different opinion about how they could figure that out.

- Avery said, "We can just multiply $3 \times \frac{4}{9}$."

- Remi said, "Wait, shouldn't we multiply $\frac{3 \times 4}{9}$?"

- Jaylen said, "No, I've got it! We should multiply $\frac{1}{9} \times 4 \times 3$."

Who is right? What is the total area of the black part of the floor so far?

TASK PREPARATION

- Plan for heterogeneous groups of 2 or 3. Consider partnering students in mixed-strengths groups based on observed preference for different types of representations (symbolic, physical, drawn, etc.).

STRENGTHS SPOTTING

Mixed-strengths groups position each member as a valued contributor to the learning process by inviting students to use their strengths to construct their own understanding, support one another's learning, and provide feedback to peers. Let students know that each person in the group contributes strength to the group. Together, through collaboration, they are stronger!

LAUNCH

1. Facilitate a Notice and Wonder using the image from the task.

2. Allow students to *Turn and Talk* before taking ideas from the group.

3. Record student ideas on the board.

4. Ask students to share where they might have seen similar patterned tiles before (classroom floor, hallway, their own home, etc.).

FACILITATE

1. Present the full task to students.

2. Ask, "Have you ever looked at something and thought about it differently from the ways someone else might have thought about it? What do you notice about the three different ideas that were presented?"

3. Organize students into small groups and challenge them to figure out what exactly each part of the three different expressions represents.

4. Encourage students to mark up the pictures to show connections to each expression.

5. **Show Me.** As you circulate to each group, have students show

   » Where does Avery see three groups of $\frac{4}{9}$?

   » How is that different from what Remi sees?

   » What does the $\frac{1}{9}$ that Jaylen sees represent in the picture?

6. **Hinge Question.** Della thought about it differently from everyone! Della thought of the expression $(3 \times 4) \div 9$. What was Della seeing and thinking?

CLOSE: MAKE THE MATH VISIBLE

1. Bring the class together to make connections.

2. Select and sequence groups to share how they figured out what the different people saw in the image.

   » Avery sees three 1-foot square tiles that are each $\frac{4}{9}$ black.

   3 sq. ft. $\times \frac{4}{9}$ black tiles $= \frac{12}{9}$ sq. ft. of black tile

   » Remi sees 3 groups of four $\frac{1}{9}$-square-foot-sized parts.

   $\frac{3 \times 4}{9}$ black parts of 1 square foot $= \frac{12}{9}$ sq. ft. of black tile

   » Jaylen sees that each black part is $\frac{1}{9}$ square foot. There are 4 in each tile and 3 tiles.

   $\frac{1}{9}$ square foot $\times$ 4 per tile $\times$ 3 tiles $= \frac{12}{9}$ sq. ft. of black tile

   Della's expression is similar to Remi's, using the division interpretation of a fraction. There are 3 groups of 4 black parts, and 9 parts fit in each square foot.

   3×4 black parts $\div$ 9 parts per square foot $= \frac{12}{9}$ sq. ft. of black tile

TASK 33: LAYING TILE STUDENT PAGE

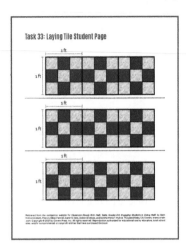

POST-TASK NOTES: REFLECTION & NEXT STEPS

_____

_____

_____

_____

_____

_____

_____

_____

Task 34
Considering Conjectures

Introduce multiplication as scaling

TASK

Considering Conjectures

A fifth-grade teacher was starting a unit on multiplying fractions and asked the class to share their ideas about multiplication. Kamari said, "I have a conjecture. I think multiplying by a fraction will always make a number smaller. Like, one half of six is three. Half of something is smaller than all of it!" Guadalupe said, "I disagree. If we do three halves of six, we'd have more than six, and $\frac{3}{2}$ is a fraction too. I don't think you can tell if the number is going to get bigger or smaller until you figure out the answer."

Help Kamari and Guadalupe test their conjectures.

TASK PREPARATION

- Plan to organize students into heterogeneous pairs.

- Make sure students have ready access to whatever manipulatives and other tools they might choose to use as they test out these conjectures.

LAUNCH

1. Write the word *conjecture* on the board.

2. Say the word aloud and have students say it with you.

3. Ask students to *Turn and Learn* from a partner what they know about conjectures.

4. Have students share what they learned and record ideas on the board.

5. Make sure students recognize that conjectures are

   » Based on evidence: Mathematicians cite true mathematical statements to support their claims.

! PRODUCTIVE STRUGGLE

In order to develop a culture in which students are comfortable grappling with mathematical ideas, it is important to normalize the feeling of being uncertain. Teachers must celebrate the learning that happens through the process of making and testing conjectures—whether the evidence supports or contradicts the conjecture.

Mathematics Standard(s)

- Interpret multiplication as scaling (resizing), by:

   a. Comparing the size of a product to the size of one factor on the basis of the size of the other factor, without performing the indicated multiplication.

   b. Explaining why multiplying a given number by a fraction greater than 1 results in a product greater than the given number; explaining why multiplying a given number by a fraction < 1 results in a product smaller than the given number; and relating the principle of fraction equivalence $\frac{a}{b} = \frac{(n \times a)}{(n \times b)}$ to the effect of multiplying $\frac{a}{b}$ by 1.

Mathematical Practices

- Look for and express regularity in repeated reasoning.

- Construct viable arguments and critique the reasoning of others.

Vocabulary

- conjecture
- evidence
- product

Materials

- manipulatives students could use to represent whole number sets and fractional amounts (color tiles, counters, fraction strips, fraction circles, dimes, pennies, etc.)

- marker boards or paper

- sticky notes in two easily distinguishable colors (one for agree, one for disagree)

» Not yet proven to be true: Conjectures are based on incomplete information and need to be tested and proven.

FACILITATE

1. Present the task to the class.

2. Ask, "What evidence does each student give to support their conjecture? How could we test their conjectures?"

3. Organize the class into pairs and challenge them to find examples that support and/or counterexamples that refute Kamari's and Guadalupe's claims.

4. **Observe/Interview.** Monitor the work of the pairs and, in particular, make note of the tools and/or representations students are using to test the claims. Encourage varied representations.

   » How could you represent Kamari's/Guadalupe's example with a manipulative/physical model? With a drawn representation? An equation? A pattern of answers to related problems?

   » What is your initial thinking about Kamari's and Guadalupe's conjectures? Do you agree or disagree? Why?

   » What is another example you could try out to verify your initial thinking?

   Note: Consider using the Observation and Interview (small group) tools for monitoring the work of the pairs and recording responses to the questions above (see Appendix B).

5. Record both Kamari's and Guadalupe's conjectures in separate places on the board. As each pair determines if they agree or disagree with the conjectures, have them put the appropriate color of sticky note up. Students should be encouraged to change these choices as desired based on new evidence.

STRENGTHS SPOTTING

Recognize students who take risks, try out new ideas, and revise their thinking. These students are exhibiting strengths in conceptual understanding. Be sure to note students' actions or behaviors for revision rather than focusing only on correct answers.

CLOSE: MAKE THE MATH VISIBLE

1. When most pairs have tested several additional multiplications and are prepared to defend a position, bring the class back together.

2. As a class, review the sticky notes posted.

   » If the class is generally in agreement, select and sequence pairs to share evidence to support the class position.

   » If the class is split, select and sequence pairs from each side of the argument to share their evidence in turn.

3. As needed, ask students to test additional specific cases to clarify the evidence. Specifically:

   » A natural (counting) number multiplied by a fraction less than one.

   » A natural number multiplied by a fraction equal to one.

» A natural number multiplied by a fraction greater than one.

» Zero multiplied by any fraction.

4. Facilitate a class discussion around the conjectures and generate a class conjecture based on the examples the class has come up with.

5. **Hinge Question.** Will our class conjecture still be true if *both* factors are fractions less than one? Provide evidence (examples) as proof.

POST-TASK NOTES: REFLECTION & NEXT STEPS

_____

_____

_____

_____

_____

_____

_____

_____

_____

_____

Mathematics Standard

- Add and subtract fractions with unlike denominators (including mixed numbers) by replacing given fractions with equivalent fractions in such a way as to produce an equivalent sum or difference of fractions with like denominators.

Mathematical Practice

- Reason abstractly and quantitatively.

Vocabulary

- whole
- numerator
- denominator
- equivalent

Materials

- Pizza Problem student page 1 (consider having several copies available for each group)
- Pizza Problem student page 2 (each group will need one "whole" pizza for comparison)
- scissors
- pizza rounds (optional)
- plastic circular fraction pieces (optional)

Task 35
The Pizza Problem

Visualize adding fractions with unlike denominators

TASK

The Pizza Problem

After a party, Ellis and Leia had leftover slices from two pizzas (see Figure 10.13). Both pizzas were originally the same size. One pizza had been cut into six slices and there were four slices left. The other pizza had been cut into eight slices and there were three slices left.

Figure 10.13 Sliced Pizzas

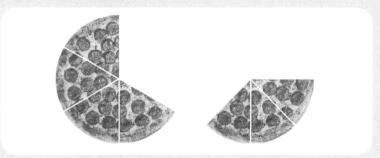

Source: nitrub/iStock.com

Ellis said, "We have $\frac{4}{6}$ of one pizza and $\frac{3}{8}$ of another pizza. When I add that together, I get $\frac{4}{6} + \frac{3}{8} = \frac{4+3}{6+8} = \frac{7}{14}$ but that doesn't make sense! I know that $\frac{7}{14}$ is equal to $\frac{1}{2}$ but we definitely have more than half a pizza left!" Leia agreed with Ellis, "Look, when I try to put the leftover slices together it looks like there is more than 1 whole pizza!" (See Figure 10.14.)

Figure 10.14 Putting the Sliced Pizzas Together

Source: nitrub/iStock.com

Exactly how much pizza do Ellis and Leia really have left?

TASK PREPARATION

- Check at local pizza places to see if they will donate two cardboard pizza rounds and two pizza boxes. Cut one of the rounds into sixths and the other into eighths. These can be used to show students that the "wholes" are equivalent, but the unit fractions are different.

- Be sure to plan sufficient time for the Close phase of the task. While you want each group to have an opportunity to make decisions about process (e.g., how will they cut apart one or both pizzas to regroup and show how much pizza there really is), you should feel comfortable stopping the work before every group actually reaches a final solution.

LAUNCH

1. Present the first half of the task to students (Figure 10.15).

2. Have students *Turn-and-Talk*. Ask, "About how much pizza do the students have left all together?" Record predictions on the board.

Figure 10.15

The Pizza Problem

After a party, Ellis and Leia had leftover slices from two pizzas. Both pizzas were originally the same size. One pizza had been cut into six slices and there were four slices left. The other pizza had been cut into eight slices and there were three slices left.

Source: nitrub/iStock.com

FACILITATE

1. Present the second part of the task.

2. Ask students to revisit the estimates they made. Were their estimates closer to what Ellis found with computation or what Leia found when she put all the slices together?

3. Organize the students into small groups and provide materials to each group. Challenge them to determine the exact amount of pizza the students have left by cutting and rearranging the pizza slices.

4. **Show Me.** As students work, visit each group, and ask them to show you how they know what unit fraction they are making when they cut apart slices.

> ### ! PRODUCTIVE STRUGGLE
>
> This will be a messy process and that's okay! Provide extra copies so that students are able to try different cuts as needed. Consider providing each group with an extra copy of Pizza Problem Student Page 1 to keep uncut for comparison purposes. Students can check to be sure they still have the same amount of pizza by layering slices over the original image and also over the "whole" pizza.

CLOSE: MAKE THE MATH VISIBLE

1. When the whole class has rearranged the pizza slices to show one whole pizza plus a bit more, conduct a Something Similar and Something Different Gallery Walk.

2. Ask, "How did each group decide to name the amount of pizza that Ellis and Leia have together as a fraction?"

3. Display student work to highlight the different strategies for cutting and rearranging. Look for the following:

   » Trimming enough off of one slice to fit together a whole composed of different-sized slices (see Figure 10.16).

   » Cutting all the slices into a common size so that the twenty-fourths are visible in the whole.

   » Identifying the size of the extra slice by comparing it to one of the other unit fractions (e.g., "The extra slice is $\frac{1}{3}$ of $\frac{1}{8}$, so it must be $\frac{1}{24}$ of a whole pizza.").

Figure 10.16 The Rearranged Pizza Slices

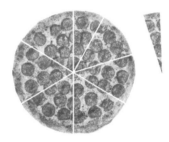

---

4. When students have concluded that there are $1\frac{1}{24}$ pizzas left, Ask, "If we cut this pizza into slices that are all the same size as this remaining slice, how many slices would there be? How could we represent that as a fraction?" If there is a student pizza already partitioned into twenty-fourths, use that as an example. Otherwise, use a marker to partition a copy of the pizzas to show the twenty-fourths.

> **STRENGTHS SPOTTING**
>
> As you highlight and discuss student work, call out specific strategies and ideas that you observed during the facilitate section. By strengths spotting the strategies and dispositions you observe, you help students connect those behaviors and strategies to mathematical thinking that they can leverage to build new mathematical understanding.

5. Write this equation on the board: $\frac{4}{6} + \frac{3}{8} = \frac{25}{24}$

6. Ask students, "Where do we see the $\frac{4}{6}$ pizza in our model? How many twenty-fourths are represented by that part? Where do we see the $\frac{3}{8}$ pizza? How many twenty-fourths are represented by that part?"

7. Add to the equation on the board: $\frac{4}{6} + \frac{3}{8} = \frac{16}{24} + \frac{9}{24} = \frac{25}{24}$

8. **Hinge Question.** Compare our equation $\frac{4}{6} + \frac{3}{8} = \frac{16}{24} + \frac{9}{24} = \frac{25}{24}$ to Ellis's equation $\frac{4}{6} + \frac{3}{8} = \frac{4+3}{6+8} = \frac{7}{14}$. Why didn't Ellis's computational strategy work?

TASK 35: PIZZA PROBLEM STUDENT PAGES

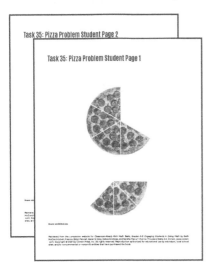

POST-TASK NOTES: REFLECTION & NEXT STEPS

_____

_____

_____

_____

_____

_____

_____

_____

Measurement

Knowing, Converting, Using

GETTING STARTED

TASK 36: GRADE 4: LET'S BUILD A CHICKEN COOP!

Know relative sizes of measurement units within one system of units, including *km, m, cm; kg, g; lb, oz.; l, ml; hr, min, sec.* Within a single system of measurement, express measurements in a larger unit in terms of a smaller unit. Record measurement equivalents in a two-column table.

TASK 37: GRADE 5: GROWING CORN

Convert among different-sized standard measurement units within a given measurement system (e.g., convert 5 cm to 0.05 m), and use these conversions in solving multistep, real world problems.

TASK 38: GRADE 4: HOW MANY METERS IS THAT?

Know relative sizes of measurement units within one system of units, including *km, m, cm; kg, g; lb, oz.; l, ml; hr, min, sec.* Within a single system of measurement, express measurements in a larger unit in terms of a smaller unit. Record measurement equivalents in a two-column table.

TASK 39: GRADE 4: A NURSE'S SCHEDULE

Use the four operations to solve word problems involving distances, intervals of time, liquid volumes, masses of objects, and money, including problems involving simple fractions or decimals, and problems that require expressing measurements given in a larger unit in terms of a smaller unit. Represent measurement quantities using diagrams such as number line diagrams that feature a measurement scale.

Anticipating Student Thinking: Measurement is a mathematics content strand that defines *doing math*. Each task in this chapter engages students in measurement applications of prior work with concepts and operations involving whole numbers, fractions, and decimals and depending on the task, involves either customary or metric measurement. As you plan for implementing the chapter's task lessons, consider how you will organize learners into small groups in which your students can collaboratively plan how to solve a task's problem. Also, ensure student access to the materials necessary for the measurement-based activities within a task. Given that measurement tasks naturally engage students, make sure to use observation, interviewing, or Show Me to note and validate how easily your students understand expectations, get involved in the mathematical ideas, and work toward determining and implementing the solution strategies for the tasks.

THINK ABOUT IT

This chapter's measurement tasks should engage your students in productive struggle. Make sure to provide time for student groups to plan and work through their task solutions, share solution strategies, and do a Gallery Walk to view the work of the other student groups.

Mathematics Standard

- Know relative sizes of measurement units within one system of units including *km, m, cm; kg, g; lb, oz.; l, ml; hr, min, sec*. Within a single system of measurement, express measurements in a larger unit in terms of a smaller unit. Record measurement equivalents in a two-column table.

Mathematical Practices

- Look for and express regularity with repeated reasoning.
- Attend to precision.

Vocabulary

- convert
- conversion
- yards
- feet
- inches
- yardstick
- tape measure
- ruler

Materials

- Let's Build a Chicken Coop student page, one for each group
- posters for Launch
- butcher paper
- markers
- yardsticks
- rulers
- tubs of 1-inch tiles (one for each group)
- sturdy cardboard or heavy card stock strips cut 1 foot long

Task 36
Let's Build a Chicken Coop!

Relate units within the customary system

TASK

Let's Build a Chicken Coop

Min showed her dad a picture of a chicken coop that she would like to build with him. He found a simple plan with measurements (Figure 11.1) and wanted to make sure that the chicken coop would be large enough to suit their needs, but he forgot to purchase a tape measure.

Figure 11.1 Coop Plan

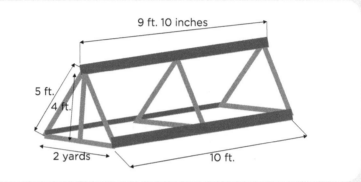

Min said, "I have some one-inch tiles and cardboard strips in my room. Maybe we can use these." Help Min and her dad measure out a pattern for the chicken coop using the tools she found. Start by recording the measurement equivalencies on the following tables.

Feet	Inches
1 ft	
2 ft.	
3 ft.	
4 ft.	
5 ft.	
8 ft.	
9 ft. 10 in.	
10 ft.	

Yards	Feet	Inches
1 yard		
2 yards		

TASK PREPARATION

- Consider grouping students in heterogeneous groups to best promote collaborative work.

- Consider areas in the school where you could lay butcher paper for students to work on the task (groups will need to measure out a 10-foot-long side, so a nearby hallway, lobby, cafeteria, or pod area might be needed in addition to space in the classroom).

- Prepare one-foot long cardboard strips (one for each group member) and gather tubs of one-inch tiles.

- Prepare three posters for the launch of the lesson: In the center of each poster write, "Things that can be best measured in inches." "Things that can be best measured in feet." "Things that can be best measured in yards."

LAUNCH

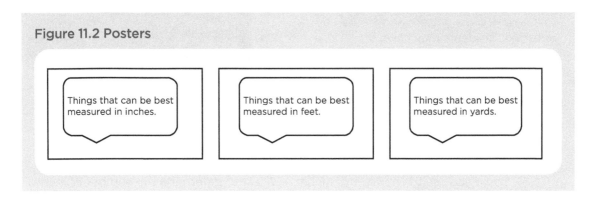

Figure 11.2 Posters

Things that can be best measured in inches.

Things that can be best measured in feet.

Things that can be best measured in yards.

1. Post the posters shown in Figure 11.2 around the classroom. Lay some yardsticks near the poster "Things that can be best measured in yards," in case some students need a benchmark for the length of a yard. Lay a one-foot ruler near the sign "Things that can be best measured in feet," and lay some one-inch tiles near the poster "Things that can be best measured in inches."

2. Organize students into three groups by having them count out loud, assigning themselves as 1s, 2s, or 3s. Direct each group to walk to a particular poster and to brainstorm as many things as they can that can be best measured in the units specified. Distribute markers to group-appointed recorders.

3. After some time, have students rotate to a different poster until all groups have generated ideas for the 3 posters.

4. Bring students back together for a whole-group discussion.

   » Ask, "What were some observations you made?"

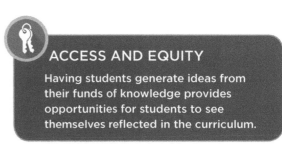

ACCESS AND EQUITY

Having students generate ideas from their funds of knowledge provides opportunities for students to see themselves reflected in the curriculum.

   » Ask, "Was there a difference between the objects that you could best measure in feet versus what you could best measure in yards? Why might measuring _____ in yards be more appropriate?" Have rulers and yardsticks nearby in case students want to use these tools to defend their thinking.

» Ask, "Were there objects that you discussed that could be measured in both inches and feet, or feet and yards?"

» Ask, "Why might it be more appropriate to measure some objects in inches rather than in feet?"

FACILITATE

1. Organize students into heterogeneous groups, and distribute the student page, the tub of 1-inch tiles, and cardboard strips.

2. Project the task on the board and read along with students. Ask, "What is a chicken coop? Why might Min want to build one with her father?"

3. Direct students to areas around the classroom where you have laid butcher paper for them to measure out a pattern and clarify any questions students may have.

4. As groups work, observe whether they notice patterns as they make conversions from feet to inches.

> **PRODUCTIVE STRUGGLE**
>
> Students who may be developing emerging understanding that 1 foot is 12 times the length of 1 inch, or that 1 yard is 3 times the length of 1 foot, may benefit from using rulers and yardsticks to convert from one unit to physical models.

5. **Show Me.**

   » How could you show me the number of inches in 2 feet?

   » How could you use the number of inches in 2 feet to determine the number of inches in 4 feet?

6. **Hinge Question.** How could you find the number of inches in 2 yards?

CLOSE: MAKE THE MATH VISIBLE

1. Bring students back together as a whole group.

2. Set aside time for a brief Gallery Walk of the chicken coop patterns that groups measured and outlined.

3. On the board create tables like those shown in Figure 11.3.

Figure 11.3 Converting Feet to Inches and Yards to Feet

Feet	Inches	Yards	Feet
1	_____	1	_____
2	_____	2	_____
3	_____		
4	_____		

4. Have students *Turn and Talk* to discuss what they discovered about the equivalencies on the board.

5. Invite students to share their thinking (based on Show Me) and to defend their reasoning (observe the tools students use to justify their thinking).

6. Affirm the following:

   » 12 inches = 1 foot

   » 3 feet = 1 yard

   » 1 yard = 36 inches

   » We can abbreviate yard as "yd.," feet as "ft.," and inches as "in."

   » Rulers, yardsticks, and tape measures are tools for measuring length in the customary system.

   » We can multiply the number of feet by 12 because there are 12 inches in 1 foot. So, $n \times 12$ represents n groups of 12 inches. (See Figure 11.4.)

Figure 11.4 Converting Feet to Inches

Feet	Inches
1 ft.	12 in.
2 ft.	24 in.
3 ft.	36 in.
4 ft.	48 in.
5 ft.	60 in.
8 ft.	96 in.
9 ft. 10 in.	118 in.
10 ft.	120 in.

» We can multiply the number of yards by 3 because there are 3 feet in 1 yard. So $n \times 3$ represents n groups of 3 feet. (See Figure 11.5.)

TASK 36: LET'S BUILD A CHICKEN COOP STUDENT PAGE

online resources To download printable resources for this task, visit **resources.corwin.com/ ClassroomReadyMath/4–5**

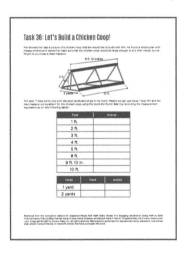

POST-TASK NOTES: REFLECTION & NEXT STEPS

Task 37
Growing Corn

Review measurement conversions in a real-world context

TASK

Growing Corn

A corn farmer measured the height of the corn when the first leaf appeared.

It was 15 centimeters high. When the corn was ready for harvest 75 days later, it measured $2\frac{1}{4}$ meters high (see Figure 11.6).

1. How much did the corn grow?

2. If it grew about the same amount each day, about how much did it grow each day?

Figure 11.6 Corn

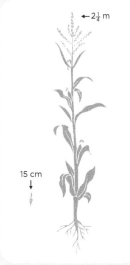

$\leftarrow 2\frac{1}{4}$ m

15 cm

Source: ilyakalinin/iStock.com

TASK PREPARATION

• Plan for heterogeneous groups of 2 or 3.

• Collect enough meter sticks to have 3 meter sticks for each student group.

• If possible, have rolls of butcher paper available so students can construct physical models of the corn stalks.

• Consider bringing an ear of corn in to show students.

ACCESS AND EQUITY

Consider also providing each group a strip of paper that is $2\frac{1}{4}$ meters long and another that is 15 centimeters long. These materials will enable students to make visual comparisons of the lengths to test for reasonableness of their solutions. Additionally, such models would enable students to draw and label partitions when determining growth per day.

LAUNCH

1. Facilitate a *See, Think, and Wonder* using the task image.

Mathematics Standard

• Convert among different-sized standard measurement units within a given measurement system (e.g., convert 5 cm to 0.05 m), and use these conversions in solving multistep, real world problems.

Mathematical Practices

• Make sense of problems and persevere in solving them.

• Model with mathematics.

Vocabulary

• harvest
• farmer
• metric system
• meters
• centimeters
• acre
• stalk
• partition

Materials

• Growing Corn Exit Task student page, one per student
• paper or marker boards
• meter sticks
• calculators

2. After giving students an opportunity to *Turn and Learn* what a partner is thinking, ask, "Who recognizes the kind of plant in this picture?"

3. If students are unsure, tell them, "This is called a corn stalk. It's the plant we get corn from."

4. Record student wonders on the board.

FACILITATE

1. Display the full task and read it with students.

2. Ask, "Did hearing the story answer or change any of our wonders?"

3. Organize students into groups and let them begin working on the task.

4. **Observe.**

   » Do students convert the 15 cm to 0.15 m, or do they convert the $2\frac{1}{4}$ m to 225 cm to find the overall growth?

   » How are students reasoning about the expected results?

   » Are students estimating or trying to find an exact answer?

5. **Interview.**

   » Ask, "Where did this value come from? Why did you make that change?"

   » Ask, "Would it be reasonable to say that the corn probably grew 200 cm per day? Why or why not?"

Note: Consider using the Observation and Interview (small group) tools for monitoring and recording responses to the questions above (see Appendix B).

CLOSE: MAKE THE MATH VISIBLE

1. Provide a place on the board for each group to record their answers to both questions in the task.

2. Ask, "What do you notice about our answers to the task's two questions? Do you think the answers on the board are reasonable? Explain."

3. Elicit from students that the first question has a precise answer, but the answer can be written in more than one way (210 cm or 2.1 m) while the second question asked for an estimate. Student estimates may vary slightly but should be in the range of 2 to 3 cm per day.

4. Select and Sequence groups to share their approaches to answering the second question based on observations during the facilitate phase of the task. Highlight how students move between units within their reasoning.

TASK 37: GROWING CORN EXIT TASK

 To download printable resources for this task, visit **resources.corwin.com/ ClassroomReadyMath/4–5**

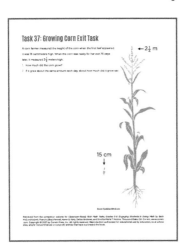

POST-TASK NOTES: REFLECTION & NEXT STEPS

Mathematics Standard

- Know relative sizes of measurement units within one system of units, including *km, m, cm; kg, g; lb, oz.; l, ml; hr, min, sec.* Within a single system of measurement, express measurements in a larger unit in terms of a smaller unit. Record measurement equivalents in a two-column table.

Mathematical Practices

- Look for and make use of structure.
- Look for and express regularity with repeated reasoning.

Vocabulary

- meter
- kilometer
- equivalent

Materials

- How Many Meters Is That? Exit Task student page, one for each pair
- meter sticks (enough for pairs)
- premeasured lengths of yarn (10 m)
- measuring tape (metric)
- yardstick (1)
- chalk, one for each pair
- centimeter cubes

Task 38
How Many Meters Is That?

Develop benchmarks for metric units of length

TASK

How Many Meters Is That?

Figure 11.7 Runners

Source: tomazzl/iStock.com

Liz announced, "Did you know that Rakesh just ran his best time in the 5-kilometer race?" Judi asked, "How many meters is that?" Liz said, "I'm not sure, but I do know that the prefix 'kilo' means one thousand."

Create a table that displays kilometer and meter equivalencies. Use the information you generate to determine the number of meters equivalent to 5 kilometers.

What if Rakesh runs 1.5 kilometers? How many meters would he run?

TASK PREPARATION

- Think about where you might be able to take students to measure lengths (such as the perimeter of the school playground) or to draw different lengths using chalk (such as on a blacktop surface). You may also consider having students compare who jumps the farthest (standing jump) and measure the distance using a meter stick.

LAUNCH

1. Display both a meter stick and a yardstick in front of the class for comparison. Facilitate a *See-Think-Wonder*. Ask, "What do you see? What are you thinking about? How does that idea connect with what you see?"

2. Have students compare both the yardstick and the meter stick. Some ideas that may surface include the following:

   » A yardstick and meter stick are both longer than the length of two 12-inch rulers or longer than 2 feet.

   » You can use both tools to measure the length of longer objects.

   » A yardstick and meter stick are close in length.

   » A meter stick is longer than a yardstick by about 3 inches.

3. Call on a few students to line up centimeter cubes (approximately 20) alongside the meter stick for comparison.

4. Ask, "What are you curious about? Where have you seen centimeters before? How many centimeter cubes do you think it will take to match the length of the meter stick? Could it take more than 50 centimeter cubes? How do you know?"

5. Some ideas students may share include the following:

   » Centimeters are also located on the opposite side of the location of inches on some rulers.

   » There could be more than 50 centimeter cubes needed to match the length of the meter stick because 20 cubes match to less than $\frac{1}{4}$ of the length.

6. Affirm the following:

   » A yardstick is a tool for measuring length using the U.S. customary system, while the meter stick is a tool for measuring length using the metric or "standard international" system.

   » A yardstick is 3 feet in length, while a meter stick is 3 feet and 3.37 inches in length.

   » It will take 100 centimeter cubes to match the length of a meter stick.

STRENGTHS SPOTTING

Students may also make connections to their real-world experiences with measurement or compare yardsticks and meter sticks to objects that they know about. Call attention to these students' observations by recognizing their strength in making connections.

FACILITATE

1. Organize students into heterogeneous triads and distribute measuring tools (e.g., meter sticks, measuring tapes [metric], or even premeasured lengths of yarn).

2. Explain to students that the class will be going outside to estimate and measure lengths in meters. Students can either measure the perimeter of the school playground or track (Figure 11.7), estimate, measure and compare who can jump the farthest, or draw different lengths on the blacktop in meters.

ACCESS AND EQUITY

Providing students with opportunities to use tools such as a meter stick supports their understanding and ability to apply their experiences to future mathematical work. This will assist students in developing a benchmark and visual image of a meter.

3. After a reasonable amount of time to explore, bring students back to the classroom to debrief their experiences.

4. Ask these questions:

   » What might be some other objects that have a length of about 1 meter? 10 meters?

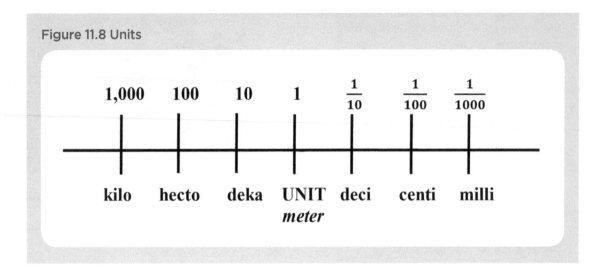

Figure 11.8 Units

5. Project Figure 11.8 to students.

6. Ask, "How does this picture relate to our study of place value? How many meters would equal the length of a hectometer? How many centimeters would equal the length of a meter?" Reinforce for students the idea that the prefix "deka" in dekameter means 10 times as much as the unit, so a dekameter is 10 times as much as 1 meter while a decimeter is one-tenth as much as a meter, . . ."

7. Distribute and review the task with students.

8. **Observe** how students organize the kilometer to meter equivalencies using a table.

9. Ask these questions:

   » What did you notice as you recorded information in your table?

   » How many meters would be equivalent to 2 km? How do you know that?

   » How could you determine the number of meters equivalent to 1.5 km?

CLOSE: MAKE THE MATH VISIBLE

1. Gather students back together to discuss the task.

2. Have students *Share* information in their tables.

3. Reaffirm the following:

   » A meter is the base unit of length in the metric system.

   » The key to the organization of the metric system and to converting metric units is to pay attention to the prefixes (refer back to the Figure 11.8 image in Facilitate).

   » Through repeated reasoning, students may determine that 5 kilometers = 5,000 meters. Additionally, 1.5 kilometers = 1 × 1,000 m + 500 m = 1,500 meters. See Figure 11.9.

Figure 11.9 Converting Kilometers to Meters

1.5 km = 1,500 m

Kilometer	Meter
1 km	1,000 m
2 km	2,000 m
3 km	3,000 m
4 km	4,000 m
5 km	5,000 m

TASK 38: HOW MANY METERS IS EXIT TASK

 To download printable resources for this task, visit **resources.corwin.com/ClassroomReadyMath/4–5**

POST-TASK NOTES: REFLECTION & NEXT STEPS

Mathematics Standard

- Use the four operations to solve word problems involving distances, intervals of time, liquid volumes, masses of objects, and money, including problems involving simple fractions or decimals, and problems that require expressing measurements given in a larger unit in terms of a smaller unit. Represent measurement quantities using diagrams such as number line diagrams that feature a measurement scale.

Mathematical Practices

- Make sense of problems and persevere in solving them.
- Reason abstractly and quantitatively.

Vocabulary

- elapsed time
- work "break"
- AM
- PM
- tape diagram

Task 39
A Nurse's Schedule

Apply understanding of intervals of time

TASK

A Nurse's Schedule

Elijah's mom is a nurse in a hospital. She loves taking care of her patients $3\frac{1}{2}$ days a week, but she works very long hours. Figure 11.10 shows her weekly schedule.

Figure 11.10 Weekly Schedule

Monday	Tuesday	Wednesday	Thursday
Off	7:30 a.m. to 8:45 p.m. **1 hr. 15 min. break**	*off*	7:30 a.m. to 8:45 p.m. **1 hr. 15 min. break**

Friday	Saturday	Sunday
1:00 p.m. to 5:30 p.m. **30-min. break**	7:30 a.m. to 8:45 p.m. **1 hr. 15 min. break**	*off*

How many hours does Elijah's mom work on Saturdays? How many hours does she work each week?

On Saturdays, Elijah's mom spends $\frac{1}{3}$ of her time completing paperwork, $\frac{1}{2}$ of her time attending to patients, and $\frac{1}{6}$ of her time training new nurses. How many hours does she spend on each of these duties on Saturdays?

TASK PREPARATION

- Think about how you will organize students in heterogeneous groups of 3.

- Consider how you might scaffold learning for students who are still developing proficiency solving multi-step word problems. Review representations such as tape diagrams, to support student understanding.

LAUNCH

1. Project the first statement of the task and calendar image on the board.

2. Facilitate the Three-Read Protocol. For the first read, have students visualize the problem as you read the task. Then ask, "What is going on in the problem?" Direct students to *Turn and Talk* to discuss the context of the task.

3. For the second read, have students read the task out loud, and ask, "What are the quantities in this situation?" Record the quantities that students offer.

4. Direct students to partner read for the third read, and ask, "What mathematical questions might you ask about the situation?" Ask partners to discuss their ideas.

5. As students share their questions, write several on the board. Have students *Pair-to-Pair Share* which questions could be answered with the information from the task.

FACILITATE

1. Organize students into heterogeneous triads.

2. Project the rest of the task to the class. Ask, "What additional information are we given?" Record additional quantities on the board.

3. Then ask, "What questions do we need to answer?" On the board, list the ideas students offer. Discuss and affirm that the breaks listed in Elijah's mom's schedule need to be considered when calculating the total number of hours she works each day.

4. Distribute chart paper, number lines, graph paper (for the tape diagrams), small clocks, and markers for each triad.

5. **Observe.** Circulate around the room, listening to student discussions about strategies they will attempt to use, questions they will tackle next, etc.

Materials

- A Nurse's Schedule student page, one for each triad
- number lines (laminated sentence strips)
- chart paper
- markers
- dot stickers in two different colors
- graph paper for tape diagrams
- two color counters (optional)
- small clocks (to be shared by groups of 3)

! PRODUCTIVE STRUGGLE

Support students in reasoning about fractional parts of a number, such as finding the product of $\frac{1}{3} \times 12$, through physical representations such as counters, or visual representations using graph paper.

6. Ask the following **Show Me** questions:

» Do you think Elijah's mom worked more than 10 hours or less than 10 hours on Saturday? Show me how you know.

» Do you think she worked more or less than 30 hours for the week? Show me how you know.

» How could you determine the number of hours Elijah's mom worked on Saturday?

» How could you figure out $\frac{1}{3}$ of 12?

STRENGTHS SPOTTING

Recognize students who use multiple representations to demonstrate their understanding, particularly when they connect representations to procedures. Specifically call attention to how the students use the representation rather than using general praise.

Note: Consider using the Show Me tool for monitoring and recording student responses to the questions above (see Appendix B).

CLOSE: MAKE THE MATH VISIBLE

1. Bring students back together as a whole group and ask them to leave their chart paper on their tables for peers to view.

2. Invite students to a Gallery Walk of triad work. Have students use stickers of one color to denote strategies that were similar to what their group used and to use stickers of another color to denote strategies that were different.

3. Encourage students to share their observations.

4. Some strategies that may surface include the following:

» Using a number line to calculate the number of hours Elijah's mom worked in one day (Figure 11.11). For example, to calculate the number of hours she worked on Saturday, students may have used length units of 1 hour on a number line, starting at 7:30 a.m. in order to calculate 13 hours and 15 minutes (some students may have moved on the number line from 7:30 am to 7:30 p.m., knowing that this is equivalent to 12 hours). Then, they may have moved back or subtracted 1 hour and 15 minutes to account for her break time. *So the total amount of time Elijah's mom worked on Saturday was 12 hours.*

Figure 11.11 Number Line Strategy

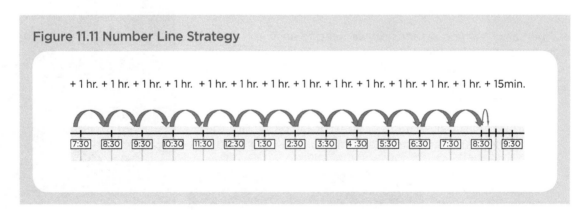

» To calculate the number of hours Elijah's mom worked on Friday, students may have moved in units of 1-hour intervals starting at 1:00 and ending at 5:00 and then moved 30 minutes to get to 5:30, for a total of 4 hours and 30 minutes. Then, they may have subtracted or moved back 30 minutes for her break time (Figure 11.12). *The total amount of time Elijah's mom worked on Friday was 4 hours.*

Figure 11.12 Interval Strategy

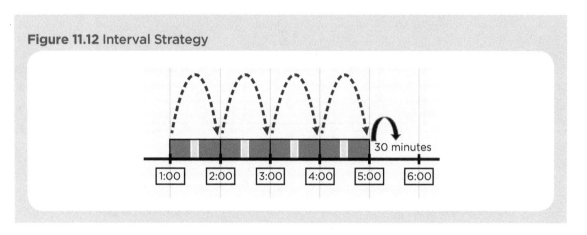

» Using equations to calculate the total amount of time worked in one week. For example,

12 hours × 3 = 36 hours (Tuesday, Thursday, Saturday)

36 + 4 hours = 40 hours per week.

» Using tape diagrams to make sense of fractional amounts of time. For example, to figure out $\frac{1}{3}$ of 12, $\frac{1}{2}$ of 12, and $\frac{1}{6}$ of 12, students may have drawn three separate tape diagrams, each 12 units long.

  » Figure 11.13 shows $\frac{1}{2}$ of 12 = 6. *Elijah's mom spends 6 hours attending to patients on Saturdays.*

Figure 11.13 Tape Diagram Strategy 1

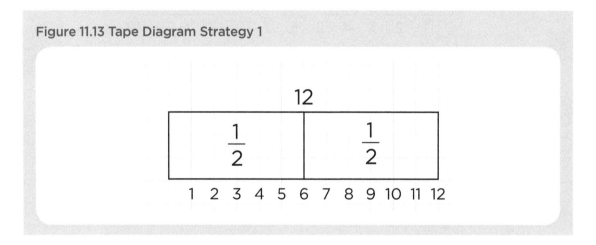

» Figure 11.14 shows $\frac{1}{3}$ of 12 = 4. *Elijah's mom spends 4 hours completing paperwork on Saturdays.*

Figure 11.14 Tape Diagram Strategy 2

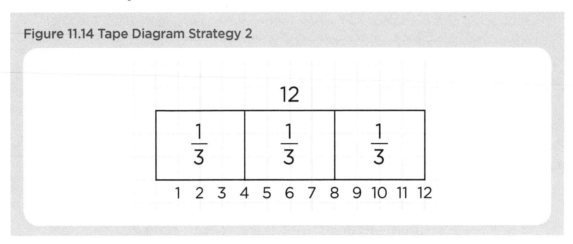

» Figure 11.15 shows $\frac{1}{6}$ of 12 = 2. *Elijah's mom spends 2 hours teaching new nurses on Saturdays.*

Figure 11.15 ape Diagram Strategy 3

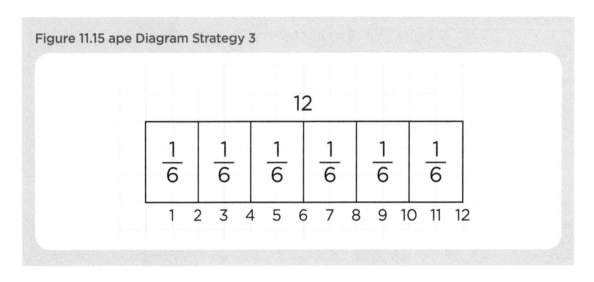

TASK 39: A NURSE'S SCHEDULE STUDENT PAGE

online resources ↖ To download printable resources for this task, visit **resources.corwin.com/ ClassroomReadyMath/4–5**

POST-TASK NOTES: REFLECTION & NEXT STEPS

Measurement

Represent and Interpret Data

Task 40: Grades 4–5: Stacking Shoe Boxes

Make a line plot to display a data set of measurements in fractions of a unit $\left(\frac{1}{2}, \frac{1}{4}, \frac{1}{8}\right)$.

Solve problems involving addition and subtraction of fractions by using information presented in line plots.

TASK 41: GRADE 4: FOURTH-GRADE FAVORITES

Make a line plot to display a data set of measurements in fractions of a unit $\left(\frac{1}{2}, \frac{1}{4}, \frac{1}{8}\right)$.

Solve problems involving addition and subtraction of fractions by using information presented in line plots.

TASK 42: GRADE 5: FAST FOOD

Make a line plot to display a data set of measurements in fractions of a unit $\left(\frac{1}{2}, \frac{1}{4}, \frac{1}{8}\right)$.

Use operations on fractions for this grade to solve problems involving information presented in line plots.

Anticipating Student Thinking: Data are all around us. This chapter's tasks engage students in creating and analyzing line plots. A line plot displays the frequency of a particular event or activity. Analysis of line plot data includes comparing differences and determining total amounts. The analysis of line plot data informally depicts the mode, median, and range of what's represented. Task 40 engages students in creating a line plot. Tasks 41 and 42 focus on the analysis of line plot data. All the chapter tasks involve or report data expressed as whole numbers and fractions. As you begin to plan for the chapter's line plot tasks, consider how you will determine student pairs or small groups for engaging the tasks and how you will present the context (e.g., shoe stacking; time spent working) for each task. As your students analyze the line plot data, provide time for them to create analysis questions based on their interpretation or view of what's created and represented.

THINK ABOUT IT

Like measurement, data representation and analysis tasks seem to immediately engage students in *doing math!* Use observation, interviews, and Show Me to monitor student progress as they create or analyze their line plots. Consider creating and using a hinge question directed toward overall analysis of a line plot's data or of a particular frequency within the line plot. Use of formative assessment will provide feedback to you relative to student level of engagement and understanding.

Task 40
Stacking Shoe Boxes

Represent data in a line plot

TASK

Stacking Shoe Boxes

Jay works at a sneaker store. When companies send boxes of their shoes to the store, Jay's job is to sort and stack the boxes by shoe size.

This week, a large shipment arrived, and all the different sizes were mixed up (see Figure 12.1). Jay needs your help organizing the shelf.

Figure 12.1 Boxes

Source: malerapaso/iStock.com

TASK PREPARATION

- Plan for heterogeneous groups of 2 or 3.

- The shoeboxes will need to be cut apart to arrange on the shelf (see student page). If desired, to save time during the task, teachers may wish to cut the shoeboxes apart using a paper cutter and just give each group a pile to arrange.

- If possible, consider bringing a large delivery box in with several smaller boxes inside it. This can serve as a visual aid during the Launch.

LAUNCH

1. Display the task image for the class (Figure 12.1).

2. Facilitate a *See, Think, and Wonder.*

3. Encourage students to share times when they might have seen large stacks of boxes like this. Ask, "What kinds of stores have you been to where they might have to organize boxes like this? How might you organize these boxes?"

FACILITATE

1. Display the full task and read it with students.

2. Show them the image of the shelf from the Stacking Shoes Student Page (Figure 12.2).

Figure 12.2 Student Page Shelf Image

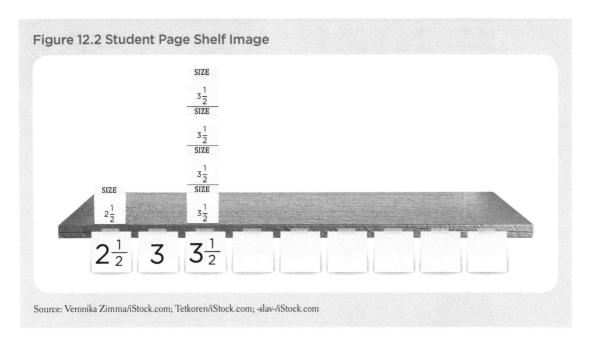

Source: Veronika Zimma/iStock.com; Tetkoren/iStock.com; -slav-/iStock.com

3. Have students *Turn and Talk* with a neighbor. Ask, "What do you think is happening in this picture? What information might be missing? What else do you notice?"

4. Organize the students into groups of 2 or 3 and distribute the Stacking Shoes Student Page.

5. **Interview.** As students work on organizing the shoe boxes onto the shelf, circulate to each group.

   » What are you noticing?

   » Do you think there are the same number of boxes of each shoe size? Why/why not?

   » Are there any sizes that are missing?

   » What is the smallest size? The largest?

   » How did you decide to organize the shoe boxes?

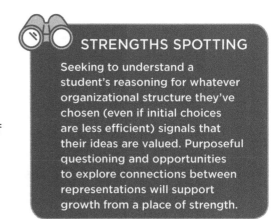

STRENGTHS SPOTTING

Seeking to understand a student's reasoning for whatever organizational structure they've chosen (even if initial choices are less efficient) signals that their ideas are valued. Purposeful questioning and opportunities to explore connections between representations will support growth from a place of strength.

CLOSE: MAKE THE MATH VISIBLE

1. Once the groups have completed their shelves, display the student work in an easy-to-see spot or conduct an Open Gallery Walk.

2. Facilitate a discussion about the data they have. Ask students to share observations they can make about the shoe collection now that it is organized.

3. If possible, compare two representations in which one has the shoeboxes stacked in such a way that it is easy to compare quantities and another that is more haphazardly stacked. Ask students to discuss which would be easier for the store manager to quickly look at and understand how many shoes of each size are available.

   » How did you decide what numbers to write for the rest of the labels on the shelf?

   » Make a connection here to the ruler-style tool used to measure the length of a foot to determine shoe size (see Figure 12.3).

   » Does that shelf remind you of a number line?

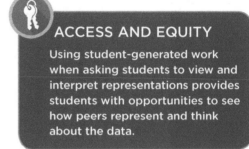

ACCESS AND EQUITY

Using student-generated work when asking students to view and interpret representations provides students with opportunities to see how peers represent and think about the data.

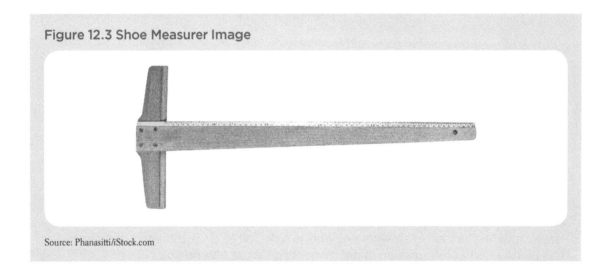

Figure 12.3 Shoe Measurer Image

Source: Phanasitti/iStock.com

4. **Show Me**. Remind students that in third grade they learned how to represent this kind of data on a line plot.

   » Show me on your paper/marker board what a line plot looks like.

   » Show me how you could represent the data from the shoe store on a line plot.

   » How did you decide on the labels for your line plot?

   Note: Consider using the Show Me tool for monitoring and recording responses to the Show Me opportunities presented above (see Appendix B).

5. **Hinge Question**. How does the way in which a line plot is constructed help you make a quick decision about the data you have organized?

TASK 40: STACKING SHOES STUDENT PAGE

 To download printable resources for this task, visit **resources.corwin.com/ ClassroomReadyMath/4–5**

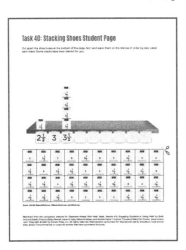

POST-TASK NOTES: REFLECTION & NEXT STEPS

Grade 4

Mathematics Standard

- Make a line plot to display a data set of measurements in fractions of a unit $\left(\frac{1}{2}, \frac{1}{4}, \frac{1}{8}\right)$. Solve problems involving addition and subtraction of fractions by using information presented in line plots.

Mathematical Practices

- Reason abstractly and quantitatively.
- Attend to precision.

Vocabulary

- line plot

Materials

- Fourth-Grade Favorites student page, one for each pair or triad
- dot stickers (one color)
- chart paper
- index cards, one for each triad

Fourth-Grade Favorites

Analyze and formulate questions from a line plot

TASK

Fourth-Grade Favorites

Mrs. Choi wondered how much time her students spent doing a favorite activity in a typical day. Figure 12.4 shows the results from her fourth-grade math class.

Figure 12.4 Fourth-Grade Favorites

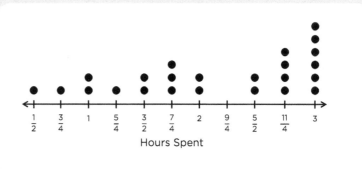

Hours Spent

What are three observations you could make by studying the information from the line plot? Develop two questions you can ask your classmates about these data.

TASK PREPARATION

- Think about how you might organize your students into heterogeneous pairs or groups of three.
- Prepare class chart for the Launch.

LAUNCH

1. Project the introductory statement from the task on the board:

   Mrs. Choi wondered how much time her students spent doing a favorite activity in a typical day.

2. Have students *Think-Pair-Share* possible activities that Mrs. Choi's students might have identified (e.g., reading a book, being on a device, playing a sport, playing an instrument, . . .) and record these on the board.

3. Direct students to select a favorite activity from the ideas they generated and to determine, to the nearest quarter hour, how much time they spend doing this activity on a typical day.

4. Display the following chart (Figure 12.5) in the front of the room. Ask, "What do $\frac{1}{2}$ and $\frac{3}{4}$ mean or represent?" Elicit from students the idea that these represent lengths of time in quarter hours. Distribute dot stickers to each student. Have groups of four students place their dot sticker on the appropriate length of time they spend on their favorite activity on the chart.

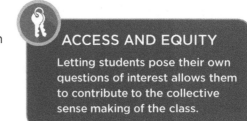

ACCESS AND EQUITY

Letting students pose their own questions of interest allows them to contribute to the collective sense making of the class.

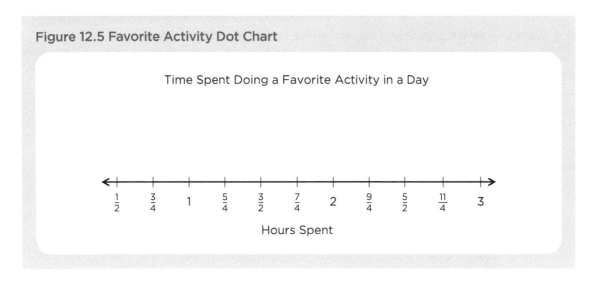

Figure 12.5 Favorite Activity Dot Chart

Time Spent Doing a Favorite Activity in a Day

$\frac{1}{2}$ $\frac{3}{4}$ 1 $\frac{5}{4}$ $\frac{3}{2}$ $\frac{7}{4}$ 2 $\frac{9}{4}$ $\frac{5}{2}$ $\frac{11}{4}$ 3

Hours Spent

5. Say, "What questions could we ask about the data we collected? Why might these be important to answer?"

FACILITATE

1. Organize students into heterogeneous pairs or triads and distribute student page and index cards.

2. Project the task on the board and direct students to compare the data generated as a class with the data from the line plot in the task. Record observations/ideas on the board.

3. **Observe** students as they record their observations and questions on the index cards provided, circulating around the room, visiting each pair or group of three.

4. **Interview.**

   » How many students in Mrs. Choi's class were occupied doing their favorite activity for less than 2 hours? How does that total compare to our class total? How do you know?

PRODUCTIVE STRUGGLE

Developing data sense, an understanding that data are more than just numbers, takes time. Allow students, through discussions, to generate questions and inferences that build on each other's ideas. It should be noted that the data presented in this graph *do* tell us about the amount of *time* students are spending doing a favorite activity but *do not* tell us what specific activities are represented.

» What was the amount of time that most of the students spent on their favorite activity?

» If we removed this data point (indicate a specific data point on the line plot) from the line plot, how might that change what we understand about the data? How would that be different from *moving* that data point to another spot in the line plot?

Note: Consider using the Interview (small group) tool for monitoring and recording responses to the interview questions presented above (see Appendix B).

CLOSE: MAKE THE MATH VISIBLE

1. Gather students back together to discuss the task.

2. Based on your Interviews and Observations, sequence pairs/triads to share the observations/questions they developed. If time permits, allow other students to respond to their classmates' questions and to signal (using hand signals) when they had a similar observation or question.

3. Highlight the following:

» A line plot is a way to display measurement data. In this task, we measured the lengths of time spent doing a favorite activity in a typical day.

» The horizontal axis displays information about the hours of time spent doing a favorite activity. In particular, time was measured using the scale of quarters of an hour, or 15-minute increments.

» Each dot on a line plot represents an individual data point. So the number of times a dot is stacked over a particular measurement represents the number of people who spent the same amount of time doing a favorite activity.

TASK 41: FOURTH-GRADE FAVORITES STUDENT PAGE

online resources: To download printable resources for this task, visit **resources.corwin.com/ClassroomReadyMath/4–5**

POST-TASK NOTES: REFLECTION & NEXT STEPS

Mathematics Standard

- Make a line plot to display a data set of measurements in fractions of a unit $\left(\frac{1}{2}, \frac{1}{4}, \frac{1}{8}\right)$. Use operations on fractions for this grade to solve problems involving information presented in line plots.

Mathematical Practice

- Reason abstractly and quantitatively.

Vocabulary

- line plot
- shift (work)

Materials

- Line Plot Cards student page, one set per group
- Data Analysis student page, one per group
- scratch paper or student marker boards

Task 42
Fast Food

Interpret data displayed in a line plot

TASK

Fast Food

Ismail runs a fast-food delivery business. Drivers for Ismail's company work anywhere from $\frac{1}{3}$ of an hour up to 2 hours each evening delivering meals from restaurants to people's homes. Each night, Ismail collects data on how many drivers worked and how many hours they worked. The line plot (Figure 12.6) shows data for each employee who worked on one night.

Figure 12.6 Delivery Driver Line Plot

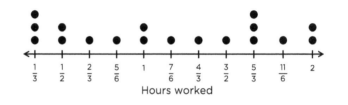

Hours worked

Ismail has asked us to analyze the data he's collected over the past ten nights. What are some things we might be able to figure out by looking at the line plots for those nights?

TASK PREPARATION

- Plan to organize students into heterogeneous groups of 3 or 4.

- Prepare one set of Line Plot Cards and one Data Analysis Worksheet per group. It will be helpful to have the line plot cards cut apart so students can rearrange them and make direct comparisons between data sets.

LAUNCH

1. Facilitate a *See, Think, and Wonder* with students using the image from the task stem (Figure 12.7).

Figure 12.7 Delivery Driver Line Plot

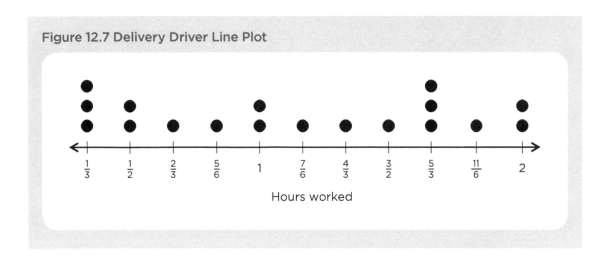

Hours worked

2. Encourage students to *Pair-to-Pair Share* before taking ideas from the class.

3. Ask, "What do you think one dot on this line plot might represent?"

4. Use the information from the task to tell students the story of Ismail's company.

5. Ask, "Were we on the right track? What does one dot on this line plot represent? How would you describe the number of hours worked by Ismail's employees on this night? What other information could you find by reviewing these data?"

FACILITATE

1. Organize students into groups and distribute a set of Line Plot Cards and a Data Analysis worksheet page.

2. **Observe.** Circulate to each group to observe strategies students are using to analyze the data sets. Pay attention to how students are calculating the total number of hours. Some strategies to watch for:

   » Students may "partner up" data points to find whole numbers of hours (e.g., notice that a driver who worked $\frac{1}{3}$ hour and a driver who worked $\frac{5}{3}$ hours can be paired to equal 2 hours).

ACCESS AND EQUITY

Students should be encouraged to make sense of the data in whatever way feels most comfortable. If the fraction notation interferes with students' engagement in the task, encourage the use of drawn representations of analog clock faces to translate the times representing fractions of an hour into numbers of minutes and/or provide fraction circle manipulatives so students can create physical representations of the times and combine amounts that make whole hours.

   » Students may convert from fractions of hours to minutes in order to use whole numbers for calculations (e.g., $\frac{1}{3}$ hour = 20 minutes).

   » Students may consider using equivalent fractions to change all the times into multiples of $\frac{1}{6}$ in order to add them more easily.

» Students may use informal reasoning strategies such as direct comparisons between two data sets or canceling out common data points and comparing only those that do not match.

3. **Show Me.**

» Is there a night when all the employees worked exactly the same number of hours? How do you know?

» Is there a night when many of the employees worked about the same number of hours? How is that different from when they worked exactly the same number of hours?

» Is there a night when none of the employees worked the same number of hours? How do you know?

Note: Consider using the Show Me tool for monitoring and recording responses to the "How do you know" portion of the Show Me responses above (see Appendix B).

CLOSE: MAKE THE MATH VISIBLE

1. Use *Two Stay, One/Two Stray* to mix up the groups. Have each group discuss the strategy they used to redistribute driving shifts (item 6 on the data analysis page).

2. Bring the class together and facilitate a discussion about the data they've analyzed. Select students/teams to share their thinking. Highlight some of the following ideas:

» If all the data points are the same, the line plot will show one tall stack of dots over the same value.

» If all the data points are different, the line plot will show no more than one dot over any given point.

» The number of workers is not always indicative of the total number of hours; the position of each data point on the graph must also be considered (e.g., a large number of shorter shifts can add up to the same number of hours as a small number of longer shifts).

» Driver shifts can be redistributed without changing the total number of hours by adding time to shorter shifts while taking the same amount of time away from longer shifts.

TASK 42: STUDENT DATA ANALYSIS WORKSHEET

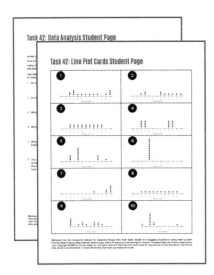

POST-TASK NOTES: REFLECTION & NEXT STEPS

CHAPTER 13

Geometric Measurement

Angles and Volume

TASK 43: GRADE 4: MEASURING AROUND

Recognize angles as geometric shapes that are formed wherever two rays share a common endpoint, and understand concepts of angle measurement:

a. An angle is measured with reference to a circle with its center at the common endpoint of the rays, by considering the fraction of the circular arc between the points where the two rays intersect the circle. An angle that turns through $\frac{1}{360}$ of a circle is called a "one-degree angle," and can be used to measure angles.

b. An angle that turns through n, one-degree angles is said to have an angle measure of n degrees.

TASK 44: GRADE 5: POOL PARTY

Measure volumes by counting unit cubes, using cubic cm, cubic in, cubic ft, and improvised units.

TASK 45: GRADE 4: ANGLES IN TIME

Measure angles in whole-number degrees using a protractor. Sketch angles of specified measure.

TASK 46: GRADE 4: THE CURIOUS CASE OF THE BLUE TRIANGLE

Recognize angle measure as additive. When an angle is decomposed into non-overlapping parts, the angle measure of the whole is the sum of the angle measures of the parts. Solve addition and subtraction problems to find unknown angles on a diagram in real world and mathematical problems, e.g., by using an equation with a symbol for the unknown angle measure.

TASK 47: GRADE 5: BOXY BASKETS

Recognize volume as an attribute of solid figures and understand concepts of volume measurement.

a. A cube with side length 1 unit, called a "unit cube," is said to have "one cubic unit" of volume, and can be used to measure volume.

b. A solid figure which can be packed without gaps or overlaps using n unit cubes is said to have a volume of n cubic units.

TASK 48: GRADE 5: VOLUME VILLAGE

Relate volume to the operations of multiplication and addition and solve real world and mathematical problems involving volume.

a. Find the volume of a right rectangular prism with whole-number side lengths by packing it with unit cubes, and show that the volume is the same as would be found by multiplying the edge lengths, equivalently by multiplying the height by the area of the base. Represent threefold whole-number products as volumes, e.g., to represent the associative property of multiplication.

Anticipating Student Thinking: Geometric measurement is the focus of this chapter, which includes six task-lessons. Three of the tasks involve angles and angle measurement, and three focus on understanding and determining volume—both informally and by multiplying height by the area of the base. Because work with angles and volume are initially introduced at the 4th- and 5th-grade levels, respectively, the chapter's tasks engage students conceptually. In the 4th-grade tasks, students will sketch and measure angles. In the 5th-grade tasks, students will use cubic units to determine volume. As you plan for implementing the chapter tasks, recognize that the pace of task implementation will vary based on student access to the tasks. Your use of the observation and Show Me techniques will help you monitor both task access and progress.

THINK ABOUT IT

Think About It: As your students engage in the particular aspects of a chapter task that promotes productive struggle, be prepared to provide the necessary wait time for students to fully engage in the task, complete their response, and be given an opportunity to share their work with others.

Task 43
Measuring Around

Recognize angles as geometric shapes; understand angle measurement

TASK

Measuring Around

Figure 13.1 Shaded Circle Picture

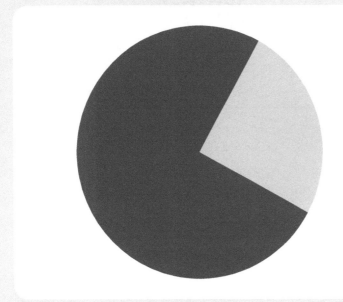

Shania and Andre studied the picture on the board (Figure 13.1). Shania whispered to her group, "I'm pretty sure I see a right angle, but I want to check." Andre shared, "I see an angle and it's greater than an obtuse angle, I don't know what kind of angle it's called, and I don't know the exact measurement, but I think it's more than 200 degrees."

Could they both be correct?

TASK PREPARATION

- Consider grouping students in heterogeneous pairs. Think about any prior knowledge they might have about angles in relation to geometric shapes.

- Prepare circular protractors using card stock paper (use any color for the solid circle—sample illustration Figure 13.2 shows blue); the protractor with markings should be copied on white paper using the template provided. Laminate if possible. Cut around both circles. Put the unmarked solid colored circle behind the protractor circle. Cut across the radius of both circles (one at a time)

Mathematics Standard(s)

- Recognize angles as geometric shapes that are formed wherever two rays share a common endpoint, and understand concepts of angle measurement:

  a. An angle is measured with reference to a circle with its center at the common endpoint of the rays, by considering the fraction of the circular arc between the points where the two rays intersect the circle. An angle that turns through $\frac{1}{360}$ of a circle is called a "one-degree angle," and can be used to measure angles.

  b. An angle that turns through n, one-degree angles is said to have an angle measure of n degrees.

Mathematical Practices

- Reason abstractly and quantitatively.
- Construct viable arguments and critique the reasoning of others.

Vocabulary

- ray
- point
- vertex
- angle
- rotate/rotation
- acute angle
- right angle
- obtuse angle
- straight angle

- reflex angle
- degrees
- protractor

Materials

- Measuring Around student page, one for each pair of students
- laminated circular protractors

on the line representing 0 degrees to the center of the circle. Slide both pieces together through the openings.

- Anticipate spending time with developing the mathematics vocabulary within the lesson. Some of the terms are new for this grade level.

LAUNCH

Figure 13.2 Shaded Protractor Circle

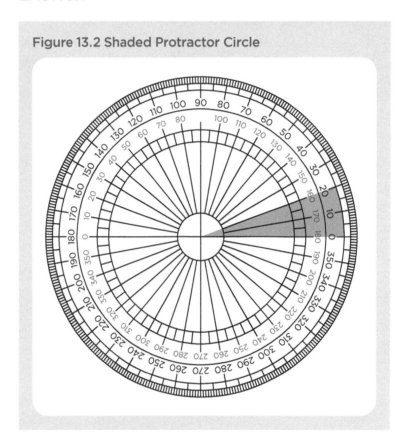

1. Project the image in Figure 13.2. Facilitate Notice and Wonder.

2. Have students *Think-Pair-Share* their observations. Record their notices and wonderings on the board.

3. Some ideas that may surface include the following:

   » The ray on the top edge of the blue "wedge" is touching 20 on the protractor.

   » The two rays on the sides of the wedge create a space inside called an *acute angle*.

   » The white circle is like a ruler and has numbers that go from 0 to 360.

4. Sketch the rays of the wedge on the board. Affirm that we can think of the wedge as formed by two rays that create a space called an *angle*. The point where both rays meet is called a *vertex*, and the numbers that mark the scale on the circular protractor can measure the space shown by the rotation of a ray in *degrees*.

5. Distribute circular protractors to students. Provide a few minutes for students to examine/manipulate this tool. Have them rotate the rays, forming different angle sizes in the space between the rays.

   » When does the space or distance between the rays of the wedge form an acute angle?

   » Could you use the protractor to show me an angle that measures 6°? 90°?

   » Could you use the protractor to show me an angle that measures 120°?

   » What would we call this type of angle?

6. Students may share that they can also create angles that measure 180°, 350°, . . . Let several students demonstrate this for the class.

ACCESS AND EQUITY

Providing opportunities for students to reason, test, and build on their prior ideas about angles strengthens their conceptual understanding of the concept of angle and angle measure.

FACILITATE

1. Organize students into heterogeneous pairs and distribute student page.

2. Review the task with students.

3. **Observe** pairs manipulating the circular protractors to make sense of the problem. Circulate around the room and listen in on student conversations.

4. Take note of students who may still express confusion about Andre's observation.

5. **Interview.**

   » How can you tell that the angle in the picture is 90°?

   » Can you Show Me a 90° angle using the protractor?

   » What angle do you think Andre sees in the picture? How is it related to the angle that Shania sees?

PRODUCTIVE STRUGGLE

Let students wrestle with an idea. At times, their partner may be better able to explain or help them visualize a problem than a teacher intervening.

CLOSE: MAKE THE MATH VISIBLE

1. Bring the class back together.

2. Invite students (based on Interview) to share their thinking about Shania and Andre's observations.

3. Highlight the following:

   » An angle that rotates $\frac{1}{360}$ of a circle is called a one-degree angle. Have students show this with their protractors.

   » Every pair of rays that share an endpoint forms two angles with measures adding up to 360°.

   » A full rotation is 360°.

   » Angles measuring 180° are called *straight angles*.

» Angles whose measure is between 180° and 360° are called *reflex angles*.

» Through student demonstrations, the angle that Shania sees in the picture (Figure 13.3) is a right angle and has a measure of 90°

Figure 13.3 Shaded Protractor Circle

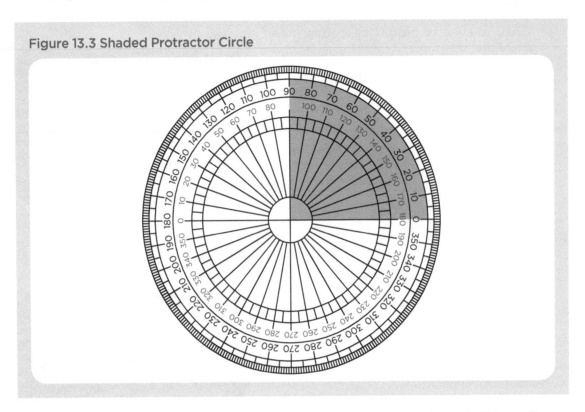

» Through student demonstrations, the angle that Andre sees (Figure 13.4) is a reflex angle and has a measure of 270°.

Figure 13.4 Shaded Protractor Circle

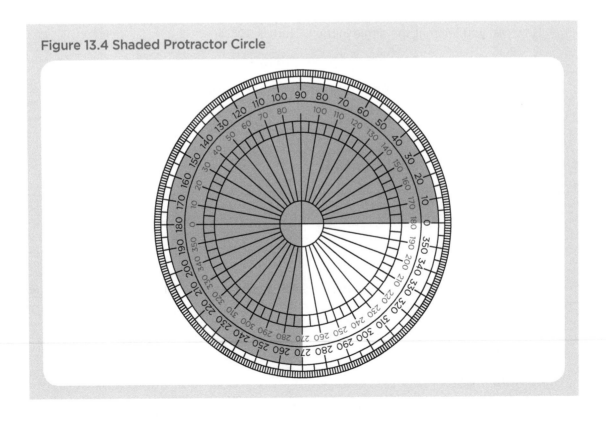

TASK 43: MEASURING AROUND STUDENT PAGE

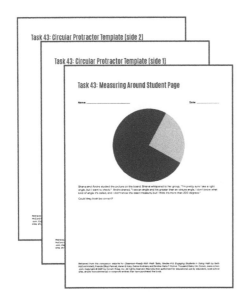

POST-TASK NOTES: REFLECTION & NEXT STEPS

Mathematics Standard

- Measure volumes by counting unit cubes, using cubic cm, cubic in, cubic ft, and improvised units.

Mathematical Practices

- Model with mathematics.
- Use appropriate tools strategically.

Vocabulary

- volume
- cubic centimeter
- cubic yard

Materials

- Pool Party student page, one per group
- scissors
- tape
- centimeter cubes (base ten unit cubes)
- 12 yardsticks or a model of a square meter

Task 44
Pool Party

Extend understanding of volume

TASK

Pool Party

The city is planning to install a new pool at the public park (Figure 13.5). They need to know about how many cubic yards of water it will take to fill the pool.

Figure 13.5 The Empty Pool

Source: alekime/iStock.com

The pool being installed will have a sloped floor. Your job is to use the scaled model of the pool and unit cubes to find an estimate of the volume of water the city will need to fill the pool. One cubic centimeter in the model represents 1 cubic yard in the real pool.

TASK PREPARATION

- If possible, gather together 12 yardsticks. Lay out four on the floor to show what a square yard looks like, then have students help you hold four of them vertically and four more over the top to show a cubic yard. (See Figure 13.6.)

Figure 13.6 Demonstrating With Yardsticks

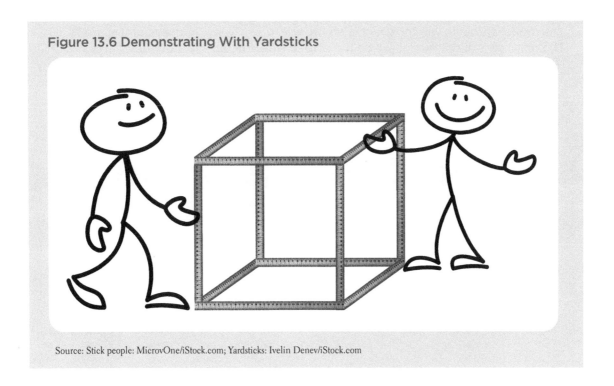

Source: Stick people: MicrovOne/iStock.com; Yardsticks: Ivelin Denev/iStock.com

- A "back up" plan may be to take a picture of an object that looks like a cubic yard.

- Think about a local pool that has a sloped floor. Find an image of the pool online to show students and activate their prior knowledge about shallow and deep ends of a pool.

- Plan for heterogeneous groups of 3 or 4.

LAUNCH

1. Bring students together and show them the image of the pool from the task (see Figure 13.5). Have students *Turn and Talk* with a partner. Ask, "Have you ever gone swimming at a public pool?"

   There may be students in your class who haven't been to a public pool before. These students will benefit from local contexts. Use Google Earth (https://www.google.com/earth/) to take a virtual field trip to a local pool. Ask students who have been to a large pool to share their prior knowledge about the varied depth of the water at each end of the pool.

2. Present the full task to students. Ask, "Why might we need a scaled model to solve this problem?"

FACILITATE

1. Organize students into small groups and provide each group with a student page and supplies for constructing the model. Students should also have ready access to as many unit cubes as they might need.

PRODUCTIVE STRUGGLE

Resist the urge to give directions about how students should go about finding an estimate. Encourage students to try out different ideas and discuss as a team which one they feel gives the best estimate of the actual volume.

2. The model students will construct is an "upside-down" view of the pool (Figure 13.7). The open part of the model will be the sloped side. Encourage students to physically flip the model over to visualize how it might look buried in the ground.

Figure 13.7 The Pool Model

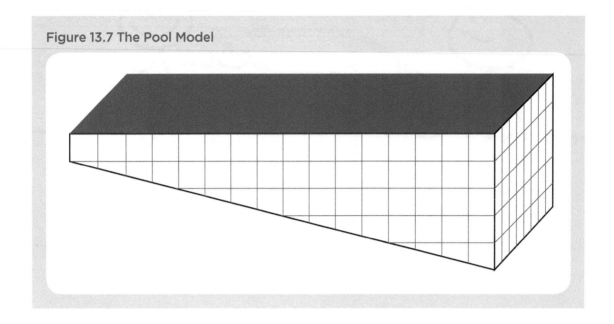

3. **Observe.** Circulate to each group, noting strategies they are using to fill the pool model with cubic centimeters.

   » Students may imagine that the floor is really flat and find the full volume as if the depth is 5 yards in the whole pool ($8 \times 16 \times 5$) and then make an estimate based on the fraction that they feel is the volume of the actual pool.

   » Students may create graduated layers: $(8 \times 16 \times 1) + (8 \times 12 \times 1) + (8 \times 8 \times 1)$, etc. to show how many full cubes can fit in the pool, slightly underfilling the pool's volume.

   » Students may create graduated layers that slightly overfill the pool's volume: $(8 \times 16 \times 1) + (8 \times 15 \times 1) + (8 \times 11 \times 1)$, etc.

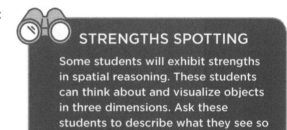

STRENGTHS SPOTTING

Some students will exhibit strengths in spatial reasoning. These students can think about and visualize objects in three dimensions. Ask these students to describe what they see so that their peers can hear their ideas.

4. **Interview.**

   » What would be a reasonable estimate you might make right now about the volume of this pool? What would be an unreasonable estimate? Explain using cubic yards in your estimate.

   » What are you noticing about the layers of cubes in your model?

   » If this pool had a flat floor, what would you know about the volume?

   » With the strategy you are using, are you able to know if your estimate will be greater or less than the actual volume of the pool?

   Note: Consider using the Interview (small group) tool for monitoring and recording responses to some or perhaps all the interview questions above (see Appendix B).

CLOSE: MAKE THE MATH VISIBLE

1. Have each group write their estimate for the volume of the pool on the board.

2. Bring the class together and look at the various estimates. Ask, "Look at all our estimates. Is it okay that they aren't all exactly the same?"

3. Discuss reasonableness and ask the class to come to a consensus on what would be a good recommendation to make to the city. "What range might we give them? Could we say the volume will be at least _ and not more than _? How might that be helpful for the city to know?"

4. Select and sequence students to share some of the strategies observed during the Facilitate phase of the task.

5. As each strategy is shared, ask students to discuss how it is related to the other strategies used. "What was the same? What was different? Is that estimate greater or less than the actual volume? How do we know that?"

TASK 44: POOL PARTY STUDENT PAGE

 To download printable resources for this task, visit **resources.corwin.com/ ClassroomReadyMath/4–5**

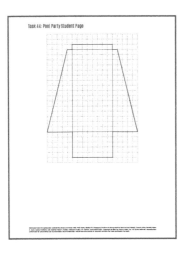

POST-TASK NOTES: REFLECTION & NEXT STEPS

Mathematics Standard

- Measure angles in whole-number degrees using a protractor. Sketch angles of a specified measure.

Mathematical Practices

- Use appropriate tools strategically.
- Attend to precision.

Vocabulary

- angle measure
- reflex angle
- straight angle
- protractor
- ray
- degree
- acute
- obtuse
- clockwise

Materials

- Angles in Time Cards on card stock paper, one for each pair
- protractors
- laptops (optional for students who may want to use the online tool: https://www.visnos.com/demos/clock)
- index cards for student explanations

Task 45
Angles in Time

Measure and sketch angles

TASK

Angles in Time

In the school cafeteria, as Arsala was eating lunch while studying an analog clock on the wall, she had an idea. She turned to Kori and said, "You know, there's a lot we can learn about angles by measuring time!" Kori looked at Arsala in disbelief.

Work with your partner to explore the Angles in Time cards. Then, help Arsala convince Kori that there are connections between angles and time.

TASK PREPARATION

- Organize students in heterogeneous pairs.
- Consider laminating and cutting the Angles in Time cards (A–J) for continued use.
- Familiarize yourself with using the virtual protractor and Interactive Clock at https://www.visnos.com/demos/clock.

LAUNCH

Figure 13.8 Angle in Time

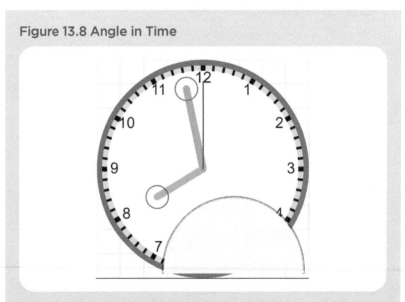

Clock Image; eliflamra/iStock.com Protractor; Eyematrix/iStock.com

1. Project the image in Figure 13.8 and facilitate a Notice and Wonder.

2. Encourage students to discuss their ideas in a *Pair-to-Pair Share* before taking ideas from the class.

3. Ask, "What is similar about the analog clock and the protractor?"

4. Use the information from the task to explain Arsala's situation. Ask, "If we start at 12 o'clock, how many hours would it take for the hour hand to turn 360°? How many minutes would it take for the minute hand to turn 360°?"

FACILITATE

1. Organize students into heterogeneous pairs and distribute a set of Angles in Time cards (A–J) and protractors.

2. **Observation.** As students work, circulate around the room, observing their comfort level with measuring angles or drawing angles using a protractor. Confirm that they are seeing the measure of the angle as the spread between the two rays and as unrelated to the length of the two rays. As you do so, have students complete the following:

3. **Show Me.**

   » How could you measure the angles shown at 3:30? (angle measure going clockwise, and reflex angle).

   » How could you prove that this time (pointing to 3:45) shows a straight angle?

   » How did you sketch the 120° angle?

   Note: Consider using the Show Me tool for monitoring responses to the Show Me questions above (see Appendix B).

4. **Hinge Question.** What are the angle measures of 1:54 and 3:00?

CLOSE: MAKE THE MATH VISIBLE

1. Gather students together to discuss the task.

2. Invite students to share their experiences measuring angles made by the two hands on a clock. Ask, "Were there any angles on the cards that were challenging to measure? Why? What did you notice about the angles on cards G and H?"

3. Highlight the following through questioning and evidence of student work during the facilitate section:

   » The difference between the measures of the angles for each hour is 30°. A 360° angle partitioned into 12 equal hour rotations would be 360 ÷ 12 = 30. For example, the measure of the angle made by the clock hands at 2 o'clock is 30° greater than the measure of the angle at 1 o'clock (Cards A, F, J).

» The minute hand moves 30° for every 5 minutes of time. A 360° angle partitioned into 12 equal 5-minute rotations would be 360 ÷ 12 = 30. From 3:20 to 3:25 is 30° and from 3:25 to 3:30 is 30°. The hour hand moves 15° for every half hour of time, so the measure of the angle between the hands of a clock at 3:30 is 75° (Card B).

» By aligning the center marker of the protractor with the vertex of the hands of a clock we are measuring and rotating the protractor to align a hand (hour or minute) with the baseline of the protractor, we can determine the measure of a given time. We can also sketch the measure of a given angle in degrees (Cards C–L).

» Because we know that the measure of one complete turn of a clock hand around a clock or a circle is 360°, we can also use the measure of the reflex angle to determine the measure of an unknown angle *n* (Cards G, H).

4. Distribute index cards to each student and have them write a brief, persuasive explanation that Arsala can use with Kori.

TASK 45: ANGLES IN TIME CARDS

online resources ↘ To download printable resources for this task, visit **resources.corwin.com/ClassroomReadyMath/4–5**

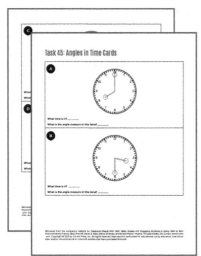

POST-TASK NOTES: REFLECTION & NEXT STEPS

Task 46

The Curious Case of the Blue Triangle

Reasoning about angles

TASK

The Curious Case of the Blue Triangle

Figure 13.9 Blue Triangles

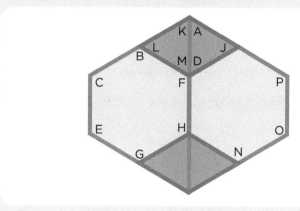

Benjamin is befuddled. He needs to find the measure of the following:

- ∠ JAD,
- ∠ LKM,
- ∠ FBC,
- ∠ CEG, and
- ∠ GHF in the picture (Figure 13.9).

His only clue is this hint card (Figure 13.10), which shows the measure of an angle of an equilateral triangle.

Figure 13.10 Hint Card

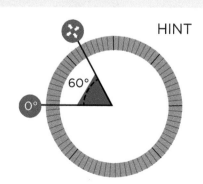

HINT

Mathematics Standard

- Recognize angle measure as additive. When an angle is decomposed into non-overlapping parts, the angle measure of the whole is the sum of the angle measures of the parts. Solve addition and subtraction problems to find unknown angles on a diagram in real world and mathematical problems, e.g., by using an equation with a symbol for the unknown angle measure.

Mathematical Practices

- Look for and make use of structure.
- Reason abstractly and quantitatively.

Vocabulary

- angle
- interior angles
- regular hexagon
- isosceles triangle

Materials

- The Curious Case of the Blue Triangle student page, one for each triad
- pattern blocks (hexagons, Blue triangles)
- protractors
- tangrams

Help Benjamin find the measure of the given angles. Can you also help him find the sum of the 6 interior angles of a regular hexagon (Figure 13.11)?

Figure 13.11 Hexagon

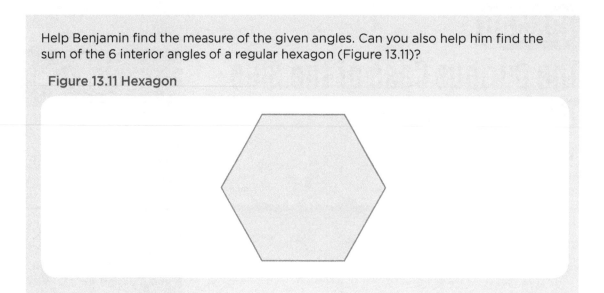

TASK PREPARATION

- Think about how you might organize your students into heterogeneous groups of three.

- Survey your class collection of pattern blocks to ensure that you have enough hexagons and triangles for each triad.

LAUNCH

Figure 13.12 Blue Triangles

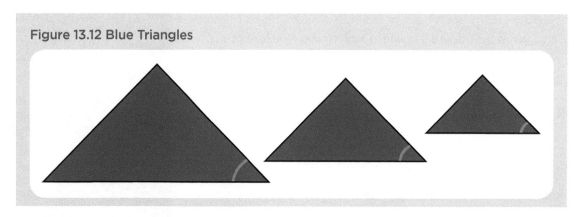

1. Project the image from Figure 13.12.

2. Have students *Pair-to-Pair Share* what they See, Think, and Wonder about the image.

3. Some ideas that may surface include the following:

   » Each of the 3 triangles are isosceles triangles.

   » An isosceles triangle has 2 angles of equal measure.

   » There is a small, medium, and large-sized triangle.

   » The triangles are part of a tangram set.

4. Ask, "Do you think the measure of this angle (point to gray mark) of the large triangle is greater than or less than the measure of the angle (point to gray angle mark) of the small triangle?" Record student ideas on the board.

5. Then, invite a student to use a protractor to measure the angle of the large triangle. Have another student measure the angle of the medium-sized triangle. Call on another student to measure the angle of the small triangle.

6. Affirm that although the sizes of the triangles differ, the angles formed on the right side of the isosceles triangles in the examples above each have the same measure—45°. Note that not all isosceles triangles have 45° angles at the base, such as in Figure 13.13.

ACCESS AND EQUITY

Providing students with opportunities to compare shapes of different sizes, with the same attributes and of equal angle measure, allows them to develop a more accurate and complete conception of angle measure.

Figure 13.13 Isosceles Triangle

FACILITATE

1. Organize students into heterogeneous triads and distribute the student page and pattern blocks.

2. Project the task on the board and clarify any questions students may have. Confirm that the word "interior" means inside, the interior angles of a regular hexagon are the six inside angles of a hexagon.

3. **Observe**. Circulate around the room, visiting and monitoring the progress of each group of three.

4. **Interview.**

> » How do you know that the measure of JAD is 60°?

> » What do you know about the total measure of angles in an equilateral triangle?

> » How are ∠JAD and ∠FBC related?

> » What are the attributes of a regular hexagon? How can this information help us find the sum of its interior angles?

PRODUCTIVE STRUGGLE

Encourage students who are still developing an understanding of angle measure to consider some attributes of an equilateral triangle and a regular hexagon. Using pattern blocks, they might also notice relationships between the measure of an angle in a regular hexagon and compare this to the measure of an angle of an equilateral triangle.

CLOSE: MAKE THE MATH VISIBLE

1. Gather students back together to discuss student solutions to the task.

2. Ask, "How did the information on the hint card help you find the measure of the other angles in the task?" Listen carefully to student explanations that you may want to refer back to when highlighting specific ideas later on.

3. Students may share the following:

   » Arranging two blue triangles, one on top of another, then rotating the triangle on top around the angle they know to be 60° (from the hint card), helped them determine that the measure of every angle of the equilateral blue triangle is 60°. Thus, the measure of ∠ JAD and ∠ LKM is 60°.

   » You can arrange ∠ JAD and ∠ LKM side by side to find the measure of angles ∠ FBC, ∠ CEG, and ∠ GHF, which is 120°.

4. Distribute protractors to students. Let them measure the angles of a blue triangle and an angle in a regular hexagon. Note: They can use a protractor not only to check their reasoning but also to develop mental images of benchmark angles such as 60°, 90°, etc.

5. Highlight the following:

   » Equilateral triangles have 3 sides of equal length, and 3 angles of equal measure. Using these attributes, we can reason that angles of an equilateral triangle each measure 60°.

   » Refer to Figure 13.4. $m\angle$ JAD + $m\angle$ LKM = x
   60° + 60° = 120°,
   so ∠ FBC, ∠ CEG, and ∠ GHF each measure 120°

Figure 13.14 Measuring Triangles in a Hexagon

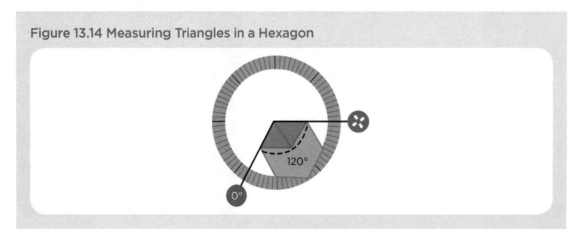

   » Regular hexagons have 6 sides of equal length and 6 angles of equal measure. To find the sum of the six interior angles of a regular hexagon, we can reason that angles of a regular hexagon each measure 120° (see Figure 13.14).

   » $m\angle$ FBC + $m\angle$ CEG + $m\angle$ GHF = x
   120° + 120° + 120° = 360°, the sum of the measure of 3 angles in a regular hexagon.
   360° + 360° = 720°, the sum of the measure of the interior angles of a regular hexagon.

TASK 46: THE CURIOUS CASE OF THE BLUE TRIANGLE STUDENT PAGE

online resources · To download printable resources for this task, visit **resources.corwin.com/ ClassroomReadyMath/4-5**

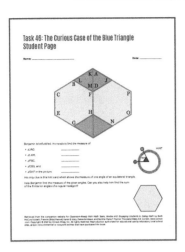

POST-TASK NOTES: REFLECTION & NEXT STEPS

Task 47
Boxy Baskets

Determine the volume of a solid figure

Mathematics Standard(s)

- Recognize volume as an attribute of solid figures and understand concepts of volume measurement.

   a. A cube with side length 1 unit, called a "unit cube," is said to have "one cubic unit" of volume, and can be used to measure volume.

   b. A solid figure which can be packed without gaps or overlaps using *n* unit cubes is said to have a volume of *n* cubic units.

Mathematical Practice

- Attend to precision.

Vocabulary

- volume
- rectangular prism
- cubic centimeters

Materials

- Boxy Baskets Prism Nets student pages
- centimeter cubes (base ten unit cubes)
- scissors
- tape
- sticky notes

TASK

Boxy Baskets

Mr. Garza has challenged his class to make boxes to store collections of 1-centimeter cubes. The students created lots of different sized boxes! Mr. Garza thinks some of the students have built boxes that have the same volume, but the students think all the boxes are different.

Figure 13.15 A Box and a Cube

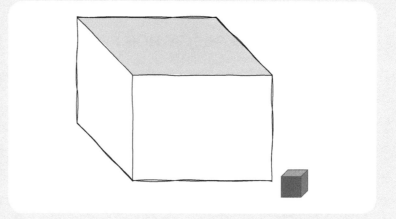

TASK PREPARATION

- Organize students into heterogeneous pairs.

- Prepare enough rectangular prism nets from the Boxy Baskets student pages for each pair to have 2 or 3 nets of different sizes.

ALTERNATE LEARNING ENVIRONMENT

To facilitate this task remotely, consider using the NCTM Illuminations "Cubes" app (https://www.nctm.org/Classroom-Resources/Illuminations/Interactives/Cubes/).

LAUNCH

1. Facilitate a *Notice and Wonder* showing students the image from the task (Figure 13.15).

2. Encourage students to *Pair-to-Pair Share* before taking ideas from the class.

3. Record students' wonders on the board.

FACILITATE

1. Organize students into pairs and distribute supplies.

2. Ask students to construct each of their box patterns and then pack them with unit cubes to find the volume of each.

3. **Observe** the students as they construct their box patterns and pack their boxes. Provide assistance, as needed.

4. After they've filled the box with unit cubes, students should write the dimensions and the volume of their box on a sticky note for display. See Figure 13.16.

PRODUCTIVE STRUGGLE

Encourage students to use any strategy they choose to pack and count unit cubes. It's okay if they start out counting one by one. Efficiency will come as students begin to internalize the relationships between box dimensions and volume.

Figure 13.16 Sticky Note Label on a Box of Cubes

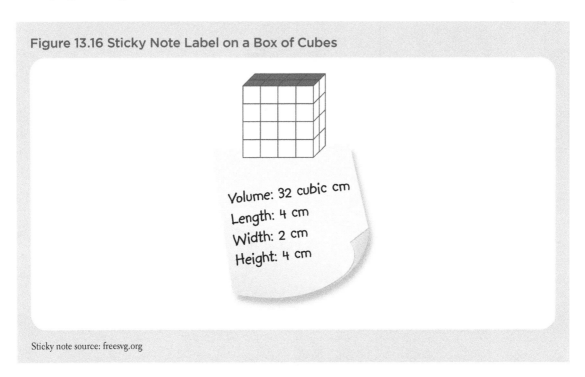

Volume: 32 cubic cm
Length: 4 cm
Width: 2 cm
Height: 4 cm

Sticky note source: freesvg.org

5. When students have completed some of the boxes, begin having student pairs meet to *Pair-to-Pair Share* to compare their different box dimensions and volumes.

CLOSE: MAKE THE MATH VISIBLE

1. Once a sufficient collection of boxes with varied dimensions are complete, conduct an Open Gallery Walk to allow students to see boxes and the measures of the volumes from all other pairs.

2. Bring the class together and ask, "What did you notice?" Revisit some of the wonders recorded on the board at the start of the task.

3. Display boxes with equivalent volumes for the class. Ask, "What do you notice about our boxes that have the same volumes? What is the same or different about each of them?"

4. Elicit from students that although the orientation of the boxes is different, the dimensions of some boxes are the same. Encourage students to physically rotate the boxes to show the relationships.

5. **Hinge Question.** Is it possible for two boxes to have the same volume but not have the same dimensions?

6. **Exit Task.** I have a collection of 32 one-centimeter cubes. What length, width, and height dimensions could I use to make a box that exactly fits all 32 cubes?

TASK 47: BOXY BASKETS PRISM NETS STUDENT PAGES

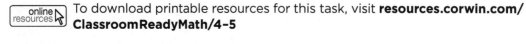 To download printable resources for this task, visit **resources.corwin.com/ ClassroomReadyMath/4–5**

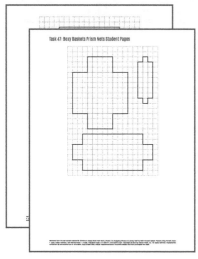

POST-TASK NOTES: REFLECTION & NEXT STEPS

Task 48
Volume Village

Relate the volume of a rectangular prism to stacked area "layers"

Mathematics Standard(s)

Relate volume to the operations of multiplication and addition and solve real world and mathematical problems involving volume.

a. Find the volume of a right rectangular prism with whole-number side lengths by packing it with unit cubes, and show that the volume is the same as would be found by multiplying the edge lengths, equivalently by multiplying the height by the area of the base. Represent threefold whole-number products as volumes, e.g., to represent the associative property of multiplication.

TASK

Volume Village

A group of city planners need your help designing a new neighborhood! Your job is to design one building for the village. Your building must meet the following guidelines:

1. All buildings in the village must be rectangular prisms.

2. Buildings in the village must have a volume no less than _____ cubic units.

3. Buildings in the village may not exceed _____ units in any dimension.

TASK PREPARATION

• Take stock of your resources (number of cubes of the same size, available space for the village, etc.). Use this information to determine the specifications you will provide (within the task) for the volume and dimensions of students' buildings.

  » Enter the specification information on the Building Registration Forms before running copies.

• Consider how you will organize students into heterogeneous pairs or small groups. If buildings are larger, it may be helpful to have slightly larger groups to assist with building construction.

LAUNCH

1. Bring the whole class together and present the task.

2. Ask students to *Turn-and-Talk* to share their ideas about the buildings they may build.

3. Ask questions to encourage students to make sense of the guidelines:

  » When it says that all the buildings must be rectangular prisms, what do you picture in your mind?

Mathematical Practices

• Look for and make use of structure.

• Construct viable arguments and critique the reasoning of others.

Vocabulary

• volume
• rectangular prism
• dimension
• specifications
• cubic units

Materials

• 1-inch or 1-cm cubes

• Building Registration Forms student page, one per group

» Based on the specifications you have for your buildings, what are some examples of dimensions or volumes that would be unacceptable? What are some examples of volumes that are possible?

» Why do you think the planners limited the building dimensions? What might happen if we built a group of buildings that were wider than those limits? Or taller than those limits?

FACILITATE

1. Organize students into heterogeneous pairs/small groups.

2. Provide students with ready access to a supply of same-sized cubes.

3. **Observe.** As groups work on constructing their buildings, circulate from group to group to observe strategies being used to create their rectangular prisms. In particular, watch for the following:

   » Counting cubes one at a time as the building is constructed

   » Creating "layers" by building one story at a time

   » Deciding on and constructing three dimensions: a length, a width, and a height; then constructing the building using the dimensions

4. **Interview.**

   » How do you know that your building meets Guideline 3?

   » How do you know that your building is a rectangular prism?

   » Do you know the volume of your building? How are you going to figure that out?

   » What will you do if the volume of your building is too small or too great for the specifications?

   » If the height of 1 cube represents 1 story in the building, how many stories are in your building?

   Note: Consider using the Observation and Interview (small group) tools for monitoring and recording student responses (see Appendix B).

5. As groups get close to finishing their buildings, distribute Building Registration Forms.

ACCESS AND EQUITY

Consider setting up a consistent space in your classroom where students are able to access mathematics tools and manipulatives without needing to ask permission. Ready access to resources helps to normalize their use and demonstrates a belief that manipulatives are something all mathematicians use—not just something for remediation.

STRENGTHS SPOTTING

This task is an opportunity for students to showcase their geometric and spatial strengths. As you observe and interview, give explicit feedback about how students are building, imagining, and designing their buildings.

CLOSE: MAKE THE MATH VISIBLE

1. When students have completed their buildings, facilitate an Open Gallery Walk so students can admire buildings created by other groups.

2. Bring the class together again to discuss the strategies they used to calculate the volume of their buildings. Highlight the various strategies you observed during the Facilitate phase of the activity.

3. Encourage students to make connections between the building dimensions and the area of the base.

   » How would the volume of your building change if you added one more story?

   » How would the volume change if you removed a story?

   » What different building volumes could you make with the same base area? Why?

4. **Hinge Question.** If you knew the area of a building's base, what else would you need to know to figure out the volume? Why?

TASK 48: VOLUME VILLAGE STUDENT PAGE

 To download the printable resource for this task, visit **resources.corwin.com/ ClassroomReadyMath/4–5**

Task 48: Volume Village Student Page

POST-TASK NOTES: REFLECTION & NEXT STEPS

CHAPTER 14

Geometry

Two-Dimensional Shapes and Symmetry

TASK 49: GRADE 4: CAN YOU BUILD IT?

Classify two-dimensional figures based on the presence or absence of parallel or perpendicular lines, or the presence or absence of angles of a specified size. Recognize right triangles as a category, and identify right triangles.

TASK 50: GRADE 5: POLYGON POSSIBILITIES

Understand that attributes belonging to a category of two-dimensional figures also belong to all subcategories of that category.

TASK 51: GRADE 5: AGREE OR DISAGREE?

Classify two-dimensional figures in a hierarchy based on properties.

TASK 52: GRADE 4: GEOBOARD EXPLORATIONS

Recognize a line of symmetry for a two-dimensional figure as a line across the figure such that the figure can be folded along the line into matching parts. Identify line-symmetric figures and draw lines of symmetry.

Anticipating Student Thinking: An important component of the geometry strand at the elementary school level is the analysis of shapes and their properties. In this chapter, three of the four tasks focus on understanding attributes of two-dimensional figures and classifying such figures based on their properties. The chapter's final task engages students in recognizing and drawing lines of symmetry. As you anticipate how your students will respond to the chapter's tasks, recognize that geometry as a content strand naturally engages all students as they explore, compare, and discuss the properties and relationships of figures. Note that lines of symmetry help define particular relationships and properties related to such figures. As your students engage in the productive struggle that each task provides, they will need time to think about and complete task responses, which will include small-group interaction or whole-class discussion. Plan for this.

THINK ABOUT IT

How might you adapt one or more of the chapter tasks so that students could complete the task or tasks from home. How would you review their work and provide feedback? Also consider an online geoboard adaptation of the chapter's symmetry task for students to complete or as an extension to the existing task.

Mathematics Standard

- Classify two-dimensional figures based on the presence or absence of parallel or perpendicular lines, or the presence or absence of angles of a specified size. Recognize right triangles as a category, and identify right triangles.

Mathematical Practices

- Model with mathematics.
- Use appropriate tools strategically.

Vocabulary

- conjecture
- parallel
- perpendicular
- adjacent
- line segments
- right angle
- quadrilateral
- parallelogram
- triangle
- rectangle
- trapezoid
- polygon
- properties

Task 49
Can You Build It?

Recognize parallel and perpendicular lines in polygons

TASK

Can You Build It?

The students in Ms. Stolp's math class were making conjectures about attributes of polygons. Figure 14.1 shows four of the conjectures students made.

Figure 14.1 Students' Conjectures

Khadija's conjecture:	"It's impossible to make a triangle with parallel sides."
Jesse's conjecture:	"It's impossible to make a parallelogram with perpendicular sides."
Kira's conjecture:	"It's impossible to make a trapezoid with perpendicular sides."
Alfie's conjecture:	"It's impossible to make a rectangle with only one pair of parallel sides."

Ms. Stolp challenged the class to test these conjectures by trying to make the figures the students described. Is it possible to make these figures? If not, explain why not.

TASK PREPARATION

- Organize the students into heterogeneous pairs. Consider planning for each pair to explore a different conjecture for the task such that two or three pairs are working on each conjecture and those smaller groups can work together during the Close phase of the task.

- Gather (see materials) a collection of rigid or semi-rigid materials students might use to construct models of two-dimensional shapes. If possible, plan to provide a variety of tools in a place where students can easily access the resources and make individual choices about which tools they will use.

• Make a few copies of the student pages, which are provided as a resource for students to check their conjectures. For example, students may wish to use the circular protractor to measure the angles and the parallel lines to test if the lines are truly parallel.

LAUNCH

1. Show only the image from the task (Figure 14.2).

Figure 14.2 Students' Conjectures

Khadija's conjecture:	"It's impossible to make a triangle with parallel sides."
Jesse's conjecture:	"It's impossible to make a parallelogram with perpendicular sides."
Kira's conjecture:	"It's impossible to make a trapezoid with perpendicular sides."
Alfie's conjecture:	"It's impossible to make a rectangle with only one pair of parallel sides."

2. Ask students to *Turn-and-Learn* what their partner is thinking about these conjectures.

3. If the word *conjecture* is unfamiliar to students: Ask, "What do you think the word *conjecture* means?" Use the students' statements as context clues. . . .

4. Use student language to develop and record a definition on the board. For example, students might say, "A conjecture is when someone thinks something is true, but they haven't proven it yet."

5. Ask students what shape names they see in the list of conjectures. Don't define these at this time, but remind students that they have seen these shapes before.

! PRODUCTIVE STRUGGLE

Students have experience working with and naming two-dimensional figures. Although they may not have familiarity with the formal definitions and list of properties, they likely have working knowledge of the appearance of the shapes. Encourage students to work together to identify key properties of the shapes as they build their own examples.

Materials

• pieces to use for constructing figures (craft sticks, straws, pipe cleaners, etc.)

• Can you Build It? student pages, one per student

• poster paper (one per conjecture—write the conjecture at the top of the poster in advance)

• markers

• tape/glue

FACILITATE

1. Display the whole task and read it with students.

2. Organize students into pairs and distribute copies of the student page to each student.

3. Make sure student pairs know which conjecture they will test and where they can access available tools for modeling figures to prove or disprove the conjecture.

4. **Observe/Interview/Show Me.**

   - Groups testing Khadija's conjecture: "It's impossible to make a triangle with parallel sides."

     » "How do you know that is a triangle?"

     » "Show me what parallel sides look like."

     » If students have concluded that the conjecture is true: "What has to be true in a triangle's definition that makes this impossible?"

     » If students create parallel segments and then "bend" the ends to connect: "Show me three more, different triangles. Look at the sides of those new triangles. Why did you draw those line segments straight? If polygons have to have straight sides, how could you change this triangle to make it have straight sides?"

   - Groups testing Jesse's conjecture: "It's impossible to make a parallelogram with perpendicular sides."

     » "How do you know that is a parallelogram? What properties do parallelograms have?"

     » "Show me what perpendicular sides look like."

     » If students have constructed a rectangle: "Wait, that is a rectangle. The conjecture is about a parallelogram. Can you explain?"

   - Groups testing Kira's conjecture: "It's impossible to make a trapezoid with perpendicular sides."

     » "How do you know that is a trapezoid? What properties do trapezoids have?"

     » "Show me what perpendicular sides look like."

     » If students have constructed a right trapezoid: "How many right angles are in your figure? Is it possible to make a trapezoid that has only one right angle?"

   - Groups testing Alfie's conjecture: "It's impossible to make a rectangle with only one pair of parallel sides."

     » "How do you know that is a rectangle?"

     » "Show me what parallel sides look like."

   - If students have concluded that the conjecture is true: "I noticed that in your rectangle all the adjacent sides are perpendicular. Can you make a rectangle that has some adjacent sides that aren't perpendicular?"

5. As students begin to draw their conclusions, encourage pairs testing the same conjecture to *Pair-to-Pair Share.* Give each group a poster with the conjecture written at the top. The group should complete the poster showing if the conjecture is true or not. If true, provide reasoning. If not, display counterexamples.

STRENGTHS SPOTTING

Students are likely to show various strengths throughout this activity such as creative and novel thinking and logical reasoning. Note explicit student moves and help them understand how these strengths support them to be mathematical thinkers.

CLOSE: MAKE THE MATH VISIBLE

1. Conduct an Open Gallery Walk.

2. Bring the class together to discuss each of the conjectures using the student posters to seed the discussion.

3. Some ideas to highlight include:

   » Because a triangle has only three sides, each of the sides has to connect with both of the other sides. That makes it impossible to have any parallel sides.

   » The definition of a parallelogram does not preclude right angles, but when one pair of adjacent sides in a parallelogram is perpendicular, all other pairs of adjacent sides must also be perpendicular.

   » The definition of a trapezoid does not preclude right angles, but when one angle is a right angle, another angle must also be a right angle.

4. Encourage students to share defining attributes of the figures that help them recognize and name the shapes.

5. **Exit Task.** Is it possible to make a triangle with exactly one acute angle? Write a conjecture and provide reasoning to support your thinking.

TASK 49: CAN YOU BUILD IT? STUDENT PAGE

 To download printable resources for this task, visit **resources.corwin.com/ ClassroomReadyMath/4–5**

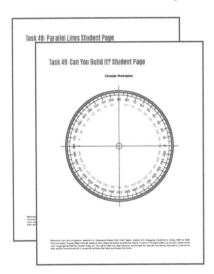

POST-TASK NOTES: REFLECTION & NEXT STEPS

Mathematics Standard

- Understand that attributes belonging to a category of two-dimensional figures also belong to all subcategories of that category.

Mathematical Practices

- Look for and make use of structure.
- Attend to precision.

Vocabulary

- polygon
- property
- parallel
- perpendicular
- obtuse angle
- acute angle
- right angle
- equilateral triangle
- scalene triangle
- isosceles triangle
- right triangle
- quadrilateral
- right trapezoid
- trapezoid
- square
- rectangle
- pentagon
- rhombus
- hexagon

Task 50
Polygon Possibilities

Consider properties of a polygon

TASK

Polygon Possibilities

Directions:

1. Each student pair will use two sets of the Polygon Possibilities Cut-Out Template (one set for each player) and one set of Polygon Possibilities Clue Cards.

2. Each player will take turns drawing a clue card. The player who draws the card will read the clues to their partner. The clues should be read slowly, one bullet at a time.

3. The other player will have all the shapes spread out across a table or carpet. Listen to each clue to determine which shapes will be eliminated and which shapes are still under consideration.

4. Players must identify the answer or possible answers by displaying the shape card(s) and calling each shape by its proper name.

5. Each clue card can have one or more than one possible answer. One point is awarded for a correct answer, regardless of whether there is one or more than one answer.

6. The winner is the player with the most points after five rounds.

TASK PREPARATION

- Consider grouping students in heterogeneous pairs to best promote collaborative work.

- Prepare two copies of the Polygon Possibilities Cut-Out Template and one copy of the Polygon Possibilities Clue Cards.

- This task provides students with opportunities to reason about two-dimensional shapes and to analyze their properties. This task should be implemented after students have had multiple opportunities to learn about the attributes of two-dimensional shapes.

LAUNCH

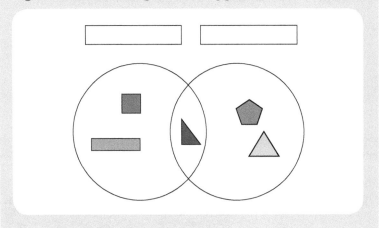

Figure 14.3 Venn Diagram of Polygons

1. Project the task image (Figure 14.3) on the board.

2. Say, "This picture is called a two-ring Venn diagram. Each ring contains polygons that share at least one property."

3. Have students huddle in groups of three or four to discuss the properties shared by the shapes inside the left circle and compare them with the characteristics shared by the shapes inside the right circle.

4. Then, have students *Turn and Learn* to discuss possible titles for each circle in the diagram.

5. Ask students to share what they learned from their peer and record all suggestions for titles on the board. Possible ideas (correct and incorrect) that surface may include the following:

   - Left circle:

     » Polygons with at least two perpendicular lines

     » Shapes with at least one right angle

     » Quadrilaterals

   - Right circle:

     » Polygons that are not quadrilaterals

     » Shapes with acute angles

ACCESS AND EQUITY

Record all ideas on the board; this supports students' ability to see themselves as active participants in the class' collective sense making. In turn, this contributes to students' development of agency.

Materials

- task directions
- Polygon Possibilities Cut-Out Template, two sets for each student
- Polygon Possibilities Clue Cards, one set for each student
- document camera

6. Address any misconceptions students may have about the shapes inside the Venn diagram, such as the location of the right triangle. Ask, "Does this shape belong in the left or the right circle?" This may alert other students that the title of the left circle cannot be Quadrilaterals because the right triangle is not a four-sided polygon.

7. Ask, "What other shape can you put in the same area (the overlap of the two circles) as the right triangle?"

FACILITATE

1. Explain to students that this time they will be given several properties of a polygon and they will need to identify the shape(s) that meet the attributes. Have students brainstorm possible properties that can be used to describe shapes.

2. Group students into pairs, then project the Polygon Possibilities game directions on the board.

3. Read and review the directions with pairs, allotting time for clarifying questions about the game.

4. Share with students that if they have a question about the solution to a clue card, they may consult with another nearby pair or discuss their question with the teacher.

5. **Observe**. Visit each pair in the class to monitor student conversations as they play the game.

PRODUCTIVE STRUGGLE

If students are stuck or confused, invite them to explain their thinking before you pose any questions. Scaffold your support by tackling one clue at a time. Ask which shapes they would eliminate and why. Then have students think about the next clue and the shapes they have left.

6. **Interview** As you visit student pairs, ask the following Interview questions:

   » Why did you eliminate this shape (point to specific polygon)?

   » Which shapes are equilateral? How do you know?

   » Why is this triangle called scalene? What other name can this triangle have?

   » What are the properties of a right trapezoid?

   Note: Consider using the Interview (small group) tool for monitoring and recording responses from the student pairs (see Appendix B).

CLOSE: MAKE THE MATH VISIBLE

1. Bring students back together as a whole group.

2. Debrief the game with students and ask, "Which clue cards made you think the most? Why? Which clues were you certain about? Why is that the case? What did you enjoy about the game?"

3. Call on students to share which figures they found to fit all the clues on each card (use document camera).

4. Reiterate that we can compare two-dimensional shapes by the number of sides, sizes of the angles, and the length of sides. We can also determine specific properties of shapes by considering their classification. For example, if parallelograms have two pairs of parallel sides, and a square is a parallelogram, then all squares must have two

pairs of parallel sides. Or if a square has two pairs of parallel sides, then it must be a parallelogram.

5. **Hinge Question**. What is the name of one of the quadrilaterals that you compared that does not have four right angles?

TASK 50: POLYGON POSSIBILITIES STUDENT PAGE

online resources ➜ To download printable resources for this task, visit **resources.corwin.com/ ClassroomReadyMath/4–5**

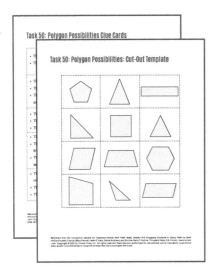

POST-TASK NOTES: REFLECTION & NEXT STEPS

Task 51
Agree or Disagree?

Classify two-dimensional shapes

TASK

Agree or Disagree

Directions: Create a T-chart on your chart paper. Label the left side Agree and the right side Disagree. Cut out Agree or Disagree task cards. Read each statement and as a group, discuss and analyze the shapes' properties. Decide whether each statement goes in the Agree or Disagree column (see Figure 14.4). For any cards that you put in the Disagree column, sketch a counterexample on a sticky note and add it to the chart. Be prepared to defend your decisions.

Figure 14.4 Example Card and T-Chart

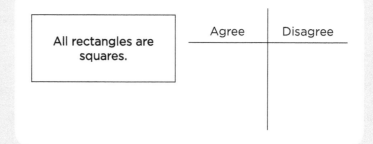

TASK PREPARATION

- Think about how you will heterogeneously organize students in groups of four to promote productive discussions about quadrilaterals.

- Ensure that there is ample space for groups to lay down their chart paper and to view the statements they will be discussing.

LAUNCH

1. Distribute dot paper for the entire class. Write the following statement on the board:

   All rectangles are squares.

2. Have students draw a rectangle on their dot paper, then have them *Turn and Talk* discussing the statement on the board.

3. Have students show you, thumbs up or down, whether they agree or disagree with the statement on the board.

4. Ask for volunteers to defend their answers. Ask students who disagree to draw counterexamples to justify their thinking. Reinforce both through drawings and definitions that while rectangles have two sets of parallel sides and four right angles, they do not always have four congruent sides, so not all rectangles are squares.

5. Direct students to draw a parallelogram, quadrilateral, trapezoid, and rhombus on their dot paper. **Observe** the students as they work to complete their drawings.

6. Have students *Pair-to-Pair Share* their drawings and describe and compare the attributes of each shape drawn.

7. Call on students to share their drawings and explanations. Affirm the following:

   » A parallelogram has two pairs of parallel sides and two pairs of congruent sides.

   » A square has two pairs of parallel sides, four congruent sides, and four right angles (90°).

   » A rectangle has two pairs of parallel sides, two pairs of congruent sides, and four right angles.

   » A rhombus has two pairs of parallel sides and four congruent sides.

   » A trapezoid has at least one pair of opposite sides parallel. (Note: This is the inclusive definition of trapezoids.)

   » A quadrilateral is a polygon with four sides.

ACCESS AND EQUITY

It is important for students to have opportunities to construct/draw visual images of various two-dimensional shapes and connect them to verbal definitions, supporting their conceptual understanding and ability to communicate geometric ideas and recognize defining attributes.

STRENGTHS SPOTTING

As students are sharing, notice students who listen well to their peers and explain how this strength helps everyone understand math better. Ask students to share what they heard their peers explain highlighting the importance of this strength.

FACILITATE

1. Organize students into heterogeneous groups of four. Distribute the remaining materials.

2. Review with groups the directions for creating the T-chart on their chart paper, then let them dive into discussions about the statements they have been given. Encourage students to use the quadrilateral images to support their mathematical arguments.

3. Circulate around the room, ensuring that you have allotted enough time to visit each group.

4. **Observe** student conversations and record any statements/questions that you may want to refer back to during the close.

Note: Consider using the Observation tool for recording the statements/questions noted above (see Appendix B).

PRODUCTIVE STRUGGLE

Some students may have difficulty reasoning about hierarchal relationships. Support students by having them create drawings. For example, when discussing whether all rectangles are parallelograms, ask, "What would a rectangle that is not a parallelogram look like? Can you draw one?"

5. **Interview.** Visit the student working groups and ask the following:

   » Is a rhombus always a parallelogram?

   » Are all squares rectangles?

   » Are all trapezoids quadrilaterals?

CLOSE: MAKE THE MATH VISIBLE

1. Gather students back together to discuss the task.

2. Ask, "Which statements did your group come to unanimous agreement on right away? Why?"

3. **Hinge Question.** "Which statements were more problematic for your group? Why?"

4. As you review each statement, reaffirm the following (see Figure 14.5):

   » *All rectangles are quadrilaterals.* Quadrilaterals are polygons with four sides, and rectangles have four sides (Agree column).

   » *A rhombus is always a parallelogram.* Rhombuses are subsets of parallelograms. They have two sets of parallel sides and they are a special kind of parallelogram because they have four congruent sides (Agree column).

   » *All rectangles are squares.* While rectangles have two sets of parallel sides and four right angles, they do not always have four congruent sides, so not all rectangles are squares (Disagree column).

   » *All squares are rectangles.* Rectangles have two sets of parallel sides and four right angles. Squares have two sets of parallel sides and four right angles, so all squares are rectangles (Agree column).

   » *Trapezoids are not quadrilaterals.* Trapezoids are polygons with four sides, so all trapezoids are quadrilaterals (Disagree column).

   » *All squares are rhombuses.* Squares are subsets of rhombuses (Agree column).

   » *All quadrilaterals are trapezoids.* While trapezoids have four sides, so do parallelograms (Disagree column).

   » *All rhombuses are squares.* Rhombuses can sometimes be squares, when they have four right angles, but not all rhombuses are squares (Disagree column).

Figure 14.5 Hierarchical Shape Diagram

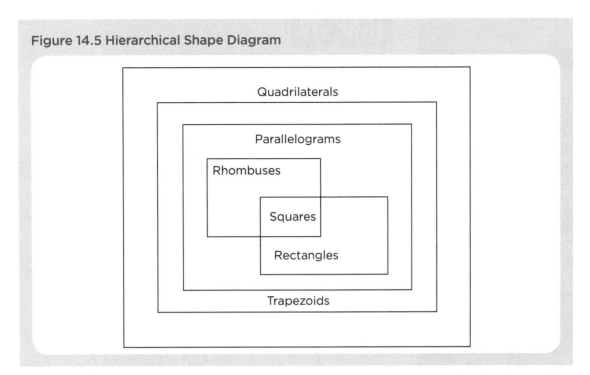

TASK 51: AGREE OR DISAGREE TASK CARDS

online resources

To download printable resources for this task, visit **resources.corwin.com/ClassroomReadyMath/4–5**

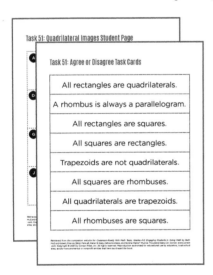

POST-TASK NOTES: REFLECTION & NEXT STEPS

Mathematics Standard

Recognize a line of symmetry for a two-dimensional figure as a line across the figure such that the figure can be folded along the line into matching parts. Identify line-symmetric figures and draw lines of symmetry.

Mathematical Practice

- Attend to precision.

Vocabulary

- symmetry, symmetrical
- lines of symmetry
- quadrilateral
- vertical
- horizontal
- diagonal

Materials

- Geoboard Explorations student page, one for each pair
- geoboards
- rubber bands
- laptops (one for each pair, optional)
- dot paper
- rulers
- scissors

Task 52
Geoboard Explorations

Explore lines of symmetry

TASK

Geoboard Explorations

Mr. Suarez created four quadrilaterals on a geoboard. Find the lines of symmetry for each shape (Figure 14.6).

Figure 14.6 Quadrilaterals on a Geoboard

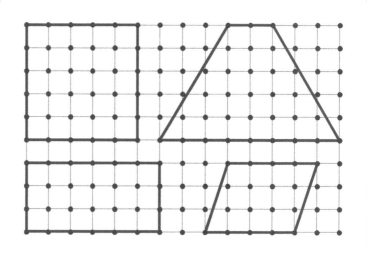

Use a geoboard or dot paper and re-create the shapes to help you identify all the possible lines of symmetry in each shape. Then create a new shape and ask a classmate to re-create it and draw the new shape's lines of symmetry.

ALTERNATE LEARNING ENVIRONMENT

Alternate Learning Environment: Teachers facilitating this task outside the classroom may wish to use a digital geoboard such as the free version from the Math Learning Center (https://apps.mathlearningcenter.org/geoboard/).

TASK PREPARATION

- Think about how you will heterogeneously organize students in pairs to work collaboratively when using a geoboard or the geoboard app by the Math Learning Center.

- If you decide on using the geoboard app, ensure that there are enough computers/laptops for each pair of students. Practice demonstrating how to use the rubber bands on the virtual tool, how to use the drawing tool to identify the lines of symmetry on each shape, and the functions of the other tools on the app.

LAUNCH

1. Project the image shown in Figure 14.7 on the board.

2. Facilitate *See-Think-Wonder*. Ask, "What do you see? What do you think about what _____ (their partner) said? Would you like to add to their idea? What does what _____ (their partner) said make you wonder about?"

3. Using a classroom drawing of a rectangle, discuss, define, and create lines of symmetry. Then, note that the butterfly's wings are symmetrical by asking students to note the characteristics. A vertical line can be drawn in the center of the image of the butterfly such that folding along this line results in matching parts. Ask for a volunteer to draw the line of symmetry on the butterfly.

4. Ask, "Where do you see symmetry in our world?"

Figure 14.7 Butterfly

Source: Photograph by Gregory Phillips, December 2003. CC BY-SA 3.0. https://creativecommons.org/licenses/by-sa/3.0/deed.en

FACILITATE

1. Organize students into heterogeneous groups of four. Distribute materials to each group.

2. Read the task along with the students, and then direct them to start working on the task.

3. If working on laptops using the geoboard app (https://apps.mathlearningcenter.org/geoboard/): Demonstrate for students how to use the various tools on the app's dashboard.

4. If using classroom geoboards, have students create the quadrilaterals shown in the task or use a rubber band to create each shape one at a time on a geoboard. Students can also sketch their figures on dot paper and cut/fold to prove the line of symmetry.

5. **Observation.** Monitor pair work, listening for how students determine where to draw a line of symmetry.

ACCESS AND EQUITY

Symmetry is something that can be observed in our daily lives and occurs in both nature and architecture. Allow students to generate examples from real life to support their growing understanding about symmetry and lines of symmetry.

STRENGTHS SPOTTING

Highlight students who use problem-solving skills to explore the app. Ask these students to share how they used multiple trials to learn the program and call attention to how this strength helps them be good mathematical thinkers.

6. **Show Me** the lines of symmetry you located for the square. How can you prove that this line creates two matching shapes? How many lines of symmetry does a square have?.

7. **Show Me** where the line of symmetry can be drawn for the trapezoid. How do you know if this line can be the only line of symmetry for this shape?

Note: Consider using the Show Me tool for monitoring and recording responses for sequencing student sharing in the Close (see Appendix B).

8. **Hinge Question.** Do you think every trapezoid will have a line of symmetry? Represent a trapezoid that has no lines of symmetry.

9. If time permits, have pairs exchange their shape designs with another pair and allow them to identify possible lines of symmetry.

CLOSE: MAKE THE MATH VISIBLE

1. Gather students back together to discuss the task.

2. Sequence student sharing (based on Show Me responses) and have students share where they drew lines of symmetry for each shape and explain why these can be the only lines of symmetry for the given shape.

3. Through questioning, elicit the following ideas about the particular shapes shown on the geoboard (Figure 14.8):

   » The square has four lines of symmetry—a vertical line can be drawn, a horizontal line, and two diagonals.

   » The isosceles trapezoid has one line of symmetry—a vertical line can be drawn to create two congruent pairs.

   » The rectangle has two lines of symmetry—a vertical line and a horizontal line can be drawn to create two halves that match up.

   » The parallelogram has no lines of symmetry.

Figure 14.8 Quadrilaterals on a Geoboard With Lines of Symmetry

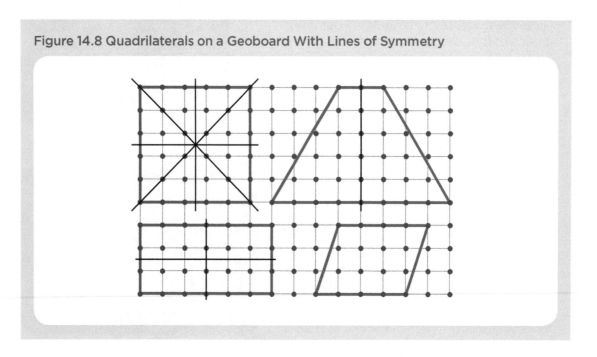

4. Direct students' attention to the shapes represented on the geoboard and the lines of symmetry drawn. Ask, "Can you represent a parallelogram that has a line(s) of symmetry? Are there parallelograms with no lines of symmetry? Can you represent a parallelogram that has a line(s) of symmetry?"

TASK 52: GEOBOARD EXPLORATIONS STUDENT PAGE

 To download printable resources for this task, visit **resources.corwin.com/ClassroomReadyMath/4–5**

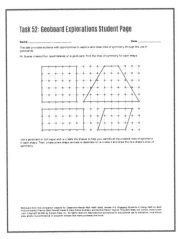

POST-TASK NOTES: REFLECTION & NEXT STEPS

Geometry

Representing Real-World Problems

TASK 53: GRADE 5: MARIA'S NEW GAME

Use a pair of perpendicular number lines, called axes, to define a coordinate system, with the intersection of the lines (the origin) arranged to coincide with the 0 on each line and a given point in the plane located by using an ordered pair of numbers, called its coordinates. Understand that the first number indicates how far to travel from the origin in the direction of one axis, and the second number indicates how far to travel in the direction of the second axis, with the convention that the names of the two axes and the coordinates correspond (e.g., *x*-axis and *x*-coordinate, *y*-axis and *y*-coordinate).

TASK 54: GRADE 5: HAPPY ABOUT HOOPS

Represent real world and mathematical problems by graphing points in the first quadrant of the coordinate plane and interpret coordinate values of points in the context of the situation.

Anticipating Student Thinking: Both tasks in this chapter engage students in graphing points on the coordinate plane. For many students, these tasks will be their first opportunity to formally experience working with a coordinate system. The real-world contexts represented in each of the chapter's tasks are applications of how plotting ordered pairs visualize change. When planning for implementation of the tasks consider how you might actually group students to engage learning pairs or small groups. As your students complete the tasks, use formative assessment to get a sense of their understanding of the coordinate system and ordered pairs. For instance, what is their thinking about the difference between the ordered pairs 4,5 and 5,4 as suggested by the Hinge Question in Maria's New Game? As your students do the mathematics, use observation to make sure that all have access to the tasks and are engaged.

THINK ABOUT IT

There are many online tools for creating coordinate systems. If you decide to use such a tool within your classroom, or for remote/online instruction, take the time to fully explore and then decide how you will help your students gain access to the online tool and use it appropriately. Try to anticipate questions students or caregivers may have about such access and use, particularly if the online tool is used in a remote location.

Mathematics Standard

Use a pair of perpendicular number lines, called axes, to define a coordinate system, with the intersection of the lines (the origin) arranged to coincide with the 0 on each line and a given point in the plane located by using an ordered pair of numbers, called its coordinates. Understand that the first number indicates how far to travel from the origin in the direction of one axis, and the second number indicates how far to travel in the direction of the second axis, with the convention that the names of the two axes and the coordinates correspond (e.g., x-axis and x-coordinate, y-axis and y-coordinate).

Mathematical Practices

- Construct viable arguments and critique the reasoning of others.
- Attend to precision.

Vocabulary

- point
- coordinate grid
- axis
- coordinates
- horizontal
- vertical
- origin
- ordered pairs

Maria's New Game

Introduce the first quadrant of a coordinate plane

TASK

Maria's New Game

Maria is designing a game that can be played on cell phones. In Maria's game, players need to round up stray animals and take them to the shelter so they can be adopted (see Figure 15.1). Maria needs to locate specific points on the screen so that she can program the game to know when someone collects a stray pet.

Figure 15.1 The Game

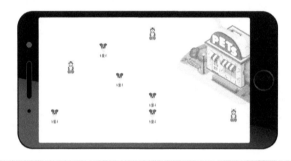

Image sources: iPhone: Pavlo Stavnichuk/iStock.com; Pet Shelter Okeksandr Pupko/iStock.com; Cat and Dog ayutaka/iStock.com

Maria decides to use a coordinate grid to identify points on the screen (see Figure 15.2). How does Maria's system work? How can you use the coordinate grid to identify the locations of all the stray animals?

Figure 15.2 Coordinate Grid Over the Game

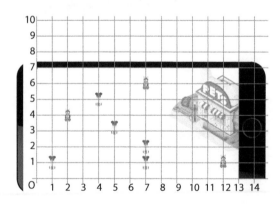

Image sources: iPhone: Pavlo Stavnichuk/iStock.com; Pet Shelter Okeksandr Pupko/iStock.com; Cat and Dog ayutaka/iStock.com

TASK PREPARATION

1. Plan to organize students into heterogeneous pairs.

2. Consider using a clear sheet protector for each student handout so students can use dry-erase markers to make annotations on the page.

LAUNCH

1. Bring the class together on the carpet or in some other common space in the room.

2. Display the first part of the task (Figure 15.3).

Maria's New Game

Maria is designing a game that can be played on cell phones. In Maria's game, players need to round up stray animals and take them to the shelter so they can be adopted. Maria needs to locate specific points on the screen so that she can program the game to know when someone collects a stray pet.

Figure 15.3 The Game

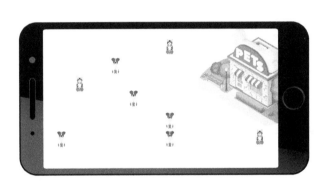

Image sources: iPhone: Pavlo Stavnichuk/iStock.com; Pet Shelter Okeksandr Pupko/iStock.com; Cat and Dog ayutaka/iStock.com

3. Ask students to *See, Think, and Wonder* about the story. After a bit of individual thinking time, have students *Pair-to-Pair Share* their ideas about how they might describe the specific locations of the various pets on the screen.

4. Take a few suggestions from students. Respond to their responses as literally as possible. For example, if a student says, "There is a cat at the right side of the screen (Figure 15.4)" point to the very rightmost center part of the screen, and ask, "Right here?"

Materials

- Maria's New Game student page, one copy of the image per student pair
- clear sheet protectors
- dry-erase markers
- extra animal pictures

Figure 15.4 Demonstrating Pointing in the Game

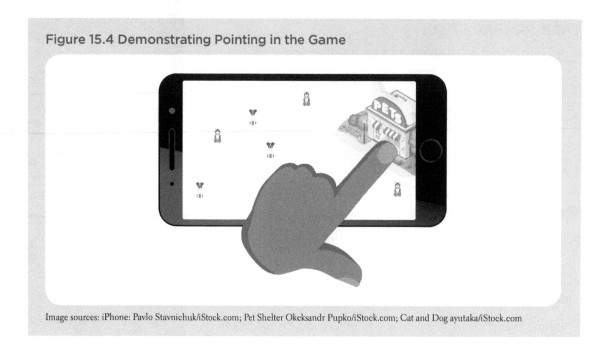

5. As soon as students recognize that describing a location relative to the edges of the screen (or to some other image on the screen) is not a generalizable way to consistently and accurately identify a specific location and a more systematic and precise approach is needed, present the second part of the task (see Figure 15.5).

Figure 15.5 Coordinate Grid Over the Game

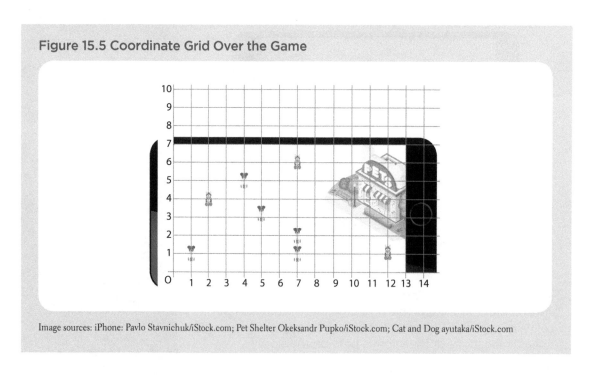

FACILITATE

1. Organize students into heterogeneous pairs and distribute a copy of the image from the task to each pair.

2. Tell students that their task is to analyze Maria's system and try to figure out how it works.

3. **Observe/Interview.** Pay attention to the language students are using to describe locations to one another. Students who begin to use the numbers from the two axes or who use words like *up* and *over* as they work with their partners will be ones you want to have share during the close phase of the task. As you circulate and observe, ask Interview questions to clarify student thinking. For example:

> **! PRODUCTIVE STRUGGLE**
>
> Do not teach students how to use a coordinate grid at this time. Instead, allow students to explore and discuss their own ideas about how the system might work. In this way, through observations and interviews, teachers can identify what funds of knowledge students already may have on this topic and leverage those ideas to develop the concept.

> » "What did you mean when you said that the cat is 'on the 12 line'? Is there another line connected to that cat?"

> » Indicate the dogs located at (7,1) and (7,2). "How is the position of these two dogs the same? How is it different?"

> » "When you say the cat is at the '2 and 4 lines,' how do I know you don't mean this point?" (point to (4,2), as shown in Figure 15.6)

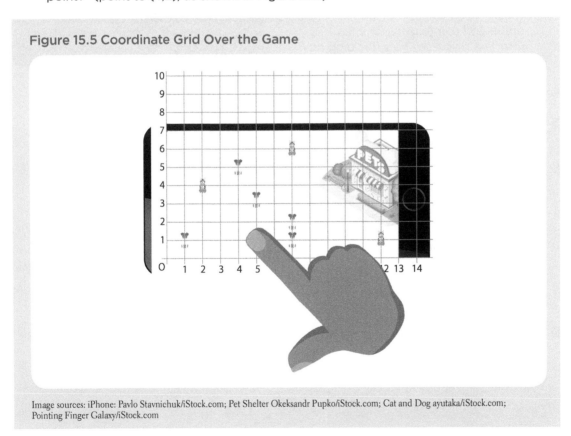

Figure 15.5 Coordinate Grid Over the Game

Image sources: iPhone: Pavlo Stavnichuk/iStock.com; Pet Shelter Okeksandr Pupko/iStock.com; Cat and Dog ayutaka/iStock.com; Pointing Finger Galaxy/iStock.com

> » Give students a cat or dog image and challenge them to use their rules to tell their partner exactly where to place it without pointing at the grid.

Note: Consider using the Observation and Interview (small group) tools for monitoring and selecting and sequencing responses that will be shared in the Close (see Appendix B).

4. As pairs are ready to share their ideas, have them meet up with another pair to conduct a *Pair-to-Pair Interview* as an opportunity to practice defending their ideas about how to place animals and how to notate where they are including critiquing the reasoning of others.

CLOSE: MAKE THE MATH VISIBLE

1. When every pair is ready to share and defend their thinking about how the coordinate grid helps Maria locate specific points on the phone screen, bring the class back together to discuss the task.

2. Select and Sequence student pairs to share their thinking based on your observations/ interviews. Consider sequencing students in a way that highlights the need for the convention of naming the distance along the *x*-axis first. For example:

   » 1st: a pair who noticed that they could use numbers to describe a location, but did not distinguish order of the numbers shares their thinking.

   » 2nd: a pair who used directions with the numbers (e.g., "up 4, over 2") shares their method; the class discusses how this is the same or different from the 1st pair's thinking.

   » 3rd: a pair who used directions with the numbers but in the opposite order of the 2nd pair (e.g., "over 2, up 4"); the class discusses how deciding on one directional language can help to eliminate confusion about which 2 and which 4 are being referenced.

STRENGTHS SPOTTING

As each pair shares, note the strengths in their work and how they contributed to the solution pathway. When students hear explicit feedback about their solutions, they understand how to call upon and use that strength again.

3. At this time, let students know that they have discovered important ideas about how a coordinate grid can be used to identify a specific location! Tell them that mathematicians also realized that they needed to make sure it was clear which lines they meant (horizontal or vertical) when they referenced a point, so they agreed to use a convention (or rule). "The rule we use is to always name the horizontal distance first. We call the horizontal number line on a coordinate grid the *x*-axis. Then we can name the vertical distance. We call the vertical number line on a coordinate grid the *y*-axis."

4. Encourage students to locate and point to the *x*-axis and the *y*-axis on their coordinate grid.

5. Demonstrate for students how to write an ordered pair to describe the location of a stray pet on the task image (see Figure 15.7).

6. **Hinge Question.** Ask, "How is this point (4,5) different from the point (5,4)?"

Figure 15.7 Demonstrating a Labeled Point in the Game

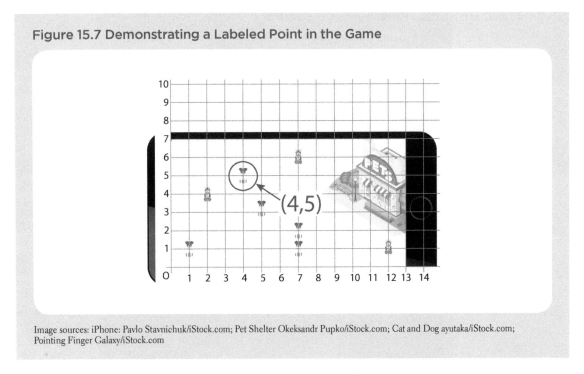

Image sources: iPhone: Pavlo Stavnichuk/iStock.com; Pet Shelter Okeksandr Pupko/iStock.com; Cat and Dog ayutaka/iStock.com; Pointing Finger Galaxy/iStock.com

7. As time allows, give each pair several extra cat and dog pictures and have them work with their partners to practice placing animals on their grid to match a point named by their partner.

8. **Exit Task.** Write an ordered pair that describes the location of the pet shelter's front door.

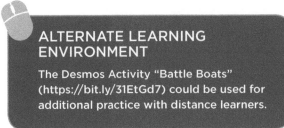

ALTERNATE LEARNING ENVIRONMENT

The Desmos Activity "Battle Boats" (https://bit.ly/31EtGd7) could be used for additional practice with distance learners.

TASK 53: MARIA'S NEW GAME STUDENT PAGE

 To download printable resources for this task, visit **resources.corwin.com/ClassroomReadyMath/4–5**

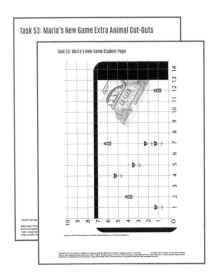

POST-TASK NOTES: REFLECTION & NEXT STEPS

Task 54
Happy About Hoops

Graph and interpret coordinate values

TASK

Happy About Hoops

Cameron's favorite sport is basketball. He practices and then keeps track of his foul shooting every day. Each day he shoots 20 foul shots at the end of his practice. The table below shows how he has done this week.

Image Source: Anna Valieva/iStock.com

Days of the Week	Foul Shots Made
Monday	6
Tuesday	12
Wednesday	11
Thursday	13
Friday	8
Saturday	17
Sunday	18

- Graph the corresponding points (days of the week and shots made) on a coordinate plane.

- What observations can you make about Cameron's foul-shooting data?

- Which days were Cameron's most successful days for foul shooting?

- What was the difference between the number of foul shots made on Cameron's most and least successful shooting days?

Mathematics Standard

- Represent real world and mathematical problems by graphing points in the first quadrant of the coordinate plane, and interpret coordinate values of points in the context of the situation.

Mathematical Practices

- Make sense of problems and persevere in solving them.
- Model with mathematics.

Vocabulary

- point
- coordinate plane
- coordinate grid
- data

Materials

- Happy About Hoops student page, one for each student

TASK PREPARATION

- Organize students into heterogeneous pairs or triads.

- Prepare copies of student page.

LAUNCH

1. Display the image of the basketball and ask students what they know about basketball. Ask, "How many of you play on a basketball team? How many of you like to watch basketball? How many of you practice your foul shooting at your team practices or have seen players practice their foul shots?"

2. Implement *Turn and Talk*. Connect student ideas with basketball, perhaps through experiences with their teams or teams of family members, or show a brief video clip of young, high school, collegiate, or professional players (e.g., basketball video about foul shooting could be used—https://bit.ly/34JbIrG).

3. Display the full task. Ask, "What do you notice about Cameron's foul shooting in the first two rows of the table? What do you wonder?"

> ### STRENGTHS SPOTTING
> As students share their ideas, take the opportunity to notice how students listen as well as how and when they share. Curiosity and the interest in others' ideas are important mathematical strengths to celebrate.

FACILITATE

1. Divide the class into heterogeneous pairs or triads. Distribute the student page.

2. Ask, "What do the headings in the columns of the table represent?" (*x*-axis and *y*-axis).

3. Direct students to graph data from the table on the coordinate grid.

4. **Show Me**. Pose the following prompts:

   » The ordered pair for shots made on Tuesday.

   » The point on the coordinate grid that represents the data for Cameron's best day of foul shooting.

5. Ask, "Based on the graph, what can you say about Cameron's foul shooting during this week of practice?"

CLOSE: MAKE THE MATH VISIBLE

1. Ask, "What observations can you make about the data?" As students offer ideas, encourage them to build on one another's ideas to further the discussion. Ask, "Who would like to add on to what _____ shared?"

2. Ask, "On which days did Cameron make fewer than half of his foul shots?"

3. **Hinge Question**. Ask, "Based on the graph of Cameron's shooting, do you think his foul shooting improved during the week, or not? Why or why not?"

4. Ensure that through information from the table and coordinate grid, students are able to note the differences in daily foul shooting totals and the range of shots made during the week, recognizing that the coordinate graph provides an immediate visual image of Cameron's progress.

TASK 54: HAPPY ABOUT HOOPS STUDENT PAGE

 To download printable resources for this task, visit **resources.corwin.com/ ClassroomReadyMath/4–5**

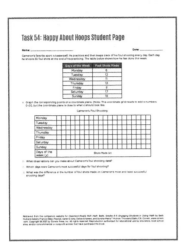

POST-TASK NOTES: REFLECTION & NEXT STEPS

Your Turn

Now that you have had an opportunity to implement lots of *doing-math tasks*, we imagine that you have clear ideas about what works well with your students and how these tasks have specific characteristics that truly engage them in mathematical thinking. We admire and respect the ways that teachers innovate and create to engage their students in meaningful mathematics learning experiences, and we want to provide support to you as you search for, adapt, and create more tasks with these features to address your students' specific learning strengths and needs.

So where do your mathematics tasks come from now, beyond those in this book? As you consider teaching an upcoming mathematics standard, thinking about and searching for rich tasks to engage your students in *doing-math* within the context of the lesson becomes an obvious and important concern and a daily element of your preparation. Here's what we know: The curriculum materials that you currently use, your textbook, trusted online sources, professional development seminars you've attended, and/ or supplemental materials you have acquired over the years all represent *possible* starting points, as does your own creativity in actual task creation. As you consider the tasks you encounter in curriculum resources or have gathered through other means, you may naturally want to adapt the tasks to meet your students' needs. This chapter will support you in selecting, adapting, and creating *doing-math tasks*. In addition, this chapter includes both frequently asked questions that teachers often ask when they do this work and an exploration of the responses to those questions. You will explore recommendations for selecting, adapting, and creating tasks and examine the responses to frequently asked questions that teachers ask when facilitating tasks.

Your Turn: Selecting Tasks

In Chapter 1, we explored important characteristics of *doing-math tasks* and their implications for creating high cognitive demand instruction. Now that you have had the opportunity to implement a collection of tasks, and have likely developed some of your own criteria, you can apply the research-informed decision points introduced in Chapter 1 (pages 7–8) to evaluate tasks that you would like to implement in your classroom. Let's take a look at four tasks that Margaret, a fourth-grade teacher, found in her district-supplied curriculum resources (Figure 16.1).

Figure 16.1 Example: 4th Grade

Content Standard: Measurement and Data—Apply concepts related to area and the area formula for rectangles in real world and mathematical problems.

Mathematical Practice(s): Reason abstractly and quantitatively—Construct viable arguments and critique the reasoning of others.

Task A

Ben had a small rectangular-shaped vegetable garden. He decided that it needed to be larger. He asked Sylvie and Ernesto to help him decide how large his garden would be if he doubled the length and width of his garden. Ernesto said, "Well, if you double each side, the area of the garden, the planting space, will also be doubled." Sylvie said, "I don't think so. The garden would be larger than double." Can you help Ben consider both options?

- Who's right, Ernesto or Sylvie? How do you know?
- How large would the area of Ben's garden be if he doubled the length of each side of his garden? Make a representation to represent your solution. Be prepared to discuss your solution plan.

Task B

Bernita measured 3 ft. × 2 ft. as the length and width to construct a rectangular base for her rabbit cage. What would the length and width be if doubled? What would the area of the new rabbit cage be?

Make a table to show the differences in the length, width, and area of both of Bernita's rabbit cages. Share your table with the class.

Task C

Alanna is decorating a bulletin board for the hallway. The bulletin board is 12 ft. long by 3 ft. wide. How much bulletin board paper will she need to cover the background?

Task D

The carpet in our classroom will be installed over the winter break. Each class is tasked with letting the principal know how much carpet will be needed for their classroom. Determine the amount of carpet needed, explain your reasoning, and make a final recommendation to your principal.

Next, let's take a look at how Margaret used the research-informed task selection decision points to record notes about the tasks and make a decision about the task she would implement in her own classroom (Figure 16.2).

Figure 16.2 Task Selection Decision Points

Task Selection Decision Points	Task A	Task B	Task C	Task D
Does the task connect to important mathematics content and mathematical practices, using your grade-level content standards?	Yes. The task is challenging and will definitely ensure that the students are constructing viable arguments.	Yes. This task is a simpler version of Task A.	No. This is a below grade-level task.	Yes. I will have to make sure students are attending to the mathematics in the task and using mathematics to make a recommendation.
How does the task develop, build on, or connect to important mathematical understandings?	The doubling aspect helps students understand the relationship of area and the increase of a dimension.	The doubling aspect helps students understand the relationship of area and the length of a side.	This is an area computation problem.	Students won't have an opportunity to explore the relationship of area with this task.
Does the task provide multiple solution pathways for your students?	Yes. This is very open-ended. Students will likely create and test the two suggested pathway solutions to conduct a viable argument.	Yes. There are a few solution pathways. Not as many as for Task A and Task D.	Students are likely to just multiply. The task does not invite multiple solution pathways.	Yes. There are many solution pathways. Students could use manipulatives and tools.
Does the task engage your students in *doing mathematics*?	Yes. Although some students don't have home gardens, there is a community garden that we can use to connect to this task.	Yes. The students could also use large chart paper and masking tape to build models for the rabbit cages.	No. This task is not a *doing-math task*. Students will apply a procedure.	Yes. The students will likely be very excited to inform the principal of their plan for the carpeting.
Does the task require higher level thinking and reasoning?	Yes	Yes	No	Yes
Does the task connect to additional mathematics topics (or other content areas), and if so, how?	No	No	No	Yes. Students will use tools to measure.

Given the analysis of all the information, Margaret immediately ruled out Task C, as she knew that it was not going to challenge her students to think mathematically. Although she loved Task D, she was worried that the students would get caught up in measuring the room to find the area and would not have opportunities to explore how the area changes when the dimensions change. Margaret really liked Tasks A and B and thought the students would welcome the opportunity to construct garden representations to prove which person was correct while developing mathematical practices.

As Margaret reviewed her task selection, she decided to change the context slightly on Task A to focus on the neighborhood community garden. She knew that two of her families had plots in the community garden. With their permission, she planned to take photos of the whole garden and their plots to help launch the task. She knew that drawing on students' knowledge and family experiences would both engage the students and help them focus on the mathematics they are learning.

Finally, Margaret decided to review her adaptation of Task A with particular consideration of the four special callouts used throughout this book as a lens:

- Equity and Access: Margaret determined that her decision to change the context to a community garden promoted students' access because they are familiar with and have knowledge of the community garden.

- Productive Struggle: Margaret's decision to rule out Task C was the first step in promoting productive struggle. She knew that she wanted an open-ended task that would invite students to develop multiple solution pathways.

- Alternate Learning Environment: Although this task is not specifically necessarily designed for an alternate learning environment, Margaret thought that students would enjoy working on this problem as a longer "at-home" project. She envisioned that students could share ideas during a brainstorming phase through an online discussion board and upload sketches of their ideas.

- Strengths Spotting: As in any lesson or task, there are many opportunities to spot strengths. Margaret planned to highlight her students' collaboration, strategies, solution pathways, and reasoning throughout the Launch, Facilitate, and Close portions of the task-lesson.

Your Turn: Adapting Tasks

As you consider adapting a math task, the goal is to transform a task into one that is truly a *doing-math task* and meets your students' instructional needs. One of the main reasons for adapting a task is if the task quality is low, only requiring students to memorize or implement procedures without connecting those procedures to key conceptual understanding of the mathematics they are learning. Another key reason that teachers might want to adapt a task is if the context of the task is not relatable or realistic for students. There are several ways to adapt math tasks.

ADAPTING A LOW-QUALITY TASK

You can adapt a low-quality task by making changes that provide more opportunities for students to apply prior knowledge, make connections to conceptual understanding, provide multiple solution pathways, explain their thinking, and justify their reasoning. Let's take a look at how a team of fourth- and fifth-grade teachers adapted a low-quality decimal task to be something much more. On the left is the original task, and on the right is the adaptation (Figure 16.3).

Figure 16.3

> Order the following decimal values.
>
> 10.326, 10.3, 10.302, 10.032

→

> The track coach recorded times in seconds for the 50-yard dash and needs your help organizing them from slowest to fastest. Who came in first through fourth? Justify your reasoning with a detailed explanation.
>
> Amaya 10.326
>
> Maria 10.3
>
> Laney 10.302
>
> Reya 10.032

Another reason a teacher might adapt a task is to strategically design contexts that incorporate students' experiences and funds of knowledge to promote student access. By changing the problem setting to a familiar and relevant context, students can focus on exploring and learning the mathematics. Teachers can do this by changing the task context using students' shared experiences such as a common field trip they took in a prior grade or are preparing for, community events such as a farmer's market or community yard sale, or neighborhood landmarks or businesses that are explicitly linked to the mathematics that students are learning. Let's take a look at how the fourth- and fifth-grade team changed the context of the problem to promote their students' access (Figure 16.4). The teacher thought the task was—well, boring—and wouldn't inspire students to want to solve the problem. The community arts festival was coming up and that seemed a perfect context for the problem. Again, the original task is on the left and the adaptation is on the right.

Figure 16.4

> The length and width of Rectangle B are $1\frac{1}{2}$ times greater than rectangle A.
>
> The dimensions of Rectangle A are $3\frac{1}{2}$ cm by $5\frac{1}{4}$ cm.
>
> What are the dimensions of Rectangle B?

→

> Arlo the Artist was planning to sell some of his favorite art pieces at the Art Festival. He knows from past history that people tend to buy the larger prints. Therefore, he decides to make 20 prints that are the length and width of Rectangle A and 40 prints that are $1\frac{1}{2}$ times greater than the length and width of Rectangle A. The dimensions of Rectangle A are $3\frac{1}{2}$ cm by $5\frac{1}{4}$ cm. What will the dimensions of the bigger prints be?

Finally, you may wish to adapt a task by engaging the students in a task preparation activity that ensures all students can move quickly into actually *doing the math* that the task requires. This groundwork can include providing a quick review of vocabulary related to geometric measurement for a task that involves perimeter, area, and volume before students actually complete a task that involves these concepts. Another possibility is assembling and discussing the use of the representations or tools that students will be expected to use as they engage in the task. You may also consider adapting a task in such a way that small groups of students are better able to work collaboratively on the task. Such an adaptation could include the use of a group response form designed in such a way that all students provide "evidence" of their involvement in the task's solution strategies.

As these examples demonstrate, there are many ways to adapt a task to promote student engagement, interest, and mathematical understanding. In each instance, you will want to ensure that the task adaptations will support your students' access to the task without reducing the cognitive rigor.

Your Turn: Creating Tasks

There is no end to the creative possibilities that emerge from a teacher's mind! The more experience teachers have in facilitating *doing-math tasks,* the more comfortable they become with creating their own tasks. Use the template we have provided in this book (Appendix A) to guide your task construction. Allow us to provide a few recommendations for creating your own *doing-math tasks.*

1. Start with the content standard and the mathematical practices used in your setting as your guide-posts. Consistently check the task against these standards to ensure they are being addressed.

2. Determine your students' learning strengths and challenges. Make your own list and make sure the task adequately addresses what students do well, what they are learning, and particular challenges they may be experiencing.

3. Consider your students' interests, experiences, and funds of knowledge. What contexts would interest your students in the task?

As you begin the process of creating your own *doing-math tasks* or adapting tasks from textbooks, online locations, or your school or school district's curriculum resources, find the time to try out your "new" tasks with your colleagues first. Such peer reviews at the pre-implementation stage are always helpful. As tasks are successfully implemented, consider creating shared online files of all tasks so that they can be adapted and revised as needed and used by your team in the future.

Finally, as you think about the actual use of a task you have located, adapted, or created from curriculum materials or related resources, recognize that as you actually implement the task, things change! You may decide to suggest a different representational tool to be used, you may decide to adjust the task to address particular student needs, you may decide to have the class start the task today and finish that night on their own or to provide time for task completion tomorrow. Such adaptation and flexible implementation-related decisions are based on the needs and developmental stages of your students and your own instructional awareness and expertise.

As you consider selecting and adapting tasks, we suggest that you begin by starting with the tasks in this book as they are written. Notice how you select and modify the tasks through planning or during your actual implementation of the task. Next, seek tasks that have similar characteristics and adapt tasks that need tweaking by using the task selection decision points. Finally, create your own tasks! Go for it!

Frequently Asked Questions

In this work, some questions surface more than others. Here, we address popular questions we receive.

Q 1. How can I use the tasks in alternate learning environments (e.g., online, off-site, high level of family support)?

A *Now that many schools are facing a variety of ways to implement instruction, these tasks can fulfill multiple roles. Of course, they can be used in face-to-face settings, but many of the tasks can be adapted for use in alternate learning environments as noted throughout the task chapters. Consider assigning a task to students in a Google slide or through Jamboard. Multiple students can collaborate on the task by typing or drawing directly into the slide and uploading pictures. Students can also bring family members into the solution process and have them contribute their ideas. We encourage you to adapt tasks to meet these situations in your own creative ways!*

Q 2. How can I monitor student progress using the formative assessment techniques presented within the tasks?

A *Formative assessment tools have been provided for you in Appendix B. Download the tools and adapt them, if needed, to use with the tasks provided in this book or any of the tasks you adapt or create.*

Q 3. What are some ways that I can provide feedback to my students regarding their task performance?

A *We agree that feedback is critical for students to move learning forward. Use the formative assessment tools to record your observations, student interviews, and Show Me responses as well as notes about the student strategies observed and heard to frame and guide the feedback you provide.*

Q 4. I notice that the tasks provided don't address *all* the mathematics standards for a grade level. Why is that?

A *These tasks are meant to be a catalyst and empower you as you are selecting, imagining, and creating additional tasks that meet ALL of your standards. As much as we wanted to provide tasks that address all the standards, we simply did not have enough room! We selected those standards that are most often emphasized or highlighted as essential standards for fourth and fifth grades. These are meant to help you get started and empower you to select, adapt, or create additional tasks that meet ALL of the standards you will teach.*

Summing Up

You began this work on developing a collection of high-quality lessons by considering the important characteristics of a *doing-math task*. By now, we hope you have had many opportunities to see your students become energized as they engaged collaboratively in rich mathematical discourse while developing strategies and solution pathways for the tasks. You have also likely made strategic decisions about the selection and adaption of these tasks as well as others you will create on your own, always with your students' mathematical strengths at the forefront of your decision making. You have likely developed some very specific ideas about what works well with *your students* in *your classroom*, and frankly, this is what this work is all about! And hopefully, you may have also noticed that this process helped solidify your own purpose and intentions for teaching *doing-math tasks*.

As you continue this journey, we suggest the following:

- Find collaboration partners. Seek teachers in your school, across your district, or even across the country to cocreate and share task-related ideas. This process is often more rewarding and fun when shared with others.

- Determine how you will document and store your task selection, creation, and adaptation decisions. If you collaborate with others, consider virtual sharing platforms such as Google Docs.

- Celebrate your success by showcasing your students' thinking and reasoning. Make sure you share these success stories with your leadership!

Finally, as we began to think about the need for this book and the importance of engaging students in *doing-math tasks*, we felt a resource that helped define the importance of such tasks and provided exemplars would both assist and stimulate practitioners like you to take the next step and "own" the task creation, adaptation, and implementation process. You see now, as Stein and Smith (1998) note, you surely "know a good task when you see one" (p. 347). Go for it!

Professional Learning/Discussion Questions

- Provide an example of a time when you adapted a math task on the spot during a lesson. What did you do? Are there particularly important representation tools that your students would use regularly as they engage in *doing-math tasks*? What are they?

- What are some particularly helpful sources for mathematics tasks that seem, for the most part, to address the book's task selection decision points?

- How do you, or how will you, use formative assessment to monitor student progress as you implement *doing-math tasks*?

- What are some of the particular challenges you have faced when preparing for and implementing *doing-math tasks* online/virtually?

Appendix A

TASK LESSON TEMPLATE

*The task lesson template provided is the template used for the tasks provided in Chapters 4–15.

Grade Level

Task Title

Task Topic

Mathematics Standard(s):
Mathematical Practice(s):
Task

Vocabulary	**Materials**

Task Preparation:
Launch:
Facilitate:
Close: Make the Math Visible
Post-Task Notes: Reflection & Next Steps

Appendix B

FORMATIVE ASSESSMENT TOOLS*

* Tools are provided for recording student responses to task activities which involve the following formative assessment techniques: Observations, Interviews (individual and small group), and Show Me.

Observations: Small Group or Class

Intent of the Observation	What Was Observed?	Observation Comments; Next Steps
Mathematics Content	(Indicate the mathematics of the task activity)	(What were the students doing math-wise? Quick comment about next steps)
Mathematical Practices	(What processes/practices were students engaged in?)	(What were the students doing with regard to the processes/ practices? Next steps?)
Student Engagement	(How were the students engaged in doing the math? Consider: tools and representations grouping: pairs; small groups; communication: discussions; sharing activities; notice and wonder; etc.)	(How was the level of engagement? Did the task truly engage the students in doing math? Next steps?)
General Comment: (Overall comments about the task activities and student involvement in the activities. Particular thoughts about individual, group, or class needs, as observed.)		
Feedback to Students: (How and when will you provide feedback to the students based on your observations of their task performance? This may include interviewing some students or using the Show Me technique based on what you have observed.)		

Source: Adapted from Fennell, Francis (Skip), Kobett, B., & Wray, J. (2017). *The Formative 5: Everyday Assessment Techniques for Every Math Classroom.* Thousand Oaks, CA: Corwin. permission conveyed through Copyright Clearance Center, Inc.

Interview: Individual Student

Student Name:	Date:	Math Topic:
Student Questions:		**Student Responses** (Provide notes regarding student responses for each of the questions)
1. How did you solve that?		
2. Why did you solve the problem/task that way?		
3. What else can you tell me about what you did?		

Note: If available, attach completed work sample(s).

Source: Adapted from Fennell, Francis (Skip), Kobett, B., & Wray, J. (2017). *The Formative 5: Everyday Assessment Techniques for Every Math Classroom*. Thousand Oaks, CA: Corwin. permission conveyed through Copyright Clearance Center, Inc.

Interviews: Small Group

Student Name	Mathematics Content Focus	Mathematical Practice(s)	Task	Interview Question #1 *(For example: How did you solve that?)*	Interview Question #2 *(For example: Why did you solve the problem that way?)*

Note: Add more rows as needed, for additional students.

Source: Adapted from Fennell, Francis (Skip), Kobett, B., & Wray, J. (2017). *The Formative 5: Everyday Assessment Techniques for Every Math Classroom*. Thousand Oaks, CA: Corwin. permission conveyed through Copyright Clearance Center, Inc.

Show Me

Mathematics Content/Standard:	
Task Focus: (title and/or brief description of the content)	**Anticipated Student Show Me Responses:**
Student: (Brief description of the student's Show Me response and/or a picture of the response)	Student:
Student:	Student:

Source: Adapted from Fennell, Francis (Skip), Kobett, B., & Wray, J. (2017). *The Formative 5: Everyday Assessment Techniques for Every Math Classroom*. Thousand Oaks, CA: Corwin. permission conveyed through Copyright Clearance Center, Inc.

References

Aguirre, J., Mayfield-Ingram, K., & Martin, D. (2013). *The impact of identity in K–8 mathematics: Rethinking equity-based practices*. NCTM..

Anderson, N., Chapin, S., & O'Connor, C. (2011). *Classroom discussions: Seeing math discourse in action, Grades K–6*. Math Solutions.

Baker, K., Jessup, N. A., Jacobs, V. R., Empson, S. B., & Case, J. (2020). Productive struggle in action. *Mathematics Teacher: Learning and Teaching PK–12, 113*(5), 361–367.

Ball, D. L. (1992). Magical hopes: Manipulatives and the reform of math education. *American Educator: The Professional Journal of the American Federation of Teachers, 16*(2), 14–18.

Ball, D. L., & Forzani, F. M. (2011a). Building a common core for learning to teach, and connecting professional learning to practice. *American Educator, 35*(2), 17–21.

Ball, D. L., & Forzani, F. M. (2011b). *Identifying high-leverage practices for teacher education*. Panel paper presented at the State Higher Education Executive Officer Association Conference, Chapel Hill, NC, May.

Barousa, M. (2013). *Which one doesn't belong?* https://wodb.ca/

Bay-Williams, J. M., & Livers, S. (2009). Supporting math vocabulary acquisition. *Teaching Children Mathematics, 16*(4), 238–246.

Bloom, B. S. (1956). *Taxonomy of educational objectives, Handbook I: The cognitive domain*. David McKay.

Boaler, J. (2006). How a detracked mathematics approach promoted respect, responsibility, and high achievement. *Theory Into Practice, 45*(1), 40–46.

Boaler, J. (2014). *Setting up positive norms in math class*. Stanford Graduate School of Education. http://www.youcubed.org/wp-content/uploads/Positive-Classroom-Norms2pdf

Boaler, J., & Staples, M. (2008). Creating mathematical futures through an equitable teaching approach: The case of Railside School. *Teachers College Record, 110*(3), 608–645.

Carbonneau, K. J., Marley, S. C., & Selig, J. P. (2013). A meta-analysis of the efficacy of teaching mathematics with concrete manipulatives. *Journal of Educational Psychology, 105*, 380–400.

Cavanaugh, R. A., Heward, W. L., & Donelson, F. (1996). Effects of response cards during lesson closure on the academic performance of secondary students in an earth science course. *Journal of Applied Behavior Analysis, 29*(3), 403–406.

Chapin, S. H., & O'Connor, M. C. (2012). Project Challenge: Using challenging curriculum and mathematical discourse to help all students learn. In C. Dudley-Marling & S. Michaels (Eds.), *High-expectation curricula: Helping all students succeed with powerful learning* (pp. 113–127). Teachers College Press.

Chapin, S. H., O'Connor, C., & Anderson, N. A. (2013). *Talk moves: A teacher's guide for using classroom discussions in math*. Math Solutions.

Danielson, C. (2008). *The handbook for enhancing professional practice: Using the framework for teaching in your school*. Alexandria, VA: Association for Supervision and Curriculum Development.

Danielson, C. (2016). *Which one doesn't belong? A shapes book and teacher's guide*. Stenhouse.

Danielson, C., & McGreal, T. L. (2000). *Teacher evaluation to enhance professional practice*. Association for Supervision and Curriculum Development.

Dewey, J. (1933). *How we think: A restatement of the relation of reflective thinking to the educative process*. D. C. Heath.

Dougherty, B., Bryant, D. P., Bryant, B. R., & Shin, M. (2016). Helping students with mathematics difficulties understand ratios and proportions. *Teaching Exceptional Children, 49*(2), 96–105.

Doyle, W. (1988). Work in mathematics classes: The context of students' thinking during instruction. *Educational Psychologist, (23)*2, 167–180.

Drake, C., Land, T. J., Bartell, T. G., Aguirre, J. M., Foote, M. Q., Roth McDuffie, A., & Turner, E. E. (2015). Three strategies for opening curriculum spaces. *Teaching Children Mathematics, 21*(6), 346–353.

Ellis, M. W. (2008). Leaving no child behind yet allowing none too far ahead: Ensuring (in) equity in mathematics education through the science of measurement and instruction. *Teachers College Record, 110*(6), 1330–1356.

Erikson Institute. (2018). *Exploring the three-reads math protocol for word problems.* https://earlymath .erikson.edu/exploring-3-reads-math-protocol-word-problems/

Fennell, F., Kobett, B. M., & Wray, J. (2015). Classroom-based formative assessments: Guiding teaching and learning. In C. Suurtamm and A. Roth McDuffie (Eds.)., *Annual perspectives in mathematics education—2015* (pp. 51–62). NCTM.

Fennell, F., Kobett, B. M., & Wray, J. (2017). *The formative 5: Everyday assessment techniques for every math classroom.* Corwin and NCTM.

Fennell, F., & Rowan, T. (2001). Representation: An important process for teaching and learning mathematics. *Teaching Children Mathematics, 7*(5), 288–292.

Flynn, M. (2017). *Beyond answers: Exploring mathematical practices with young children.* Stenhouse.

Franke, M. L., Webb, N. M., Chan, A. G., Ing, M., Freund, D., & Battey, D. (2009). Teacher questioning to elicit students' mathematical thinking in elementary school classrooms. *Journal of Teacher Education, 60*(4), 380–392.

Fyfe, E. R., McNeil, N. M., Son, J. Y., & Goldstone, R. L. (2014). Concreteness fading in mathematics and science instruction: A systemic review. *Educational Psychology Review, 26*, 9–25.

Ganske, K. (2017). Lesson closure: An important piece of the student learning puzzle. *The Reading Teacher, 71*(1), 95–100.

Goffney, I., Gutiérrez, R., & Boston, M. (Eds.). (2018). *Rehumanizing mathematics for Black, Indigenous, and Latinx students.* NCTM.

Gonzalez, J. (2018, December 2). 10 ways educators can take action in pursuit of equity [Blog]. *Cult of Pedagogy.* https://www.cultofpedagogy.com/10-equity/

Harbin Miles, R., Kobett, B. M., & Williams, L. (2018). *The mathematics lesson-planning handbook, Grades 3–5: Your blueprint for success.* Corwin.

Hattie, J. (2009). *Visible learning: A synthesis of over 800 meta-analyses relating to achievement.* Routledge.

Heddens, J. W. (1986). Bridging the gap between the concrete and the abstract. *Arithmetic Teacher, 33*(6), 14–17.

Heick, T. (2019). 10 ways to be a more reflective teacher [Blog post]. *Teachthought.* https://www .teachthought.com/pedagogy/reflective-teacher-reflective-teaching/

Hiebert, J., Carpenter, T. P., Fennema, E., Fuson, K., Human, P., Murray, H., Olivier, A., & Wearne, D. (1996). Problem solving as a basis for reform in curriculum and instruction: The case of mathematics. *Educational Researcher, 25*(4), 12–21.

Hiebert, J., & Wearne, D. (1993). Instructional tasks, classroom discourse, and students' learning in second-grade arithmetic. *American Educational Research Journal, 30*(2), 393–425.

Illustrative Math. (2019). Co-creating classroom norms with students [Blog]. https:// illustrativemathematics.blog/2019/08/02/co-creating-classroom-norms-with-students/

Institute for Mathematics and Education. (2007). *Progressions documents for Common Core Math Standards.* http://ime.math.arizona.edu/progressions/#about

Jackson, K. J., Shahan, E. C., Gibbons, L. K., & Cobb, P. A. (2012). Launching complex tasks. *Mathematics Teaching in the Middle School, 18*(1), 24–29.

Jilk, L. M. (2016). Supporting teacher noticing of students' mathematical strengths. *Mathematics Teacher Educator, 4*(2), 188–199.

Kapur, M. (2010). Productive failure in mathematical problem solving. *Instructional Science, 38*(6), 523–550.

Karp, K. S., Dougherty, B., & Bush, S. (2020). *The math pact, elementary: Achieving instructional cohesion within and across grades.* Corwin and NCTM.

Kasberg, S. E., & Frye, R. S. (2013). Norms and mathematical proficiency. *Teaching Children Mathematics, 20*(1), 28–35.

Kazemi, E., & Hintz, A. (2014). *Intentional talk: How to structure and lead productive mathematical discussions.* Stenhouse.

Keeley, P., & Tobey, C. R. (2011). *Mathematics formative assessment, Volume 1: 75 Practical strategies for linking assessment, instruction, and learning.* Corwin.

Kelemanik, G., & Lucenta, A. (2016). *Routines for reasoning: Fostering the mathematical practices in all students.* Heinemann.

Kobett, B. M., Harbin Miles, R., & Williams, L. (2018). *The mathematics lesson-planning handbook, grades K–2: Your blueprint for building cohesive lessons.* Corwin.

Kobett, B., & Karp, K. (2020). *Strengths-based teaching and learning in mathematics: 5 teaching turnarounds for Grades K–6.* Corwin and NCTM.

Laski, E. V., Jor'dan, J. R., Daoust, C., & Murray, A. K. (2015). What makes mathematics manipulatives effective? Lessons from cognitive science and Montessori education. *SAGE Open, 5*(2), 1–8.

Lempp, J. (2017). *Math workshop: Five steps to implementing guided math, learning stations, reflection, and more.* Math Solutions.

Livers, S., & Bay-Williams, J. M. (2014). Vocabulary support: Constructing (not obstructing meaning). *Mathematics Teaching in the Middle School, 20*(3), 152–159.

Lortie, D. C. (1975). *Schoolteacher: A sociological study.* University of Chicago Press.

Lott Adams, T., Thangata, F., & King, C. (2005). Weigh to go! Exploring mathematical language. *Mathematics Teaching in the Middle School, 10*(9), 444–448.

Lynch, S. D., Hunt, J. H., & Lewis, K. E. (2018). Productive struggle for all: Differentiated instruction. *Mathematics Teaching in the Middle School, 23*(4), 194–201.

Marshall, A. M., Superfine, A. C., & Canty, R. (2010). Star students make connections: Discover strategies to engage young math students in competently using multiple representations. *Teaching Children Mathematics, 17*(1), 38–47.

Math Forum. (2015). Beginning to problem solve with "I notice and wonder." https://www.nctm.org/Classroom-Resources/Problems-of-the-Week/I-Notice-I-Wonder/

Murata, A., & Stewart, C. (2017). Facilitating mathematical practices through visual representations. *Teaching Children Mathematics, 23*(7), 404–412.

National Council of Teachers of Mathematics. (1991). *Professional standard for teaching mathematics.* Author.

National Council of Teachers of Mathematics. (2000). *Principles and standards for school mathematics.* Author.

National Council of Teachers of Mathematics. (2014a). *Access and equity in mathematics education.* Author. https://www.nctm.org/Standards-and-Positions/Position-Statements/Access-and-Equity-in-Mathematics-Education/

National Council of Teachers of Mathematics. (2014b). *Principles to actions: Ensuring mathematical success for all.* Author.

National Council of Teachers of Mathematics. (2017a). *Principles to actions: Professional learning toolkit.* NCTM. https://www.nctm.org/PtAToolkit/

National Council of Teachers of Mathematics. (2017b). *Taking action: Implementing effective mathematics teaching practices in Grades 6–8.* NCTM.

National Council of Teachers of Mathematics. (2020a). *Catalyzing change in early childhood and elementary mathematics: Initiating critical conversations.* Author.

National Council of Teachers of Mathematics. (2020b). *Classroom practices that support equity-based mathematics teaching.* Research brief. https://www.nctm.org/Research-and-Advocacy/Research-Brief-and-Clips/Classroom-Practices-That-Support-Equity-Based-Mathematics-Teaching/

National Council of Teachers of Mathematics & National Council of Supervisors of Mathematics. (2020, June). *Moving forward: Mathematics learning in the era of COVID.* https://www.nctm.org/uploadedFiles/Research_and_Advocacy/NCTM_NCSM_Moving_Forward.pdf

National Governors Association Center for Best Practices & Council of Chief State School Officers. (2010). *Common Core state standards for mathematics.* Author.

National Research Council. (2001). *Adding it up: Helping children learn mathematics.* National Academies Press.

National Research Council. (2012). *Education for life and work: Developing transferable knowledge and skills in the 21st century.* Committee on Defining Deeper Catalyzing Change in High School Mathematics.

O'Connell, S., & SanGiovanni, J. (2013). *Putting the practices into action: Implementing the Common Core standards for mathematical practice, K–8.* Heinemann.

Opfer, V. D., Kaufman, J. H., & Thompson, L. E. (2017). *Implementation of K–12 state standards for mathematics and English language arts and literacy: Findings from the American teacher panel.* RAND Corporation.

Parrish, S. (2014). *Number talks: Whole number computation, Grades K–5.* Math Solutions.

Parrish, S., & Dominick, A. (2016). *Number Talks: Fractions, decimals, percentages.* Math Solutions.

Pollock, J. E. (2007). *Improving student learning one teacher at a time.* Association for Supervision and Curriculum Development.

Raposo, J., & Stone, J. (1972). One of these things is not like the other [Song lyrics]. https://www.metrolyrics.com/one-of-these-things-lyrics-ernie.html

Resnick, L. B. (1988). Treating mathematics as an ill-structured discipline. In R. I. Charles & E. A. Silver (Eds.), *Research agenda for mathematics education: Vol. 3. The teaching and assessing of mathematical problem solving* (pp. 32–60). Hillsdale, NJ: Erlbaum.

Ritchhart, R., Church, M., & Morrison, K. (2011). *Making thinking visible: How to promote engagement, understanding, and independence for all learners.* Wiley.

Rumack, A., & Huinker, D. (2019). Capturing mathematical curiosity with notice and wonder. *Mathematics Teaching in the Middle School, 24*(7),394–399.

SanGiovanni, J. J., Katt, S., & Dykema, K. (2020). *Productive math struggle: A 6-point action plan for fostering perseverance.* Corwin.

Shor, C. (2017). Clothesline math. https://clotheslinemath.com

Silver, E. A., & Mills, V. L. (Eds.). (2018). *A fresh look at formative assessment in mathematics teaching.* NCTM.

Small, M. (2017). *Good questions: Great ways to differentiate math instruction in standards-based classrooms.* Teacher's College Press.

Smith, M. S., Bill, V., & Sherin, M. G. (2019). *The 5 practices in practice: Successfully orchestrating mathematics discussions in your elementary classroom*. Corwin.

Smith, M. S., & Stein, M. K. (1998). Selecting and creating mathematical tasks: From research to practice. *Mathematics Teaching in the Middle School, 3*(5), 344–349.

Smith, M. S., & Stein, M. K. (2018). *Five practices for orchestrating productive mathematics discussions*. (2nd ed.). NCTM.

Smith, N. N. (2017). *Every math learner, K–5: A doable approach to teaching with learning differences in mind*. Corwin.

Stein, M. K., Grover, B. W., & Henningsen, M. (1996). Building student capacity for mathematical thinking and reasoning: An analysis of mathematical tasks used in reform classrooms. *American Educational Research Journal, 33*(2), 455–488.

Stein, M. K., & Lane, S. (1996). Instructional tasks and the development of student capacity to think and reason: An analysis of the relationship between teaching and learning in a reform mathematics project. *Educational Research and Evaluation, 2*(1), 50–80.

Stein, M. K., Smith, M. S., M. A., Henningsen, M. A., & Silver, E. A. (Eds.). (2000). *Implementing standards-based mathematics instruction: A casebook for professional development*. Teachers College Press.

Stein, M. K., Smith, M. S., Henningsen, M. A., & Silver, E. A. (Eds.). (2009). *Implementing standards-based mathematics instruction: A casebook for professional development* (2nd ed.). Teachers College Press.

Stigler, J. W., & Hiebert, J. (2004). Improving mathematics teaching. *Educational Leadership, 61*(5), 12–16.

Sweller, J. (1988). Cognitive load during problem solving: Effects on learning. *Cognitive Science, 12*(2), 257–285.

Thompson, D. R., & Rubenstein, R. N. (2000). Learning mathematics vocabulary: Potential pitfalls and instructional strategies. *The Mathematics Teacher, 93*(7), 568–574.

Turner, E., Dominguez, H., Maldonado, L., & Empson, S. (2013). English learners' participation in mathematical discussion: Shifting positionings and dynamic identities. *Journal for Research in Mathematics Education, 44*(1), 199–234.

Van de Walle, J. A., Karp, K., & Bay-Williams, J. (2019). *Elementary and middle school mathematics: Teaching developmentally*. Pearson.

Van de Walle, J. A., Karp, K. S., Lovin, L. H., & Bay-Williams, J. M. (2017). *Teaching student-centered mathematics: Developmentally appropriate instruction for Grades 3–5* (3rd ed., Vol. 2). Pearson.

Van de Walle, J. A., Karp, K. S., Lovin, L. H., & Bay-Williams, J. (2018). *Elementary and middle school mathematics: Teaching developmentally*. Pearson.

White, D. Y., Gomez, C. N., Rushing, F., Hussain, N., Patel, K., & Pratt, J. (2018). Assembling the puzzle of mathematical strengths. *Mathematics Teaching in the Middle School, 23*(5), 268–275.

Wiliam, D. (2011). *Embedded formative assessment*. Solution Tree.

Wiliam, D., & Thompson, M. (2008). Integrating assessment with learning. What will it take to make it work? In C. A. Dwyer (Ed.), *The future of assessment: Shaping teaching and learning* (pp. 52–82). Lawrence Erlbaum.

Willingham, D. (2017a, Fall). Ask the cognitive scientist: Do manipulatives help students learn? *American Educator*. https://www.aft.org/ae/fall2017/willingham

Yeh, C. (2019). *Countering deficit myths of students with dis/abilities and conceptualizing possibilities: A culturally responsive and relational approach to mathematics TODOS Live!* [Webinar] https://vimeo.com/353856573

Yeh, C., Ellis, M. W., & Hurtado, C. K. (2017). *Reimagining the mathematics classroom: Creating and sustaining productive learning environments*. NCTM.

Index

h Tasks

Supporting TEACHERS | Empowering STUDENTS

PETER LILJEDAHL

14 optimal practices for thinking that create an ideal setting for deep mathematics learning to occur

Grades K–12

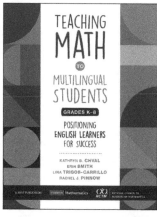

KATHRYN B. CHVAL, ERIN SMITH, LINA TRIGOS-CARRILLO, RACHEL J. PINNOW

Strengths-based approaches to support multilingual students' development in mathematics

Grades K–8

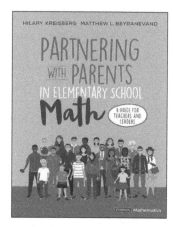

HILARY KREISBERG, MATTHEW L. BEYRANEVAND

Guidance on building productive relationships with families about math education

Grades K–5

BETH MCCORD KOBETT, FRANCIS (SKIP) FENNELL, KAREN S. KARP, DELISE ANDREWS, TRENDA KNIGHTEN, JEFF SHIH, DESIREE HARRISON, BARBARA ANN SWARTZ, SORSHA-MARIA T. MULROE

Detailed plans for helping elementary students experience deep mathematical learning

Grades K–1, 2–3, 4–5

BETH MCCORD KOBETT, KAREN S. KARP

Your game plan for unlocking mathematics by focusing on students' strengths

Grades K–6

JOHN J. SANGIOVANNI, SUSIE KATT, KEVIN J. DYKEMA

Empowering students to embrace productive struggle to build essential skills for learning and living—both inside and outside the classroom

Grades K–12

To order, visit corwin.com/math

**JENNIFER M. BAY-WILLIAMS,
JOHN J. SANGIOVANNI**

Because fluency is so much more
than basic facts and algorithms

Grades K–8

**KAREN S. KARP,
BARBARA J. DOUGHERTY,
SARAH B. BUSH**

A schoolwide solution for students'
mathematics success

Elementary, Middle School, High School

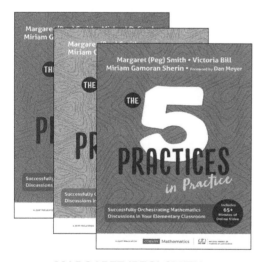

**MARGARET (PEG) SMITH,
VICTORIA BILL,
MIRIAM GAMORAN SHERIN,
MICHAEL D. STEELE**

Take a deeper dive into understanding the
five practices—anticipating, monitoring,
selecting, sequencing, and connecting—
for facilitating productive mathematical
conversations in your classrooms

Elementary, Middle School, High School

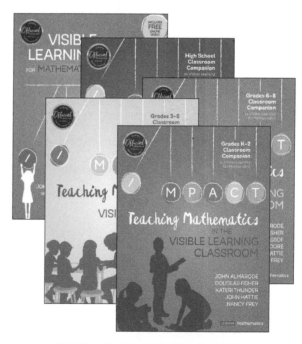

**JOHN HATTIE, DOUGLAS FISHER,
NANCY FREY, JOHN ALMARODE,
LINDA M. GOJAK, SARA DELANO MOORE,
WILLIAM MELLMAN, JOSEPH ASSOF,
KATERI THUNDER**

Powerful, precision teaching through
intentionally designed, guided, collaborative,
and independent learning

Grades K–2, 3–5, 6–8, 9–12

A SAGE Publishing Company

Helping educators make the greatest impact

CORWIN HAS ONE MISSION: to enhance education through intentional professional learning.

We build long-term relationships with our authors, educators, clients, and associations who partner with us to develop and continuously improve the best evidence-based practices that establish and support lifelong learning.

All activity sheets and online resources provided in the Materials section of each task are available for download or viewing on the companion website.

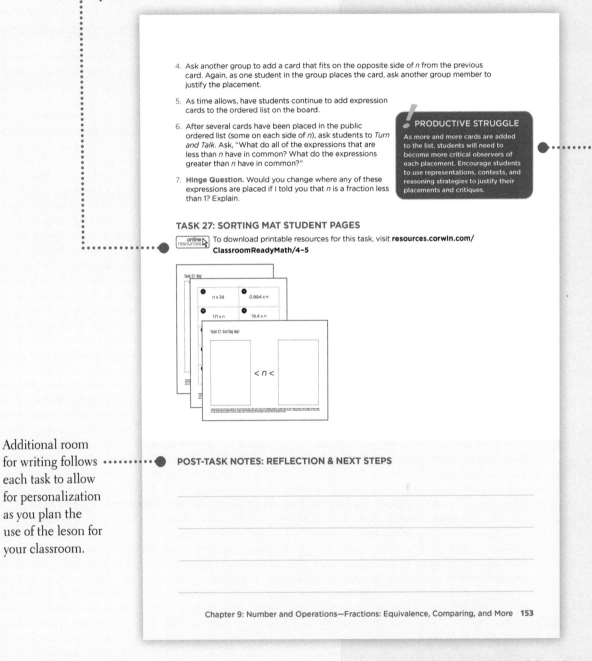

4. Ask another group to add a card that fits on the opposite side of *n* from the previous card. Again, as one student in the group places the card, ask another group member to justify the placement.

5. As time allows, have students continue to add expression cards to the ordered list on the board.

6. After several cards have been placed in the public ordered list (some on each side of *n*), ask students to *Turn and Talk*. Ask, "What do all of the expressions that are less than *n* have in common? What do the expressions greater than *n* have in common?"

7. **Hinge Question.** Would you change where any of these expressions are placed if I told you that *n* is a fraction less than 1? Explain.

PRODUCTIVE STRUGGLE

As more and more cards are added to the list, students will need to become more critical observers of each placement. Encourage students to use representations, contexts, and reasoning strategies to justify their placements and critiques.

TASK 27: SORTING MAT STUDENT PAGES

online resources ▸ To download printable resources for this task, visit **resources.corwin.com/ ClassroomReadyMath/4–5**

Task 27: Key

| $n \times 34$ | $0.894 \times n$ |
| $171 \times n$ | $19.4 \times n$ |

Task 27: Sorting Mat

$< n <$

POST-TASK NOTES: REFLECTION & NEXT STEPS

Additional room for writing follows each task to allow for personalization as you plan the use of the leson for your classroom.

The tasks in this book have been designed with student considerations in mind. Important ideas and teaching moves that will enrich students' learning experiences while engaged in *doing-math tasks* can be found in marginal boxes throughout the tasks. These ideas highlight: access and equity, productive struggle, alternate learning environments, and strengths spotting.